Through the Client's Eyes

New Approaches to Get Clients to Hire You Again and Again

Second Edition

Henry W. Ewalt

Commitment to Quality: The Law Practice Management Section is committed to quality in our publications. Our authors are experienced practitioners in their fields. Prior to publication, the contents of all our books are rigorously reviewed by experts to ensure the highest quality product and presentation. Because we are committed to serving our readers' needs, we welcome your feedback on how we can improve future editions of this book. We invite you to fill out and return the comment card at the back of this book.

Cover design by David Voigt.

Library of Congress Control Number 2001133131
ISBN 1-59031-058-6

05 04 03 02 02   5 4 3 2 1

Discounts are available for books ordered in bulk. Special consideration is given to state bars, CLE programs, and other bar-related organizations. Inquire at Book Publishing, American Bar Association, 750 N. Lake Shore Drive, Chicago, Illinois 60611.

DEDICATION

This work is dedicated to my father, H. Ward Ewalt, who, from 1929 to 1994, continually and consistently put the needs of his patients and the good of his profession, optometry, before his personal desires and self-interest.

Second Edition

My father became too sick to continue his optometric practice when he was 87 and died at 88 years of age. Many of the visitors at the funeral home were patients and former patients who expressed their heart-felt gratitude for his professional skills enabling them to enjoy better lives and for his caring personal interest in them and their families.

The lasting example he left for his patients and his family could only be achieved by Dad's continual implementation of his understanding that human needs exceeded the bounds of his defined professional responsibility. He did his best to facilitate fulfillment of those broader needs without judging them. We have an obligation to our clients to do likewise.

All this book addresses is the narrow concept of augmenting your professional training to serve others better. This is a mission that can never be completely fulfilled, even with the best of intents and greatest of efforts. But, at the very least, with sensitive effort as a lawyer, you will be more successful, and whatever level of success you achieve in client relations, it will produce many times the return in true personal satisfaction.

CONTENTS

CHAPTER 8

CHAPTER 9

CHAPTER 10

CHAPTER 11

CHAPTER 12

CHAPTER 13

ACKNOWLEDGMENTS

My government, private, corporate, and general public clients have taught me most of what you are about to read. I am grateful for their patient teaching because it often took more than one course of study from each of these "client-professors" for me to get the point. Clients' forgiveness of my failures has gratified, educated and humbled me.

Many attorneys, as well as non-lawyers, with whom I have practiced have set guideposts for me to improve my relations with clients. Some are my superstars in this category and established their reputations in Pittsburgh as well as other locales in Pennsylvania, District of Columbia, California, New York, Texas, and other states. They practice in small, medium, and large communities and in law organizations ranging from one person to those with well over one thousand lawyers. This empirically establishes that good client relations and successful, satisfying law practice are paired regardless of the location, type, or size of practice.

Another group of lawyers who are few in number but great in influence are those who have represented me as a client or a corporate client we jointly represented. They have performed at the highest professional level, charged reasonable fees and earned my personal trust and respect to the degree that I will always treasure their friendship, which grew from the client-attorney relationship.

Support staffs in the governmental, private, and corporate organizations in which I've practiced have been great teachers. While many managers, administrators, and legal assistants have positively influenced my client relations behaviors, my administrative assistants and secretaries warrant special recognition. They made a huge contribution to my being able to satisfy clients and turn out quality legal work. These fine people have my sincere gratitude and my request for forgiveness!

Some of the active members of the Law Practice Management Section of the American Bar Association have provided excellent counsel, terrific sounding boards, and insightful speeches and reading. Professor Gary Munneke has consistently championed the concepts in this book and unwaveringly urged me to update them with this Second Edition. His suggested changes in the text have resulted in clearer descriptions of concepts and improved organization of ideas. Reid Trautz, Director of Lawyer Practice Assistance for the District of Columbia Bar, has contributed numerous editorial suggestions making this Second Edition one that is easier to read and more concise.

Staff and members of the Law Practice Management Section Publishing Board have for years cajoled me, pushed me, left me alone, and made light of my lack of progress as the author of the Second Edition of this book. In so doing, each has improved the quality of and guaranteed the delivery of this final product. Beverly Loder has been terrific as the professional coordinator of this edition. Tim Johnson worked out the practical editing and printing problems in a professional manner and remained calm in the eye of the production hurricane.

All of these people share one common behavioral characteristic: commitment to service. They serve their clients, and this author, where and when it is convenient to the person being served. Like my Dad, they have wanted to be home many times when they continued working at the office. Their commitment to service and simultaneous regret of not being with family or pursuing personal interests is an established pattern in each of them. I thank and salute them all for their demonstration of what each of us strive to emulate—serving clients in a manner in which they will personally appreciate.

My wife, Mary, has expressed her strong support for my efforts. Mary has even pitched in on the typing of the Second Edition, which was a tremendous help since I sometimes have trouble reading my own writing. Our children, Andrew and Sarah encouraged me to finish by periodically asking, "how's it coming?" They also provided important professional information and insights, which I have incorporated in this edition. Since the First Edition, Kim has joined our family as Andrew's wife and they have blessed us with Chloe and Ward who, in Mary's and my opinions, are the most fabulous grandchildren. If we could treat clients as we do grandchildren, there would be no need to write this book or worry about the future of our legal profession. For over twenty-five years, Richard Martin has helped around our home, which has freed me to do projects such as this. Without his mechanical talent and loyalty my books wouldn't have been completed, nor would our marriage have lasted . . . for both, I'm deeply indebted.

The Second Edition, my first writing project since I decided to leave the full-time practice of law, attempts to capture some additional experiences and insights that have been revealed in my seven years of practice since the First Edition. My underlying concern growing from those experiences is that the legal profession is losing the market share in the competitive challenge from other professions. In my opinion, this stems chiefly from our shortcomings in client relations. It is my sincere hope that this Second Edition will help enable some attorneys to counter this trend so that clients will hire them again and again.

Henry W. Ewalt

FOREWORD

"Treat clients like people and not like cases. If you do, you will reap rewards for yourself and for your practice in the form of satisfied clients." The simplicity and strength of this message is often lost in the noise of theoretical proclamations about the lawyer client relationship. This is the message that Henry Ewalt proclaims: "Law practice is a human endeavor, involving a minimum of two people, a lawyer and a client."

Although complex matters seem to involve legions of lawyers and clients, at some level there is a one-on-one relationship between the provider and the recipient of services. Henry further postulates that the way lawyers treat their clients in this very human relationship is a key element in client satisfaction, and ultimately to success in the practice of law and lawyer satisfaction.

The new edition of *Through the Client's Eyes: New Approaches to Get Clients to Hire You Again and Again* offers readers specific, realistic ideas about how lawyers can better serve their clients by utilizing human relations skills, in all aspects of the attorney-client relationship. The book is written in an easy-to-read, informative style that will strike familiar chords in the minds of all lawyers who have represented clients. Henry Ewalt's perspective is particularly relevant, because he speaks as both a practitioner and a client, having spent time in private practice, in government, and in a corporate law department.

He recognizes the particular problems of lawyers in smaller organizations, as well as ones experienced in large firms, corporations, and government. Many lawyers received little or no skills training in law school, and picked up what they learned on the street, so to speak. *Through the Client's Eyes* provides practical answers for lawyers who want to develop their skills and practice in a manner that provides a win-win outcome for lawyer and client.

Professor Gary A. Munneke
Pace University School of Law

FOREWORD TO FIRST EDITION

For several years, Henry Ewalt has proclaimed a message to members of the legal profession: treat clients like people and not like cases. If you do, you will reap rewards in the form of satisfied clients. The simplicity and strength of this message is often lost in the noise of theoretical proclamations about the best way to practice law. Henry gets down to the basics: Law is a human endeavor, involving a minimum of two people, a lawyer and a client.

Although complex matters seem to involve legions of lawyers and clients, at some level there is a one-on-one relationship between the provider and the recipient of services. Henry further postulates that the way lawyers treat their clients in this very human relationship is a key element in client satisfaction, and ultimately to success in the practice of law.

Through the Clients Eyes: New Approaches to Get Clients to Hire You Again and Again offers readers specific, realistic ideas about how lawyers can better serve their clients by utilizing human relations skills in all aspects of the attorney-client relationship. The book is written in an easy-to-read, informative style that will strike familiar chords in the minds of all lawyers who have represented clients. Henry Ewalt's perspective is particularly relevant, because he speaks as both a practitioner and a client, having spent time in private practice and in a corporate law department.

As the author of another successful LPM Publishing title, *Practical Planning: A How-To Guide for Solos and Small Law Firms,* Henry Ewalt recognizes the particular problems of lawyers in smaller organizations, although he would argue that all lawyers need good client relations skills, regardless of the size of the firm.

This book is another strong addition to the wealth of publications by LPM Publishing that focus on practical lawyering skills. Many lawyers received little or no skills training in law school, and picked up what they learned on the street, so to speak.

Through the Client's Eyes offers an alternative for lawyers who want to develop their skills in a deliberate, organized way.

LPM Publishing is in the business of providing practical tools for practicing lawyers. The members of the Publishing Board who have reviewed this book are all enthusiastic about its positive, concrete, ground-level advice for lawyers everywhere—and they commend its contents to all lawyers who care about enhancing client relations skills.

Professor Gary A. Munneke
Chair, LPM Publishing

PROLOGUE

This is intended to be a book of practical advice. Unfortunately, there is no recipe to follow precisely to be sure client relations turn out well. You must adjust for your personality, the circumstances and the client's attitude about you and the client's situation.

There are parts of this manuscript that overlap with other parts. This does not mean that the words are repeated, but in certain sections a concept may seem to have been stated previously. These different applications of the same concept reflect that effective client relations is a complex web of communications which cannot be untangled into single strands or presented in free standing chimneys of ideas. In truth, it also means that some things are worth repeating. I learned these lessons from multiple experiences with the same concept. So, it may well take more than one presentation for me to make my point clear.

You shouldn't assume that because you know everything about or aren't affected by the subject of the chapter title that the chapter would not contain anything of interest. By way of illustration, if you work in a big law firm or corporation, Chapter 13 "Entrepreneuses and Entrepreneurs," might appear to contain no applicable material. Au contraire! That chapter has sections addressing the issues to be taken into account if you are considering leaving your organization, improving people skills, the importance of referrals and building budgets. Similarly, Chapter 14 "Corporate Counsel Client Relations," discusses information that may be useful to government laywers dealing with corporations and all those representing or seeking to represent corporations.

In any case, I sincerely hope lawyers, law students and others in the legal profession, regardless of whether they are law school graduates, will take away at least one idea from this book that will enable them to serve their clients better. The legal profession dearly needs this . . . and so do our clients.

CHAPTER 1

A WAKE-UP CALL

APPROACHING CLIENT RELATIONS

This book is intended as a resource for an individual lawyer's client relations program. Chapter 2 provides the philosophical foundation for the remainder of the book. It provides observations on why we find ourselves, as lawyers and a profession, where we are today and how we may gain greater personal satisfaction from the practice of law.

As you read the remaining chapters, underline or highlight those ideas that appeal to you and that you actually feel comfortable implementing. Then, extract those ideas by making a list of them in your own words. Next, under each idea, list specific action items necessary to execute the plan with respect to particular clients you target. After that, develop a plan of client relations that specifies the date by which you will complete each client initiative for each idea. Finally, assimilate the series of plans into a focused effort.

You need—for your future—to schedule and spend a minimum of two hours per week on client relations efforts. Your client relations plan must make sense to you and be one you will actually implement in your practice. Only thinking about ideas concerning client relations is practically useless and will add to your frustration and stress. Implementing reasonable long-term client relations goals, regardless of their success, inevitably reduces the pressures of practicing law. Besides, some of this is really fun.

If you are a member of a law firm, you may also wish to try to get your firm to adopt specific client relations approaches that you favor. Do not let you firm's lack of support become a convenient excuse not to institute your own individual client relations plan. If your individual approach is successful, it will not be long before it will spread throughout the firm. Lawyers embrace proven success, even where they won't risk failure.

YOUR PARTNERS AND SUPERVISORS ARE CLIENTS

Associates in law firms should remember to practice good client relations with partners. Lawyers in government and corporations need to develop a pattern of excellent client relations with their supervisors. After all, partners and supervisors are the sources of associates' work and should be cultivated. To simplify the next three paragraphs, I shall refer to the associate-partner relationship, but it is intended to include lawyers' relationships with supervisors too.

Naturally, the quality of associates' legal work and compliance with partners' work expectations, including writing style preferences, are more important to the associates' partner-client than to non-lawyer clients. An added element for associates' relations with partners is that partners are keenly aware of the quality of associates' legal scholarship, whereas clients would not be. This is compounded by the "master-servant" relationship which imposes a much more restricted bracket for acceptable legal products than is required by other clients. Factors like the pattern of ties, clothing styles and the bouquet from perfumes, may pack a potent impact on associates' relationships with partners. Associates are well advised to learn what their partner-clients want . . . and provide it.

Likewise, associates must handle partners' clients with the best client relations techniques. This is as critical to associates' relationships with their partner-clients as their direct dealing with partners. First, associates should ask the partner if they should communicate with the client or if the partner wishes to do that exclusively. Associates need to clarify with partners what to do about communications from and to clients in situations when partners are unavailable for extended periods, such as vacations or trials. Also, if courses of action dictated by partners turn out poorly, associates should not commiserate with clients by revealing they recommended something different than what the partner adopted. It is critical that associates keep partners fully aware of what is occurring in every matter so that the partner will be informed and fully prepared to talk with the client at all times. Each partner deals with clients differently. Each associate has the responsibility to discover how the partner-client wants client relations conducted with the partners' clients.

Associates partner-client situations present more complex challenges than dealing with clients associates have brought to the firm themselves. The goals are the same, but associates should tweak client relations methods to best serve partners and partners' clients. Such will develop associates' work sources and advance their careers.

CORPORATE ENVIRONMENT

Members of corporate law departments need to pay particular attention to both using and modifying these techniques for your clients. The corporate environment, with its greater structure and intricate communications culture, requires specially constructed approaches to client relations in order to confine communications to corporately acceptable language and methods. Forget not, your clients include the General Counsel, various corporate executives, as well as retained outside counsel. To be successful, you need all of these individuals' support, as well as the others you work within and outside the law department.

Some corporate law departments have ignored client relations to the detriment of their clients and themselves. As corporations are forced to become more competitive by declining economies, evaporating markets, and international competition, the cost of legal representation has become more prominent on the corporate decision makers' radar screen. When outside legal fees are not brought within perceived acceptable cost parameters, the executive reaction has been to change in-house or outside counsel, or even eliminate the corporate law department. These actions may indeed be logically justified. When they are not, it has usually been because the law department has failed to educate executives about the nature, cost, and importance of the work they are doing. In other words, those law departments and in-house counsel have failed to grasp the relevance and importance of client relations.

GOVERNMENT ENVIRONMENT

Government lawyers also should take note of and practice improved client relations. All too frequently government lawyers act in a self-created vacuum. They may virtually ignore supervisors' directions or the needs of the individual who has come to the government for assistance. Some define their client as "the public interest." Unknowingly, they have self-defined their client as they personally view the public interest. This, at times, causes problems with their supervisors who have the responsibility to define the public interest in that governmental office. On the other hand, as the media has pointed out, especially with respect to the Internal Revenue Service and the Federal Bureau of Investigation, some government agencies have focused too much on internal drives to please, as opposed to external taxpayer client needs.

When I served the federal and local governments as an attorney, I felt a great deal of satisfaction from representing the public. I observed then, and continue to experience today, that many government lawyers decide what the public interest is without consulting the public, the elected officials, other administrative agencies that have a responsibility to carry out their legal interpretations, or even the supervisors in their own department who are on the front lines with the public every day.

Government lawyers have multiple clients and complex relationships. They need to identify all of their true clients and then develop good client relations with each. This will add value to the political and governmental processes, and to the government lawyers' service.

SOLO AND SMALL PRACTICES

Solo and two- or three-attorney practices may initially be regarded as the easiest circumstances in which to implement an effective client relations plan. Some think obtaining buy-in is easier than in a larger organization. This is just not so. Lawyers in these practices have fewer opportunities to bat around ideas, fewer assets to spend and fewer hours to devote to client relations without dramatically adversely affecting income. The relative percentage costs are greater and the tolerances for missteps are much thinner.

These smaller scaled practices need special approaches. Client relations efforts should be better integrated into billable activities, instead of being regarded as distinct. Non-billable efforts should emphasize hobbies and things the practitioners like to do. Involving lawyers' families and clients' families in client relations activities reduces pressure at the office and at home. Carving out more time from their lives for client relations activities that aren't enjoyable is problematic at best, and sure to ferment more stress.

GOOD MORNING!

This is one of the best customer satisfaction cards I have seen in a restaurant. It is simple and direct. It made me feel welcome. I could convey my

---

WE'RE GLAD YOU'RE HERE!

YOU MAKE A DIFFERENCE

What Did You Like? _____

What Didn't You Like? _____

What Would You Like? _____

Name _____ **Phone** _____

---

reactions. I was considered intelligent enough to do more than check innocuous boxes.

Hotels, restaurants, amusement parks, car dealers, airlines, toy manufacturers, department stores, temporary employment agencies, home appliance makers, sports teams, and a myriad of other businesses actively seek customer reaction to their product or service. This information is so critical to business success that the demand for it has created such occupational specialties as pollsters, surveyors, and marketing statisticians and a diverse industry of customer information seekers and analyzers. Even internet companies have installed interactive applications to obtain information to improve their businesses through greater knowledge of the customer.

Yet, generally, lawyers studiously avoid encouraging or even accepting such client opinions and reactions. Non-lawyer law firm marketing directors are insisting that such information is necessary for them to effectively contribute so more client satisfaction surveys are being utilized. Frequently lawyers aren't comfortable with this solicitation of information unless they can be assured ahead of time that client praise will be effusively pronounced. It seems many lawyers are out of sync with virtually all others who seek to sell products and services.

We laywers really aren't unique and our business practices are not independent from all other business knowledge. For the well being of their practices and profession, lawyers need to know what clients and potential clients are thinking.

WHY LAWYERS WON'T ASK

So important is customer information to businesses, they even use an apparently benign legal means to get data from purchasers of their products. Often, if you wish to activate a warranty on a product you purchased, you must complete the warranty registration which requires personal demographic data as well as where you heard of the product, the main motivator for your purchase and the place or method of purchase. Obviously this is not necessary for the warranty, but businesses recognize that it is useful for marketing.

There are as many reasons lawyers fear asking about their performance as the total of lawyers, clients, and matters combined. More accurately, there are as many as the capacity for creative rationalization can generate. Some of the more obvious spoken and unspoken reasons and excuses include the following:

- It is not professional.
- We know we've done a great job, no matter what anyone else thinks.
- We know we haven't satisfied the client and don't want to hear someone say it out loud.
- Our gut feeling is that our fees are too high (and we don't want to hear it), but we have high costs and we have a desire for a wealthy standard of living.
- There are no clear measures and, therefore, our professional results are spotty.
- Deep down we think that time expended, the basis of hourly fees, does not equate to value for the client even though they are charged on the basis of time expended.
- We wouldn't do anything differently even if we knew what the clients thought.
- Any criticism from a client, rather than a judge, is a broadside on our fragile egos.
- We have enough to do without adding this client survey nonsense and nuisance.
- It would be dangerous if my partners or shareholders ever found out what "my" clients think of me.
- Who cares what they client says? They don't understand the law and what we have to do.

Whatever the excuses, it is very shortsighted for any provider of services not to know what the consumers or clients of those services think about it, what other services are needed and, if other services were offered, which would be purchased at what cost.

I hasten to add that I am among the myopic ones because I rarely asked a client about how I was doing as a lawyer. Nonetheless, I have shamelessly pointed out the magnitude of victory or cost savings in an attempt to provoke praise for what I've done. However, I was able to conquer the fear of asking in circumstances where I had a complete victory and my bill had not yet been presented to the client. And, oh yes, the final element was sometimes a couple of drinks for me and the client to give me the courage to ask, and the client a warm, all-is-well feeling.

I readily admit I do not know the causes of or understand the disease of "I-Won't-Ask". But I shall, like many of our scientists, concentrate in this book on the cure for those who have it and a vaccination for those who have not yet contracted the malady.

IMPROVING CLIENT RELATIONS

As a lawyer in any practice setting, you may hope that this publication will provide you a specific formula for highly successful client relations. You will not find one because the truth is that such a formula would be doomed to fail. Your style, your substantive practice, your level of comfort with a particular technique, your clients, your firm, and your community all meld into a unique combination that cannot be served by a generic client relations plan. What will work in your esoteric situation is something only you can investigate, determine and implement. The best this or any book can realistically do is present a menu of ideas, suggestions and examples from which you may choose. Even then, you must realize it is a menu of choices, not recipes with particular ingredients that, when combined, will result in a spectacular dish.

Read and think about this menu. Make considered choices based on your tastes and what you are willing to pay in time, money, and effort. Sample your selections, and if they don't taste right, are ineffective, or cost too much, send those selections back and try some others. You alone are responsible for and in charge of your relations with your clients and potential clients. This is true even if you practice in a firm that has a skilled marketing director or in a corporation with excellent public relations professionals.

The best client relations programs evolve rather than emerge by miraculous revelation. All worthwhile client relations programs for individuals and organizations are written, contain systems of accountability, and include methods of measuring the success of the program. Be sure you give yourself the advantage of having these elements in your program.

There are tens of thousands of lawyers who are superb practitioners of client relations. To them our profession owes a deep debt of gratitude, for they provide some counterbalance to our less than favorable reputation. I believe these ambassadors of good client relations would be the first to assert there are ways even they could improve their client relations techniques.

Unfortunately, many lawyers have for too many years deemed many things that constitute good client relations as mundane or beneath the dignity of our profession because it smacks of buttering up the client. Simultaneously, other newer professions such as accounting, banking, insurance, financial planning, and securities underwriters have steadily eroded the business base of the legal profession by practicing effective client relations.

THE ALARM

Lawyers have unintentionally de-emphasized the reason for the profession to exist: **to resolve problems of people and organizations.** That simply can't be done without relating well to those very people and organizations. Simultaneously, the profession has defined its mission to be technically correct, to navigate the thousands of regulations, statues and cases affecting everyday business and daily personal life. This path of elevating the means (technical correctness) above the goal (resolution of problems) inevitably minimizes the people-relationship aspect of the profession. It actually removes the vehicle through which clients can come to understand and appreciate the services lawyers provide them.

The continuation of this trend into the first couple of decade of this new century will further reduce the function and usefulness of our profession. On the present course, more and more our role will shrink to calling attention to legal technicalities both before and after implementation of decisions made by others. This is a minor part compared to the lead role lawyers used to play as respected decision advisors. It is on this former starring role that clients built the legal profession. Being barred from the process of client decision making depreciates the lawyer's value to the client, undermines the stature of the legal profession, and lowers the level of satisfaction a lawyer will be able to obtain from a lifetime of work.

The most effective vehicle to reverse the decline of the legal profession and the vocational satisfaction level of lawyers is improved client relations. It's time to wake up and go to work on client relations.

CHAPTER 2

A NEW VISION OF LAW PRACTICE

Almost fifty-five years ago, long before it became popular, I recall my father telling me about the benefits of visualization. Whether I was struggling or succeeding with academics or sports, Dad advocated that I take the time to close my eyes and picture the academic material or physical moves that were necessary for academic and athletic success. Only after that was I advised to attempt implementation. When I did that, and do this even today, I am invariably more successful because I am training my mind to "see" what has to be done to accomplish the desired result.

Visualization provides a mental road map—a plan if you will, to follow. This focuses the effort expended much better than trial and error or even reactions to a circumstance. If one creates the abstract mental map, chooses to read it, and is committed to following it, one will not easily be knocked off the course to the goal by reacting to stimuli hurled by someone else or to unanticipated occurrences.

Dad's visualization process works for organizations as well as for individuals. A shared vision within an organization will energize it, create tremendous machinery and the fuel to drive it, and will result in significant, measurable progress toward the shared visualized goal.

THE PRESENT: PERSONA NON GRATA (PNG)

In many circles and to many people, lawyers are persona non grata (PNG).

Despite being PNG, we have made many changes which are beneficial to clients. We have substantially increased and refined the body of law, thereby providing more specific guidelines for legally acceptable behavior in our society; we have become faster in response through sophisticated use of electrical technical apparatus (computers, optical scanners, e-mail, and other speed-enhancing machines); we have changed the image conveyed by our offices from files and books piled high on every available surface—floor included—to an orderly, refined, upscale one; we communicate with clients more frequently by e-mailing and faxing much of what was previously conveyed in hardcopy; we bill monthly instead of only at the end of a matter so the client knows what legal services are costing as the matter continues; we delegate to the lowest-billing, qualified timekeeper; and we have helped many in the middle and upper classes survive in modern society by using a lawyer for all but the most routine situations.

With all this modernization at a time when the use of lawyers is increasing, why are we so frequently PNG? Perhaps we have created an audience, which, after seeing a lawyer's performance it is forced to attend, doesn't like the act. Why did this happen?

One explanation is that there are too many lawyers in the United States and that the lawyers make too much money. According to this theory, the lawyers' audience is predisposed to resent them.

Some years ago, the number of lawyers in the United States per 10,000 in population was about thirty, which ranks it below countries such as Syria, Japan, France, Argentina, Germany, New Zealand, and Mexico. Even in Washington, D.C.—Lawyer Heaven—there is only about one lawyer for every forty persons. Yet, the public perception must be that in the United States about a third of the population are lawyers instead of one-third of one percent (0.003).

FEE FEAR

Most news stories about lawyer fees featured relatively rare total, huge class-action fees and costs or emphasized that the gross fee revenues per lawyer in many firms rose between 85 and 90 percent. The other side of the same coin, and what has not been published generally, is that during the same decades, the overhead costs per lawyer have grown at a rate 35 to 50 percent faster than the revenue rate growth and that the fastest rise in lawyer compensation was among those with the least experience, not the experienced partners.

It seems that much of the public perception that lawyers make too much money is driven by a few newsworthy gross fees collected by plaintiffs' counsel in the grotesque personal injury, large bankruptcy and class-action fields, such as tobacco litigation. Ignored is the fact that without contingency arrangements and class actions, individuals with high-risk litigation would be denied access to the judicial system because they couldn't afford to pay hourly rates to get their claim before a jury. The public also ignores the statistics showing that when individuals have an opportunity to join a no-risk class action, they jump at the chance.

The public belief may also be fed by generalized knowledge of attorney's hourly rates ranging from $100 to over $500. Hourly rates of this magnitude are tough for the public to digest since they seem so out of proportion to hourly wage earners' rates and the salaries of management. This is on top of the public's perception that the value received for lawyers' services is not in the same ballpark as what lawyers charge. Also, many people unknowingly assume that every penny of that hourly rate or percentage fee goes into the lawyer's take-home pay.

Usually, when people need a lawyer, they feel like they are dialing 911 for help. But, unlike the 911-services provided by emergency medical teams, firefighters, and police, a lawyer's service is not rescuing or protecting a client's physical safety. Legal rescue or prevention is abstract and not usually related to a primary human need—physical security. In addition, the municipal 911 services are prepaid through taxes and voluntary contributions while the user of legal services is sent a bill after the service fact, regardless of result, except in contingent cases. These obvious differences make lawyers' services and the payment for them much more distasteful than physical security services.

Even when providing preventive legal services, lawyers are less appreciated than other professionals. Many people go to a dentist every six months for a check-up and to have their teeth cleaned. They willingly pay—granted many times dental insurance covers some or all of the cost which changes the meaning of "pay"—for these twice yearly preventive visits because it involves their physical appearance which impacts their psychological well being.

The nature of legal services does not allow for this type of client appreciation. First, not many visit a lawyer to review traffic laws to prevent an accident so as to preserve their good looks. Second, most legal services are provided after the client has done the damage and for which the client firmly believes another is at fault. Third, even with preventive legal advice, the client may believe the result could have been achieved without the lawyers—not so with the dentist. Lawyers become for them a societally imposed necessary evil. Fourth, in numerous situations, there is no way to demonstrate the value added by the lawyer before the fact, because the circumstance contemplated in drafting the document never occurred or, in the case of estate planning, the client will die before most of the value from the lawyering will occur.

None of these factors would matter to the client if the client only understood and appreciated what was being done for him, her, or it. Even when one receives a gift, true appreciation is forthcoming only if people's physical and psychological needs are being satisfied. This creates the circumstances for one to understand and appreciate what has been provided. Client recognition that these two needs have been addressed by providing legal services is particularly difficult to achieve, unless the engagement is in the criminal or family law fields.

One sure thing is that without effective client relations, true client appreciation (personally felt gratitude) will not be generated. Without a conscientious effort at client relations, lawyers' representations of clients just do not address clients' psychological needs, except in the most tangential manner. Where the technical execution of the legal issues is perfect and the relationship with the client is sterile, the client is left to figure out how to psychologically deal with success or failure. No professional will ever generate long-lasting loyalty without actively dealing with the person's psychological side in victory and defeat.

It is quite likely that lawyers are pegged PNG, not because there are too many of us or because we make too much money, but because we do not know, understand, or act to satisfy the client's true personal needs or that the circumstances under which we ply our profession prevent the same.

LAWYERS WANT OUT

Almost every survey about and conversation with lawyers clearly conveys that the dissatisfaction level among them is high and increasing.

There are many sources of lawyers' discontent. As strange as it may seem to lawyers who have been practicing for a few years, many still enter practice to pursue service ideals . . . and circumstances don't permit them. Others do it for the money . . . and they don't find it. Some seek power and influence . . . and they can't acquire it. Associates and experienced practitioners find it necessary to deny themselves the simple pleasures of family and recreation time to satisfy billable hour requirements . . . and they resent it. Many seek freedom through law practice . . . and they become imprisoned by clients' demands, law firm requirements, and financial necessities.

Add to these frustrations the changing role of a lawyer. The traditional function of a general practitioner—trusted friend and counselor—has evolved into a narrow-based technical legal specialist, a role less understood and appreciated by the client and far less satisfying for most lawyers. For those working on large class actions or corporate litigation, the workday is filled with projects, small discrete pieces of a very large plaintiff or defense puzzle, which are neither recognized nor appreciated by the team of lawyers or the client.

Coupled with these sources of discontent is the fact that to be identified as a lawyer places one on the trust scale survey below used car salespersons—sometimes this lack of status exists even within the lawyer's own family. The chance for ego-satisfying recognition from being in the legal profession has become minimal. This low rating on the "trust scale" may be caused in part by the death of legal heroes in modern society. There are no Jeffersons, Adamses, Lincolns, or Darrows whom the general public admires for their courage and principled legal stands. Regardless of cause, positive public and private approval opportunities for lawyers are so rare that they are truly virtually nonexistent.

Likewise, the rewards of law practice are shrinking. Sure, there exist the exceptions of plaintiffs' lawyers who "hit it big," and top corporate law practitioners who make "big bucks." But for most practicing associates and partners, the income growth opportunities are shrinking. Permanent staff lawyer positions, suspended somewhere in limbo between associate and partner, are becoming more common. A partnership now does not mean automatic relative wealth or even sharing in the economic growth of the firm the partner helped to create. More non-equity partnerships and permanent salaried positions are being created and rising overhead is constricting the pipe that dumps profits into the partnership distribution pool.

Since the reasons men and women enter law practice are no longer being realized, the recognition garnered as a lawyer is mostly negative, the time required to practice is expanding, and the financial rewards and prospects are relatively on a downward course, is it any wonder that many lawyers want out of the practice?

It doesn't take any deep insight to understand that the high level of dissatisfaction among lawyers who are also under increasing stress, or even on the verge of a nervous breakdown, cause them to treat clients—knowingly or unconsciously—in a manner that is less than optimal or even minimally satisfactory.

THE LETHAL COMBO

The PNG attitude of the public and clients, combined with the dissatisfaction level of many lawyers is a lethal combination for our legal profession.

The lawyers who most enjoy practice are those with the greatest client contact. Likewise, the clients who are most content with the legal services and payments they make for legal representation are those who have greatest contact with their lawyers. Yet, ironically, all of the efficiency factors influencing current law practice dictate less personal contact between lawyers and clients.

The future of the legal profession depends upon whether lawyers, law schools, and bar associations look the current discouraging facts about the legal profession squarely in the eye. Lawyers then must commit themselves and their organizations to dramatically changing the reality of our present individual professional existences and the state of our legal profession. The only way to do this is to change clients' and potential clients' attitudes about lawyers.

THE VISION

The dramatic change required to restore the stature of the legal profession and that of individual lawyers is a total orientation, unfailing commitment, and focused action toward servicing each client's needs. Unfortunately, few lawyers are trained or positioned to even define or understand a "client's needs," let alone to service them.

The law schools, courts and firms all teach by lecture or experience that lawyers should serve the "client's needs" by being technically correct in substance and process. At the same time, clients have no earthly idea that these are their "needs."

Lawyers should take an approach closer to graphic designers and advertisers. These professionals know that to sell a service or product they must focus on the needs and desire of the audience rather than the product itself. For instance, to sell an arthritis medication they don't talk about the chemical content of the pill, but rather focus on people participating in fun activities. Likewise, when selling cars they show the vehicles in beautiful locations to create the association of the product with a pleasant surrounding and ignore the cost of the automobile, gas and maintenance and the fact that people don't have the time to go to this exciting location. This type of advertising is directly appealing to the audience's psychological, rather than rational, side of their collective brains.

Generally, the approach lawyers take with clients is to describe the technical interplay of the various statutes or Internal Revenue Code provisions and rulings, couple that with the conflicting court rulings, and apply them to the client's unclear factual situation. Then we tell them the equivalent of the worst side effects of the medication and there is at least a fifty percent chance it is going to rain the whole time they are on vacation! It isn't any wonder that clients think lawyers aren't addressing or serving their needs.

To put our profession's future on a true course to a desired destination, lawyers must communicate frequently and honestly with their clients about the results desired by the clients, as well as the technical means the lawyer is using to pursue those results. Successful communication with clients requires actions well beyond lawyers merely meeting their Model Rules 1.2 and 1.4 obligations pertaining to clients' controlling the representation and lawyers' duty to inform clients. Partnering with clients involves not only doing quality legal work, but also serving other needs—like saving clients' money. We must listen like trusted friends rather than question and lecture like an intimidating law professor.

We must proactively and tenaciously put the client's interests first—even when it is to our personal or financial detriment. Lawyers have an obligation to quickly address client matters, even if the lawyer has a planned vacation pending. If the lawyer has accepted a matter which turns out to require much more time than anticipated under its flat fee arrangement, the lawyer must continue to commit the necessary time and vigorously represent the client until the matter is closed. In such circumstances, lawyers must steel themselves against concentrating on more profitable work and looking for the shortcut that is not in the best interests of the client. Daily, lawyers face and must resolve tons of prioritizing issues to assure they put the clients' interests before their own.

When a client requests a lawyer handle a new piece of work, the lawyer must ask the questions that the client should ask, but may not know enough about the legal profession to ask. The lawyers must, at least, pose these four self-queries:

1. Am I or a member of my firm truly equipped with the skill and experience to handle this matter for the client and bring it to an acceptable resolution in a cost efficient, rapid fashion?
2. Is the fee I or my firm would charge to handle this matter appropriate for the work, or is the client better off financially being represented by someone else, either within or outside the legal profession, who could reasonably be expected to competently resolve the issue at a lower cost?
3. Do I fully understand all of the client's needs legal and non-legal with regard to this matter and am I or my firm fully prepared to do all that is possible to satisfy them?

4. Am I prepared to do whatever is necessary to find out and serve the client's needs as they change during the course of representation, regardless of what unforeseen changes occur in the client's situation and in my practice?

If you cannot answer each question with an unqualified "yes," you have a client-service obligation to discuss and resolve every reservation and qualification with the client or refer the client to another service provider. Tough medicine? Yes, but our patient—the legal profession—is very, very sick as far as clients and the public are concerned.

Some very fine people who are and have been leaders in the many bar associations have diligently tried to respond to particular criticisms of the legal profession raised by a wide variety of people, including elected officials, academics, judges, and justices, as well as public interest and corporate organizations. To some degree, we, the rank and file practitioners, have responded to the call to reform. However, as long as we react to put out individual fires instead of taking the offensive by honestly analyzing our shortcomings and initiating positive steps, not much will fundamentally change. The problems of the profession will continue to attract top billing and our response will be regarded as a weak defense of the status quo . . . which will no doubt be unacceptable to our accusers and general public. Such a course of conduct should be equally unsatisfactory to us lawyers as well.

Truly, lawyers and law organizations need a new client-oriented vision of law practice. If we develop this vision, we will not be as easily thrown off course by the slings and arrows that are constantly being used against us by a myriad of attackers. Further, if that vision is truly client-oriented and executed to each client's benefit, clients will voluntarily become lawyers' allies in defending not only our work, but also our integrity as a profession and as persons engaged in the practice of law.

OF JOY AND PAIN

One of the outstanding human beings and practicing legal thinkers I know is Jerome J. Shestack of Philadelphia, Pennsylvania, a former President of the American Bar Association. In the commencement address he delivered to the Class of 1980 of the University of Pennsylvania Law School, titled, "Of Joy and Pain in Our Profession," he provided what I believe to be excellent guidance for a vision of reviving the profession of legal service. Since we know all too well the pain of our profession, I have highlighted below excerpts from Jerry's address that to this day reflect our present state and opportunity and some of his vision of joy, which can be ours:

"You have reason to be joyful. And proud. You have traveled an arduous, sometimes even torturous path to reach this point. You have endured the angst of your first year in law school, which surely will remain vivid in memory, withstanding even the blurring of time and nostalgia. You have been peppered by acerbic tutors, salted with Socratic reasoning, spiced by the fierce competition of colleagues. And you have survived; appetites still fresh, honed intellectually, confident in your abilities and ambitions, anxious to conquer. Savor well this day. Like Goethe, we are tempted to say: "Oh moment, stay, thou art so fair."

But the moment cannot stay, or the world would end. And so you move on from the calm of your academic pond into the sea of the law's realpolitik. There is beauty in that sea, and richness. But pain and turmoil, too.

You will no longer deal with abstract issues and hypotheticals, with cases frozen in print, passionless and painless. Now you will be concerned with conflict between men and women involving the very stuff of their lives. It is an invidious business, as Llewellyn said, this shuffling, this gambling, this checker play with human rights. It is a troublesome business, this adversary system, to serve as the mouthpiece of the litigant who wins only as he tramples others down. Small wonder that the trampled do not love the lawyer. But neither do the winners. For often you will win not by affirming the justice of your cause, but through process and procedure and technique. Your clients may pay tribute to your success, but tribute of the kind one pays to the trickster or practitioner of the black art. Better than no tribute, perhaps, but painful still to be so often misunderstood.

To be unloved is perhaps not so bad if you know you have made the right choice. But if you are thoughtful and sensitive, you cannot even be confident of that. Often, you will be buffeted by conflicting cross currents, the hard choices between personal security and moral responsibility, knowledge and privacy, profit and public interest, victory and honor.

The long and short of it is that you have chosen a profession that will involve you in the antagonisms and ambiguities of human aspiration. It is not only choosing God over Caesar; often the question is which is which.

I have no answer to the moral dilemmas of our profession. It will be painful to wrestle with them. And it should be painful.

But if there is pain in the profession, there is also joy. Indeed, I believe, more joy than pain. There are few callings in the world, "Learned Hand" once wrote, that give greater opportunity for satisfaction to one's self and that are of more benefit to one's fellows. I want to speak to you today of some of the joys. Joys that I have found. That I hope you will find.

In your lifetime, you will have a thousand cases, perhaps more; some of them major, some trifling, most transitory. They will earn money for you. For some of you, a great deal of money. And that will give you certain power and certain freedom. It is not a small matter.

But if affluence and power are all you seek and all you gain, I believe you will find little joy in your profession. It all depends on one's vision, but I believe the joy comes from being involved in the drama of humanity. I hope you will see that each case is warm with life, each strong with expectation, each involved in human aspiration. In every case, there is a human struggle with all of its hope, its futility, its wonder, its grandeur. And in the background, pressing or elusive, heady or faint, but always present, is the duty to justice. The melding of human concerns and the law, I think, is part of the worthwhileness and joy of our profession.

It seems to me that where we who are practicing law get in trouble with our clients, our profession, the public, and ourselves is that we focus far too intensely on the law and neglect the human side. The eternal truth is that "the melding of human concerns and the law . . . is part of the worthwhileness and joy of our profession."

THE PREMISE

The rest of this book rests on this premise: we can be more helpful to our clients while rehabilitating ourselves and our legal profession if we put the "human concerns" first through client relations. The answer to lawyers' and the legal profession's dilemma surely is servicing each client's perceived needs.

CHAPTER 3

SOS—SAME OLD "STUFF"

NICE ISN'T ENOUGH

After your entree has been served in a restaurant and you have started to partake of the food, what is the next thing that almost invariably happens in your dining experience? Right, the server comes over and asks, "How is everything?" or "Is everything OK?"

Can you remember the first time this happened to you? I vaguely do. My recollection is that I said to Mary, my wife, "Isn't she nice!" My reaction was that this is a nice place—they care whether we think everything is to our liking.

Now, when I am asked the same question, I give a mechanical response and do not have the same feeling that the restaurant really cares what we think about the food and service. In fact, in some establishments the same question, or some minor variant of it, is asked several times during a meal. Maybe you recall these incessant questions interrupting your meal or a serious conversation. The typical reaction to this break in what you want to be doing is to wish the person would quit bothering you with that same old stuff and go away.

The point is that the same old stuff (SOS) in client relations, like asking a client to play golf, may be part of what you need to do, but it is not enough to be successful in today's world of competitive legal practice.

EXAMPLES OF LEGAL "SOS"

Although some of the law schools are addressing practice management issues, we must still rely principally on anecdotal information to define SOS in client relations.

The restaurant server's inquiry was most effective when it was novel, it didn't interrupt something that was more important to the diner, and a sincere response was desired. Meaningful information between the parties was being exchanged at a time and in a manner that was desirable to and appreciated by both parties.

Let's examine how the traditional client-relations stuff stacks up against these standards and explore some modernized modifications to make them more effective.

BROCHURES

When they were first introduced, law firm brochures were thought to be the key to bringing new clients in the doors of established law firms. Apparently, we thought that folks picked lawyers based on the dull copy and posed athletic-type team pictures of smiling lawyers that are featured in most brochures. This is clear evidence of lawyers who are out of touch.

Many brochures ballyhoo the legal capacity of the firm in such generalizations that no real information is conveyed to the client or potential client. If your firm has a brochure, read it. Ask yourself, if you presented such an argument to a jury, would a jury of reasonable people be convinced that you are with an outstanding firm? I submit that in almost all instances, the truthful answer would be "no."

The problem is that tooting one's own horn without independent facts to back up the claims, rolls off clients like water off a duck's back. They hear and read that stuff hundreds of times every day in advertising and in the political coverage. Think about how frequently even occasional consumers of legal services are exposed to such pitches on television, on radio, and in the print media and reject them without so much as a single thought being given to the pitch. If someone needs a lawyer's assistance, that someone's choice is surely going to be influenced by factors other than generalizations created by some copywriter.

The roster of lawyers found in some brochures is likewise ineffective communication. There are a couple of exceptions. First, people may recognize a lawyer they have met or the lawyer may happen to be a daughter or son of a neighbor, friend, or acquaintance. Second, if a lawyer in the firm happens to have a recognizable name like Clarence

Darrow, an unknowledgeable person may think that a famous name means he or she will get excellent legal representation. Unless there is independent name recognition, the likelihood of a person choosing a lawyer or firm as a result of seeing a person's name printed in a brochure is nil.

Whether it was for a high school yearbook, publicity for a charitable event, or a wedding, almost everyone has posed for a picture. Therefore, readers of law firm brochures know that such photographic images do not represent the reality of the event, let alone the real everyday world of law practice. The reaction to obviously staged brochure pictures showing grinning lawyers at work has got to be, "Give me a break!" The public does not know or understand how lawyers work, but they sure know it is not as depicted in most brochures.

Pictures in brochures of well-designed, impressive offices often have an undesirable impact on readers. Unsophisticated purchasers of legal services are often intimidated by imposing facades. Sophisticated users of services sometimes react by thinking, "I wouldn't spend that kind of money on my office; I wonder how they pay for that? Oh, I know, with the money the firm charges clients like me."

Unfortunately, brochures were the mainstream legal practice's attempt to stick a toe in the water of advertising. When the Supreme Court put a stamp of acceptability on lawyer advertising, great numbers of established law firms vowed not to do "that"—but they thought they should be doing something. A safer, more respectable approach was to "advertise" only among their clients or in their office with a brochure.

People involved with designing their firm's brochure often agonize over the proposed copy. "We can't say that;" or "Marketing Consultant, you don't understand—it isn't professional—we are a profession, not a common business;" or "We really need to put a footnote in the brochure explaining that point" could well have been something you said or heard. This editorial fussing can destroy the potential positive reaction to a brochure by converting it into a meaningless recitation of points irrelevant to the client and potential client.

There is obviously a place for law firm brochures in client relations. Before having one designed, the firm must think about what it wants to accomplish with the brochure and then determine what is to be put in the brochure that would cause clients to purchase legal services. Engagement of a graphic designer for this process usually reaps far more benefit than the money sown for the consultation. One must also be prepared to accept the possible answer that a brochure will not be able to bring about the desired result. In that case, it is an unnecessary waste of money to produce and distribute a brochure.

NEWSLETTERS

Some end-of-the-year holiday letters go on about a relative's or friend's family's incredible achievements during the previous year, many of which exceed those accomplished by Superman or Wonder Woman. Recall your reaction to those boasting claims. Law practice newsletters or case updates that brag about case results or boast about lawyers accomplishments are guaranteed to elicit the same negative reaction.

On the other hand, setting out neat, esoteric legal points, advice or case summaries with citations that have no widespread application is also a waste of paper and money. You or your firm may have achieved a stupendous legal victory for a client by a creative and unique argument, but do your other clients and potential clients care if they cannot use that precedent because it does not apply to their situation? If the client or potential client does not have an identical or very similar problem, the information is good for the firm's fisherman's bragging rights to other lawyers, but is irrelevant to the client's world. If irrelevant, it cannot influence the client's decision.

Some lawyers become so enthralled with their success with a technical or procedural legal victory that they fail to realize others will not understand or even care. Proof of this is within your own experience. Surely there have been occasions when you have enthusiastically described a legal victory to your spouse, a friend, or even a fellow lawyer and, to your dismay, noticed a dull glaze fogging the listener's eyes or received a cursory, "That's nice" response. Similarly, newsletter information must be relevant to the reader, not to the lawyer or law firm.

When designing a newsletter, you must ask and answer:

1. What do we want to accomplish by sending this newsletter?
2. Who is the intended reader?
3. What will the reader find interesting and practical?
4. How can we measure whether we are achieving what we set out to accomplish?

If the intended recipient of the newsletter is an individual client to whom you wish to offer tax and estate advice, the language, tone, material, and whole approach must be significantly different than if you are trying to build a RICO (Racketeer Influenced and Corrupt Organizations) defense practice among corporate executives and general counsel. All too frequently, the same plain vanilla approach to newsletters is uniformly used for all intended audiences. Such homogeneity is destined to fail to communicate to significant segments of the population receiving the letter.

Too many law firms decide they need to have a newsletter, and so they do. This is a dreadful waste of resources. If you do not know what you want to accomplish by publishing and distributing a newsletter, do not do it. Each issue of a newsletter should have a distinct purpose. The more specific the purpose of a newsletter, the greater the chance a law firm will obtain a return on its newsletter efforts and expenditures. Some of the purposes of newsletter issues could be

- To inform clients about changes in the law—a charitable service;
- To scare clients with legal horror tales into calling you with new business;
- To parade the firm's recent legal achievements before its clients;
- To make clients feel good—pictures and stories about clients (only with their express permission, of course);
- To familiarize clients with the lawyers, paralegals, secretaries, and staff of the firm with copy and pictures;
- To alert clients to pending legislation and suggest they see you before it is too late; and
- To give practical legal advice so the client will not have to call a lawyer for routine matters.

Without a clear purpose, a newsletter has no reason for being, unless it is merely to "keep up with the Joneses," which is as poor a reason for a law firm to do something as it is for a person.

Some of the most effective newsletters are purchased by solos and firms from legal newsletter services. These are "personalized" with a message about your particular practice. If done well, purchasing this service guarantees a high quality newsletter with very little time commitment. If you go this route, be sure to read each issue as soon as it comes out for you may receive a call about a story in the newsletter.

By defining the purpose for each issue of a newsletter, you will be able to assess whether the issue has been successful. For example, if the issue is intended to generate calls about real estate tax property assessments, you can tabulate the number of pertinent calls received. This data facilitates an accurate evaluation of an issue's effectiveness. Measuring in this way over a period of time will build knowledge of how to publish a more effective newsletter.

Failure to devise measurements by which the firm may assess the effectiveness of the newsletter in achieving its purpose is as irresponsible as not balancing a checkbook. Money is likely to flow out sans any return until your budget has been exhausted or exceeded. The measurements do not have to be perfect, but they should have to exist and be analyzed.

For instance, if the newsletter seeks to attract existing clients to use the firm's services in a particular legal specialty, all existing clients who, after publication of that newsletter, request services in that area should be asked if they read the pertinent newsletter article. If they did, inquiry should be made as to what in the article provoked them to action—to request legal services. Records of such responses should be maintained and then analyzed to improve the newsletter client-relations program. In this fashion, a firm may determine if it is receiving sufficient return on its investment of time and money on newsletters.

Except for sensationalized trials that exhibit human trauma, clients are not generally interested in the law as an abstract study. But, if they are told and understand how a law or case applies to their lives or to everyday business situations, their curiosity is often aroused.

If you have ever seen a gizmo on the shelf of a hardware store and had no idea of its use, you probably did not purchase it. If you took it off the shelf or pointed to it and asked the clerk, "What's that for?" you may have put your money down either for the gizmo's practical or novel characteristics. Similarly, if a legal precept has great relevance to a client, but the client does not know or understand that, the client will not buy the legal service. The newsletter must answer the client's question, "What's that for?"

Sending sophisticated corporate clients, especially lawyers in corporate law departments, newsletters that quote or paraphrase recent Supreme or appellate court decisions in the federal and state courts is usually a waste. Think about it. Does the firm really believe that corporate counsel are unaware of these decisions or that twenty other firms have not included them in their newsletters? The conscientious corporate counsel will have already read the decision, and the lackadaisical corporate counsel will not read a newsletter with decisions that he or she did not feel compelled to read in the advance sheets or from the internet. No corporate counsel, known to me, are anxiously opening their mail every day looking for a law firm's newsletter for the "latest" law.

The key to a newsletter clients will appreciate is practical advice. Telling the reader what to do about the information conveyed is more important than the underlying information. No matter how compelling the legal news is to lawyers, writing in the concluding paragraph or newsletter article that admonishes the client to call the author is simply not sufficient to satisfy the practical advice requirement. You need to finish with something that provokes the reader into seeing a lawyer.

Energizing the client to get out of an easy chair to call or visit a law firm is best accomplished by the client understanding the financial impact of the newsletter article. It is hard for newsletters to motivate people to set aside pressing business or demands on personal time to make an appointment with a lawyer. Frequently, newsletter items recite a gargantuan verdict or a superficially unjust result and suggest you come right in to protect yourself against these monsters—juries and opposing counsel. That motivates some people, usually if the factual situation is similar to their own circumstances. If the newsletter column sets out how the lawyer can save the client real money now, rather than protect against a remote potential disaster, the client has a much greater sense of immediate need for the lawyer. Restructuring businesses, adjusting to reduced personnel, postponing corporate taxes and saving employee health-care costs are a few examples of client motivating topics.

TAKING A CLIENT TO DINNER

Business people spend many nights a year going out to dinner with both colleagues and customers. Another dinner out that has any tinge of obligation is likely to be a very undesirable event for business people, even if it is with a host as scintillating as a lawyer.

Lawyers, as part of their firm's client-development program, may have an obligation to entertain a given number of times a month or to spend a client-entertainment budget. Early in my career, our small firm had a monthly entertainment budget for each lawyer. The senior partner became upset when we associates were not using the allocated amount because he believed if we spent the money it would bring in new clients. Thus, when it got toward the end of the month and the budget amount was not used, I took friends to dinner. Not much business came out of those occurrences, but we made the senior partner happy and sure had a good time with friends! If the lawyer-host feels compelled to "entertain," in most cases that emotion will show, conversation will be strained and the relationship damaged rather than enhanced.

For another night out to be an effective client-relations tool, it must be a desirable gathering for both the client and the lawyer. If the lawyer does not enjoy the company of the client, the firm should not strain the client relationship by insisting the lawyer have an obligatory dinner.

Characteristics of a good lawyer-client dinner include anticipation of an interesting conversation in a pleasant place with good food, the same as when you choose to dine with friends. By the way, this does not translate to the fanciest place in town. One of the more successful lunches I had was taking the client to a cheap, hole-in-the-wall Cambodian restaurant that I had previously enjoyed. The client had spent time working in Asia and had previously commented that he loved Asian food. When we walked in the restaurant, the client stuck his nose in the air, sniffed and said with obvious delight, "It smells right." We had a great lunch and conversation about his travels, which cemented the client relationship for less than $12.

If the main purpose of getting together is to give legal advice, exchange useful information, or close a deal, it is not a client relations event: it is a business meeting with a dinner. Confusion between the two types of encounters, either on the part of the lawyer or the client, usually results in disappointment. The evening becomes a failure, or at least not a success. The lingering image of failure and disappointment will be conjured up when the next invitation for either type of gathering is issued.

Combining support for a worthy charitable cause and a client dinner or entertainment is a good move. Often this two for one purpose for the outing helps the lawyer gain an additional night at home. This is a terrific, cost-effective way to assist charities while simultaneously building your practice. The lawyer-host need not be concerned about the atmosphere of the place or the quality of the food. A nice touch for charitable evenings is to invite the client to your home for conversation and cocktails before the dinner or for a nightcap afterward.

Make a list of the clients you enjoy as people or who you would really like to know on a personal basis. Think about the type of food, the atmosphere, and the place they might like to dine. If you do not know the person well enough to make this determination, call and ask the client or client's secretary what type of food is enjoyed. Lawyers are not perceived to have all of the answers, except perhaps by themselves. Asking will be appreciated because it reflects that the lawyer cares about the client.

Sometimes it is fun to eat at a place neither of you have been—that joins both the lawyer and client in a culinary adventure. Even if the meal is dreadful, a common nauseating experience can provide a future reference for a laugh and a bond.

Those clients and potential clients who aren't ones you would like to know better personally should be left off your clients-to-take-to-dinner list. Both you and the client will feel more comfortable eating by yourselves or confining your eating to business meetings. Nothing is static; people may move from one list to the other. The critical thing is not to get the perceptions and lists mixed up. If you do, you will probably damage your lawyer-client relationship.

GOLF AND OTHER SPORTING EVENTS

First, let me say a word about women and sports. Men, do not exclude them because you think they are not skilled or interested. Women, do not confine your sporting events to others of your own sex. Once out-dated stereotypes are set aside—including a male's fear of being beaten at a sporting event by a female—the opportunities for developing client relations through sports are just as great for heterogeneous outings as they are for homogeneous ones.

Participatory sports like golf, racquet games, and jogging can pro-vide a fine vehicle for building a relationship with a client. Golf proba-bly offers the greatest opportunity for conversation and thus the best chance of affecting, by either enhancing or damaging, the lawyer's con-nection with the client. However, one must be cautious in all participa-tory sporting encounters. If one party is extremely competitive on the course or court and the other is just out for a fun time, the game could become torturous for one or both.

Sensitivity to the client's approach to the game, regardless of the final score, is essential. An assumption that a businessperson who is energized by competition in the business world would automatically be so inclined in a sport could be fatal to a client relationship. It would be similar to a parent-child relationship where the parent pushes a reluctant child in a sport the child neither enjoys nor feels able to sat-isfy the parents' standards of performance. The object in both instances is to build the relationship, not count the strokes or points.

Spectator sports offer another opportunity to develop a better client relationship. Athletic talent is not required and understanding of the game may be limited. The sporting event can provide a means for bridg-ing communication and personal gaps. A new team in town or a new stadium or arena often piques the client's curiosity even when the client isn't particularly interested in the sport. The opportunity for con-versation exists during the game or match and it is not limited to the game being played. The game is the stated reason for getting together; however, a better personal relationship should be the result.

A friend of mine uses tickets to sporting events to build client rela-tions in a way most of us do not even contemplate. If he knows a client's child enjoys hockey, he offers both of his hockey tickets to the client and provides a parent/child outing. Likewise, he has offered the sporting tickets to two managers from a single company client. These managers were not familiar with hockey, wanted to go, but were con-cerned about asking dumb questions. They were delighted, however, to have the hockey experience together without, what they felt would be an opportunity to make fools of themselves.

Although my friend was not present at these hockey games, by pro-viding the experience to the client, he strengthened the bond with the client. He discovered that some clients appreciate, remember and talk about these events more favorably and longer than when they to go to an event with him. I always believed lawyers had to be present to develop the client relationship—such is not the case.

MIXING AND MATCHING CLIENTS

It's hard for lawyers to believe there are times when business people and other clients would enjoy each other's company, and the lawyer's more, if the lawyer contingent at the event were in the minority. In fact, with properly matched clients, they might strike a mutually beneficial commercial connection. Even better, one client might sing the praises of the lawyer-host or lawyer-hostess to the other client. This endorsement will be far more credible than the attorney singing exactly the same song solo.

Two guidelines for selecting clients for such an event are

- Match personalities
- Mix businesses

Clients who have symbiotic businesses usually work best because they have some similar experiences and concerns. Inviting business competitors to the same event is unwise. You might lose both as clients.

One skill lawyers must develop for such occasions is the ability to conversationally stay out of the way so as not to impede the clients' getting to know each other. At the same time, the hosting lawyer must make sure the conversation keeps moving along and is interesting. The lawyer becomes a facilitator, not the spotlighted performer.

WHEN "SOS" WORKS

The same old stuff works when an event has become a tradition. One of my former partners, whose father was a school district superintendent, has a clear and pleasant childhood recollection of the school solicitor's annual picnic at the solicitor's home. His father, top school administrators, school board members, and their families were invited. Annual golf outings, holiday parties, cards or gifts, and annual legal update seminars are other examples of client-relations traditions.

What constitutes a tradition? In a client's mind, it doesn't take long to create one. The same event two years in a row qualifies as a tradition for most clients. If, for financial or other reasons, the firm decides not to hold the traditional event, clients should be given an explanation. Otherwise, clients will assume the traditional event was held and they were not invited. Obviously, this does not create a desirable client state of mind.

Clients may view not holding the traditional event as a permanent cancellation. The firm's explanation for not having it this year may have to be creative. It's not in the best interests of client relations to say, "The firm is hurting for money so we aren't partying this year." That idea may convince the client that he or she is a fool to continue engaging the firm or the solo when apparently so many other clients have abandoned that ship. A more positive spin, and one that is just as truthful, could be, "The firm has decided to pursue other client development avenues this year, but if we re-institute the traditional event in the future, we surely will invite you and hope you will come."

SUMMARY

The same old stuff in client relations can work well. But it's a mistake to assume it is working well. Remember, clients are likely to be complimentary even if they did not have a good time. Be sensitive to the client's desires. It is oh-so-easy to slip comfortably into doing the same old stuff and get no return or have a net loss for your client-relations efforts and money.

The truth is that you need to do more than the SOS. What you need to do will vary from solo to solo, firm to firm and lawyer to lawyer within the firm, corporation, or government. How to decide what to do beyond the SOS is what the rest of this book is about.

CHAPTER 4

WHAT THE CLIENT SEES

As lawyers, we want to be regarded by others based on our legal abilities and stature in our community. As people, just like others, we make initial judgments based on the stimuli from our five senses, rather than on abstract concepts such as legal ability.

When you first visit someone in their house, condominium or apartment, part of your reaction to the person is formed by the surroundings in which they have chosen to live. This goes beyond location and includes the style and condition of the building, the furnishings, the details of the accessories they have chosen to place in their abode, and even whether the place is orderly. The observations and instant impression come from what a person wears.

Lawyers who pay more attention to items other than legal ability and community stature accelerate the success of their client relations program.

THE OFFICE

"Don't judge a book by its cover," is good advice, but is unlikely to be followed, any more when you visit where someone lives than when a client visits your office. This is especially for the client's office visit.

Bookstore marketers know we judge books by their covers all the time. Examine the intriguing illustrations and photographs on book covers, the colors used and the clever titles. Their purpose is to attract you to the cover and entice you to select and buy that book instead of the others on the same shelf.

So how nice does your cover—your office—have to be? The answer is, nice enough. It shouldn't be too eclectic, too elegant or too shabby. Your preference in decor is far less important to the client than the "feel" of the office. It should appear to be a professional's office, feel welcoming, and function efficiently.

If you sublease, you are somewhat painted with the same brush as your landlord. Clearly, your clients will also attribute your landlord's tastes and office appearance to you. This could be beneficial or detrimental to your practice. No matter who picked the paint color or wallpaper in the public areas of your office, the client will assume this work environment reflects your personality. When lawyers decorate their offices, they should keep the clients in mind, rather than exclusively decorating to their own taste.

There are different levels of "nice." "Nice" for the areas which clients visit is far different from what is "nice" for the storage closet. Similarly, your work area may have books upholstering the chairs and stacks of papers creating an obstacle course on the carpet, but if you don't see clients in your office, this may be "nice" enough for you. By the same token, a reception area with years of old magazines scattered on chairs and dirty coffee cups sitting on tables is not "nice" enough.

Dual-purpose areas of the office must be kept to the standards acceptable to your clients. When I was in a two-lawyer partnership, our library also served as our conference room. I'm not sure that law schools actually teach students to leave books lying about on tables, but the habit is well ingrained in virtually every law clerk and attorney. Although I had acquired that practice, I became very upset when someone else left the books they used on the library table when I was going to meet a client in that room. Note, I wasn't out of sorts about the strewn books, if a client wasn't scheduled. Unfortunately, my partner and our law clerk had no idea about when I had an appointment with a client because I didn't communicate that information. Also unfortunately, that didn't stop me from being upset with them.

Clients don't conclude that you have been working hard because they see books and papers randomly distributed on all flat surfaces in your office. Instead, they conclude that your untidiness will be carried over into sloppy legal work. That may not be logical or accurate, but it is true. Remember, when clients see your legal product, they usually are unable to judge its quality—so they form judgments based on things within their experiences. Certainly neatness and orderliness, or the lack thereof, is within clients' experiences.

When thinking about the degree of "nice" for client areas, don't neglect to consider that clients are likely to use a restroom and may want to make a private phone call. Not infrequently, when I had a client meeting in our dual-purpose library, the client wanted to place a telephone call. Since we saved money by not installing a phone in the library, I had to escort the client to my office. Mining for the phone beneath mountains of papers was an embarrassment to me and, I'm sure, a shocking revelation to clients. It is not the image I wished to convey.

Oftentimes, work areas may be visible to visiting clients. Even if your personal office is presentable and used to meet clients, they will see everything between the main entry and your office. Your secretary or assistant's work area outside your office is likely to be noted. There is no need to have the work areas meet the same neatness standards as reception areas. What is more impressive to clients is for work areas to reflect efficient operations. Orderly stacks of papers and staff members diligently attending to their duties with sufficient work area and adequate equipment will accomplish that. Lawyers could save money by creating a sweatshop appearance, but advisable that is not.

Just as you may do from time to time in your home, consider giving tours to clients visiting your offices for the first time. Highlights should include introductions to whomever will be assisting on the client's work. High-tech machines may be impressive to some clients and a matter of fact to others.

Every client will be interested in how technology will be utilized in servicing the client's matters. This explanation is far more important than looking at a bland gray box with a screen. Telling and showing the client about the technology for calendaring, automatic reminders to update estate plans, renewals for licenses and patents, alerts for court filings in pending cases, legal research database access, and tickling contract consultations with the client to prepare to give sixty-day collective bargaining termination notices will all be impressive to the client, as long as they are relevant to that client's work.

One reason that this evaluation of periodically advisable or required reviews or actions is so appreciated by clients is that it reassures them that their attorney will not forget to take care of their business. This removes some concern and worry from the client. Interestingly, it also creates a sort of reliance by the client on the attorney to meet deadlines, which in turn makes it less likely that the client will change attorneys. Finally, by taking this reminder function from the client, the attorney provides added value without additional cost.

These all work together to build trust and thus the client-to-lawyer connection. Don't fail the client on even the optional target dates, such as producing corporate minutes. For if you do miss a time commitment to a client, you fail yourself and your practice. This oversight undermines client trust.

Other possible stops on the office tour that are frequently available, even in small offices, are fireproof files for estate plans and litigation war rooms. If you are anticipating remodeling your offices or moving to larger quarters, clients are usually interested in your plans. You can show them drawings and describe how this reflects the growth in your practice and tell why you'll be able to serve them better in the new location.

A law office is not just a place for lawyers and staff to work. It is also a means for clients to connect with lawyers and a client relations opportunity. Don't miss this two-for-one opportunity to strengthen your practice.

THE LAWYER'S CLOTHES

While clothes don't make the whole person, they are significant in creating first and continuing impressions. Some will react by saying if clients can't see beyond what I wear, that is their problem. That may work at the university or if you are in the very top echelon of practicing attorneys, but for most of us this is our problem, not the client's.

You must honestly admit that when you see a person on the street in dirty rags, flamboyant colors, or an extraordinary amount of exposed skin, you immediately take note and usually form an opinion about that person that is hard to change. Many factions openly recognize that clothes make a difference. The other historic professions of clergy and medicine are expected to dress in certain ways. Whole industries calculatingly create customer impressions by regulating clothes—the uniforms of the military, airlines, fast food outlets, and the waitstaff in restaurants are examples.

The clothes lawyers wear matter to the client. Sure, the appropriateness of lawyers' clothing varies with the area of the country, the type of practice and the client. But, contrary to the opinion of some, it does matter. The client's impression of the lawyer wearing a bright sport shirt, big print slacks and flashy jewelry will be different in major metropolitan cities from that elicited in tourist destinations. Think of what impression you want your client to have and how your attire might assist the client in forming that impression.

Dressing as a lawyer used to be easy: dark suit, white shirt and conservative tie for men, and a dark dress or business suit for women. Clothing the lawyer is simple no more. In this era of "casual" there are numerous choices. Traditional, casual, and business casual dress all mean different things to some and the same thing to others. I think we all agree that shorts and flip-flops aren't appropriate for a law office. Beyond that, how should lawyers choose what to wear?

In short, wear what the client wants you to wear. There is widespread acceptability of casual dress among lawyers working with dot-coms and high-tech companies. People in those companies are used to seeing and respecting co-workers in casual dress. Caution must be exercised, however. Even among those who say you can't trust anyone over 30, a 55 year old lawyer looks pretty ridiculous wearing a tight-fitting outfit that is normally only worn by those under 30. Putting those clothes on an older body will not fool anyone into thinking the lawyer is under thirty. Besides, many of the high-tech firms now recognize the value of experience and are hiring older people to be their chief executive officers (CEOs). The way your client dresses is not necessarily the way your client wants her or his lawyer to dress.

Parameters useful in assisting you in selecting your lawyering wardrobe include what the client expects and what brings the client to your office. Basically, the client is seeking your help with a matter the client can't handle. Your client relations goal is to generate confidence in clients that you can help them by everything the client sees and in everything you do. When your sink backs up or toilet overflows, if your plumber shows up in business casual or a traditional suit, this undermines your confidence in that particular plumber. You expect and want your plumber to look like a plumber. Your potential and actual client expect to pay you a lot of money, so you need to dress to meet their expectations and look like you can effectively help them.

Your attire alone doesn't totally control the clients' impressions. Clients also observe the clothes worn by the office staff. Many offices have adopted the policy of casual all the time, if the individual is not meeting with clients. Put yourself in your client's position observing you in a traditional business suit and the others in with open collars and khakis. Reactions are as varied as, "Isn't it nice my lawyer dressed up for me" to "Who's my lawyer trying to kid? This is just more evidence that all lawyers are insincere." Or, if you dress casually to meet a "dot-com" client and the client sees people running around the office in traditional business suits, that's not really going to help you connect with the client or generate confidence in your office.

I've seen lawyers so lacking in confidence in what they are wearing that they constantly tug at their tie or smooth their slacks over their thighs or hardly breathe in a tighter fitting polo shirt. Whatever you choose to wear, you must feel comfortable. Your observed discomfort is likely to be interpreted by the worried client as stemming from the legal matter before you. This would not be good.

Cinderella lamented that she didn't have anything to wear to the ball when invited by the prince. She wasn't going to the ball in the rags she wore when she cleaned the hearth. Why? It couldn't have been the prince; he had already seen her in rags. She wouldn't go inappropriately dressed because others would regard her poorly. Cinderella wanted to make a good impression on people she didn't even know and not embarrass the one she did know, the prince. On the other hand, political candidates who are known to dress formally, look ill-at-ease on television dressed in just-bought farm duds. In both situations, the protagonists are attempting to create an impression of themselves in other people through their clothes. Like it or not, others form impressions of lawyers by what the lawyers wear.

In the end, it isn't whether the clothes are comfortable or matching the clients' style of dress, but whether the lawyer is personally comfortable in the clothes she or he wears and the client isn't uncomfortable. If the lawyer isn't comfortable—regardless of the cause—the client or potential client will pick up on it. It is virtually impossible to project confidence if your outfit makes you concerned or uncomfortable. Jurors, who are farther away from lawyers than clients in a meeting, pick up these level-of-comfort vibes even when all the lawyers are in suits. Your clients will all the more readily pick up these vibes sitting across your desk or conference table.

Sometimes, you feel you are really dressed appropriately and you spill soup on your tie, get your blouse soaked in the rain, or grease on your jacket changing your tire. Does this make a difference to other people? Absolutely. Evidence of that is abundant from the times your spouse and others who care about you discretely brush, dab, or wipe their hand on their shoulders, pearly teeth or clean face to indicate that you need to remove a dusting of dandruff from your shoulder, a piece of spinach from your front teeth, or glob of marinara sauce from your chin.

If you notice your outfit looks like it should be in the cleaners instead of on your body, it is best to acknowledge that and explain the circumstances to the client. I remember, during the course of an important new client meeting, noticing a blob of spittle on the front of the right shoulder of my best looking suit that I had worn to impress. It was dried so not to be removable by a casual wipe of my handkerchief. Because of its size, the new client couldn't have missed it. I was mortified and feared that the conclusion would be that I slobbered a lot. I decided it was best to point it out and give an explanation, since no doubt it had already attracted the attention of the client. At a break in the discussion, I exclaimed my embarrassment at the evidence showing I had burped one of our children just before I left home for the meeting. This admission actually provoked a friendly discussion, person to person as opposed to lawyer with client. The remainder of the meeting had a much more warmth.

SEEING IS BELIEVING

Lawyers are challenged to convey visible signs of trust and confidence to clients for there is not much their clients can see that would provide clients the confirmation they seek. While the lawyers' work is sometimes visible in court, during negotiations and in words on paper, practicing law remains chiefly an invisible, intellectual process. Prospective and new clients don't even have a limited opportunity to "see" a lawyer's work.

This may be why most lawyers are so focused on the result, rather than the process, to create good client impressions. It may also explain the bragging and exaggerating so many lawyers use when describing a result obtained. The chief flaws in this approach are results that are often independent from the quality of the lawyer's effort and people don't like braggarts.

We all form first, and often lasting, impressions on what we see. Since the client can see so very little of what the lawyer does or will do for the prospective client, impressions—good and bad—created by the lawyer's behavior, by the office, and by clothes that are seen by the client take on far greater importance than in most other occupations. Those impressions have an impact on the clients' perception of and relations with the lawyer. The lawyer should do everything possible to have the resulting image be positive and compliment the quality of service provided.

CHAPTER 5

WE'RE GLAD YOU'RE HERE!

How frequently have you had a client enter your office and say to you, "I'm really glad to be here"? The answer is probably never, unless the police were in hot pursuit.

Obviously, one reason this does not occur is that when a person or corporation engages a lawyer it is usually as a last resort or to handle a matter that is not understood by the client. The amazing phenomenon is that even after a lawyer has obtained an extraordinary result for a client, the return visit of the client on another legal problem still does not elicit this greeting to the lawyer.

A person—and all clients are persons whether they are individuals or corporations—usually will not enthusiastically and sincerely greet another unless there is confidence that the feeling is mutual. We attorneys must be cognizant of what we are projecting to clients. It is critical that we attorneys convey to clients "we're glad you're here."

A TYPICAL CLIENT RECEPTION

Let's listen in to a typical greeting and conversation in a lawyer's reception area. The client has been waiting a minimum of ten minutes after the time set for the client's appointment. (Note well it is the client's appointment time, not the lawyer's schedule or emergency that is important.)

[Client, dressed in a coat and tie, is sitting down in a heavily cushioned chair. The male lawyer arrives in the waiting area in a tie, but without the *coat to his suit. The female lawyer arrives in formal business attire, a business suit.]*

Lawyer:	Hi. How are you? I got tied up on the phone on an important matter.
Client:	Oh, that's okay.
Lawyer:	What's the weather doing outside?
Client:	About the same as this morning.
Lawyer:	It was sure nice yesterday. I was out on the course at the club with Mr. Big. I was really hitting them.
Client:	Had a good time, huh?
Lawyer:	Come on into the conference room and sit down.
Client:	Thanks.
Lawyer:	Do you want a cup of coffee?
Client:	Yes, thanks.
Lawyer:	I'll have someone get it. How do you take it?
Client:	A little cream, please.
Lawyer:	*[Picks up the phone and dials.]* Linda, get Mr. Client a cup of coffee with cream, and bring one for me, too, the way I usually take it. How's the typing on that other document that I want out this afternoon coming? Okay, that is real important, bring the coffee and then get that project done, it's got to be our top priority today.
Lawyer:	*[Writes date, time, and client's name on yellow pad.]* Tell me about your problem.

[Linda arrives with the coffee in styrofoam cups or with lawyer's coffee in ceramic mug and client's in styrofoam cup.]

Client:	Well . . . .

This hospitable exchange superficially reflects good client relations. There is small talk to put the client at ease, the offer of coffee, and the lawyer is preparing to write the client's comments on a yellow pad, indicating that the client's thoughts are important.

Lawyers are so busy meeting deadlines, they sometimes don't see that things aren't as they seem. Let's reexamine this apparently excellent client relations vignette to see what really might be going on in this scene. We'll do this by juxtaposing some likely thoughts that the client and the lawyer might be having with what is being said.

Lawyer:	*Speaks:* Hi. How are you? I got tied up on the phone on an important matter.

Client: *Thinks:* Lawyer doesn't really care how I am. Doesn't he think my matter is as important as the one he was discussing on the phone? Well, maybe I'm not as important. I don't know. I'm awed. Lawyer is dealing with important matters.

Or

Client: *Thinks:* I don't care who or what Lawyer was dealing with on the phone. My appointment was for ten minutes ago. I've got a sales call lined up after this. This is an insult, but I'm here now.

Speaks: Oh, that's okay.

Lawyer: *Thinks:* See, Client didn't care. Wish I could get back to handling that other matter I was dealing with on the phone.

Speaks: What's the weather doing outside?

Client: *Thinks:* Doesn't he care about me, my family, and my legal problem?

Speaks: About the same as this morning.

Lawyer: *Thinks:* Wonder how I can get that other big client's critical document deadline met when I have to spend time on this small potatoes client.

Speaks: It was sure nice yesterday. I was out on the course at the club with Mr. Big. I was really hitting them.

Client: *Thinks:* I've never been to the club, Lawyer has never invited me. He was with Mr. Big—wow—that is impressive and intimidating. Lawyer says his golf game is great. I'd be satisfied if I could find time to play and to hit the fairway with half my drives.

Or

Client: *Thinks:* The club is not as good as mine. If Lawyer only knew who I played with yesterday! I'm not even going to tell Lawyer. I'll bet he was hitting them. The last time I played with him he only got about three drives that even went half the distance of mine.

Or

Client: *Thinks:* So what? I don't care.

Speaks: Had a good time, huh?

Lawyer: *Thinks:* Wonder how long this is going to take. From what Client said on the phone, I'm going to have to finesse this until I can get an associate to look up the law on this thing.

Speaks: Come on into the conference room and sit down.

Client: *Thinks:* Holy Cow! This is fancy. This is the most expensive furniture I've ever seen. I know how much my furniture costs—this must cost a mint. Wonder how Lawyer can afford this—oh yeah, from my fees. Wonder how I should act in this room to seem natural, like . . . well, like I'm used to living this way.

Or

Client: *Thinks:* Look at this stuff! Poor taste. Probably had some decorator figure out what art and image Lawyer should have. Not nearly as nice as my office or my accountant's office. Why would anyone put that kind of money into this tasteless stuff?

Speaks: Thanks.

Lawyer: *Thinks:* Wonder if I should ask about Client's paying the last bill. I sure don't want to do more work and not get paid. I know Client has the money. Client must think I don't need it—pays us last. I really resent that when I spent all weekend six months ago on Client's legal matters and I've not been paid.

Speaks: Do you want a cup of coffee?

Client: *Thinks:* No, but I'll have one anyway. At Lawyer's rates, I'll bet it'll be the most expensive cup of coffee I ever had.

Speaks: Yes, thanks.

Lawyer: *Thinks:* Guess I'll have a cup, too. I have to remember to bill this coffee to client under refreshment costs on the bill.

Speaks: I'll have someone get it. How do you take it?

Client: *Thinks:* I've had about 30 cups of coffee in this office over the last couple of years and Lawyer still doesn't remember how I take my coffee!

Speaks: A little cream, please.

Lawyer: *Thinks:* I need this coffee to stay awake. Wonder how Linda is doing on the typing for the other client's matter?

Speaks: [*Picks up the phone and dials.*] Linda, get Mr. Client a cup of coffee with cream, and bring one for

	me, too, the way I usually take it. How's the typing on that other document I want out this afternoon coming? Okay, it is real important, bring the coffee and get that project done, it's got to be our top priority today.
Client:	*Thinks:* I don't have any document or typing being done here. Why can't Lawyer pay a little more attention to me and my needs? How can Linda type and bring coffee at the same time?
Lawyer:	*Speaks:* [*Writes date, time and client's name on yellow pad.*] Tell me about your problem.
Client:	*Thinks:* Lawyer wrote date and time—Lawyer charges for every second. Always writes things down and then asks about the same stuff later on phone. Must never look at these notes. Lawyer says "your problem"— Lawyer knew what I was doing and didn't tell me it was wrong. Lawyer will probably think I'm stupid for getting into this mess. I don't think it was all my fault.

[*Linda arrives with the coffee in styrofoam cups for everyone or with lawyer's coffee in ceramic mug and client's in styrofoam cup.*]

Client:	*Thinks:* Styrofoam! This has as much class as a fast food joint. *Speaks:* Well . . . .
Lawyer:	*Thinks:* Here Client goes again. I've got to listen and Client takes so long to get to the point. Ugh! This coffee is awful!

The point of this dialogue and the corresponding thoughts is to illustrate that many conversational exchanges in a lawyer's office that precede the discussion of the legal situation are detrimental to good client relations. The same holds for luncheon, golf and cocktail conversations.

All of us attorneys are well advised to assure we put the client first in conversation as well as in service. The surest way to do this is to always put the client first in your thoughts.

COMMUNICATING CONCERN FOR THE CLIENT

Obviously, the interest a lawyer has in the matter brought to the office by the client will vary, based in part on the matter, as well as the client. Publicized cases of great interest include that of a man who sued a property owner and won a lifetime annuity when he became paralyzed from falling through a skylight while burglarizing the premises. The key to successful lawyer-client conversations is to be as interested in the details of a routine house purchase as in the more bizarre matters. If an attorney is truly interested in the client and the client's needs, that high level of interest will be maintained regardless of how challenging or mundane the legal matter turns out to be.

Too frequently, personal communication that lawyers might have with clients falls into one or more of the following categories:

- Extending superficial hospitality;
- Trying to impress;
- Omitting inquiries about the client's interests, family or business;
- Putting the client down for getting into the situation by making the wrong decisions; or
- Discussing a subject about which the client or the lawyer does not give a twit.

The client can discuss current events in the local bar, at social gatherings, or with his or her spouse or partner. A client expects to have a sincere conversation with a lawyer that includes a demonstration of genuine concern about the client, his or her family, the client's legal matter, and/or information in which the client is interested and that will be of practical utility.

BE GENUINE

To demonstrate genuine concern, the lawyer must step out of center stage and direct the spotlight on the client. Do not panic—the lawyer may reclaim the center of attention when consideration of the legal problem commences. The best way to redirect the focus is to ask meaningful questions of concern about the client's personal life and business. Health, family, children at college, new house or car, current business cycle as it affects the client's business, and new products in the client's business are some examples. The critical element is that the question should not be generic, such as "How's the family?" Far better to inquire, "How is your son Joe getting along at State University?"

Another example is to construct a conversation around a business topic that you read in a national newspaper, a magazine, or the business pages of the local newspaper. Suppose you read that the cost of copper, a mineral your client uses in its manufacturing process or that is used in a product the client sells, is dramatically increasing in price. The lawyer could say, "I see the price of copper is going up." The client's response might be "Yep" or "Yeah, and that is really going to cost me a bundle."

Wouldn't the client be even more likely to feel that the lawyer was sincerely concerned about the client's business if the lawyer's question had been, "Client, I read the price of copper is really going sky high. Isn't that going to put a crimp in your profit picture?" It might also be that the client had not seen the article, in which case the client's reaction could be, "I hadn't heard about that. I'll have to check that out as soon as I get back to the office. Thanks for the info, Lawyer." A conversation like this is of practical import to the client and one that demonstrates the lawyer's concern about the client as a person and the client's economic welfare.

These conversational techniques to shift the center of attention to the client are important. However, the techniques simply will not succeed if the lawyer does not reflect sincere interest in the topic and genuine concern for the person, the client. Like juries, most clients quickly discern whether an individual is sincere. If you don't mean it, don't say it.

SAY MY NAME

While the above techniques will be helpful, the most effective method to convey that you are interested in a person as a unique individual is the use of a person's name.

Many lawyers greet clients with "Hello" or "Hi, how are you?" Some lawyers save the use of a person's name until the lawyer and client are at the critical juncture of a mammoth legal decision and say, "Frankly, Carolyn, you've gotten yourself into a very grave situation." This is pompous and is not an effective method to build a good relationship with a client. The more frequently you and all people in your office use a client's name in conversation, whether it is face-to-face, on the telephone, or in correspondence, the better your chances of establishing, maintaining, and developing a strong lawyer-client relationship.

We had a procedure in which the secretary or receptionist answering the phone would try to use the client's name three times before transferring the call or hanging up. We encouraged the lawyers to do the same. Does it work? Think about how you feel when someone who has just processed a charge on your credit card in a store says, "Please sign here [Mr. or Ms.] You." Use of your name makes you a unique somebody. Your client is a somebody and wants to be a special person, too. Lawyers owe it to themselves to assure that clients understand that they are important persons to their lawyers.

A dilemma arises concerning whether to use the client's first name or Mr. or Ms. Client. While there are no set rules, generally, staff and associates should use Mr. or Ms. Clients often expect younger solos and partners to use their title and last name as well. More experienced attorneys must sense how the client wishes to be addressed. Frequently when I speak with a new client for the first time, I use the more formal form. If the client uses my first name, then I reciprocate by using the client's first name. To put new clients who seem to be nervous and who address me as Mr. Ewalt at ease, I respond, "My first name is Henry, not Mister. Please call me that." Usually that gets a laugh and greatly assists in getting the relationship on more equal footing, as it should be.

Executives and managers from corporate clients usually address the lawyer as the corporate culture dictates. Most employees of corporations use first names for people occupying slots from the bottom of the organizational chart to the top. However, if the outside counsel is talking with the general counsel or chief executive officer for the first time, the safest procedure is to use Ms. or Mr. until invited to use a first name.

Internally, government lawyers will obviously comply with the culture as set by the head of the office. When I graduated from law school, I went to work for the National Labor Relations Board in Pittsburgh. Henry Shore was the Regional Director and revered nationally. I was very impressed with him, he was my senior and I called him "Mr. Shore." He told me several times to call him "Henry." From my upbringing and the respect I quickly acquired for him, this was very difficult for me to do. I persisted in calling him "Mr. Shore." Finally, another Field Attorney got me aside and said that the Regional Director didn't like being called "Mr. Shore" and told the Field Attorney that he was upset that I was calling him "Mr. Shore." I called him "Henry" ever after. The point of this is for the government lawyer to learn the culture and get with the internal custom of addressing coworkers.

Government lawyers have a slightly different issue from other lawyers when dealing with members of the public who come to the government office. First, individual members of the public or representatives of entities are not the government lawyers' clients. Second, the government lawyer must continually drive home the fact that the government is the lawyer's client. Thus, it is advisable to use the more formal names. This guideline can be carefully relaxed in circumstances where the government lawyer is seeking redress for an alleged unlawful action against an individual, such as in an unfair labor practice trial, and where there are regular encounters with people such as corporate or union representatives. The key is for the government lawyer to prevent members of the public from thinking that they are represented by or have a special relationship with the government lawyer.

SUMMARY

Give a few minutes of thought on how you could change the office decor, the receptionist's greeting, your conversation and the focus of the spotlight to elicit the client reaction, "Hey, my lawyer is truly glad I'm here. I am somebody and I really do make a difference to my lawyer!" Then, implement your conclusions—tomorrow.

CHAPTER 6

KNOW YOUR CLIENT

THE NEED

Most lawyers know the law better than they know their clients. Without clients there is no reason for lawyers to know the law. Therefore, a lawyer who wants to practice law needs to know the client better than the law.

This heavily flawed syllogism makes the point that there can be no practice of law without clients. A corollary and a factual observation is that lawyers rarely "know" the most critical element of their practice, their clients.

Most lawyers regard client relations as an undesirable extra duty. Nothing could be further from the truth. It is the most essential duty in the practice of law. Lawyers who do not know the law still practice, as long as they have clients. However, lawyers who know the law well but have no clients cannot practice law at all.

Think of your best three clients. If one or more of those are corporations, think of your chief human contact at each of those clients. Now, complete the information shown below for each of your three best clients.

"Nonsense!" you say? But, I say if you cannot correctly answer almost all of these questions about the three people (clients) who are most important to your practice, to your chosen profession, to your financial well being, you have not been nurturing your practice with good client relations. Eventually, this will adversely affect your law practice and every

---

CLIENT INFORMATION

Date of birth—if not the year, the day and month _____

Place of birth _____

Hometown where teenage years were spent _____

College(s); major and degrees _____

Spouse's or Partner's name _____

Children's names _____

Favorite foods _____

Hobbies _____

Religion _____

Favorite restaurant _____

Political persuasion _____

Type of car(s) owned _____

Club memberships _____

Favorite charities _____

Employment history _____

Entertainment preferences; theater, sports, etc. _____

---

benefit that spins off from it. Certainly it caps your ability to grow your clients. One might argue the relevance of some of the questions posed. Regardless of the questions, the point is, how much do you know about your clients?

If you disagree with the questions posed above, another way to think about this issue is: What type of personal information about yourself would you give to professionals trying to help you to give them the best insight into what drives you? Make a list of the information you perceive to be relevant to you and then convert the list to questions about your clients. Perhaps you, like me, will be amazed at how far afield that helpful information and those questions are from accounting, banking, commercial, and legal information.

You should be cautious in obtaining some of the information necessary to answer whichever questions you deem important. You need to be sure you do not accidentally offend this very important client. Whatever the list of questions, one object of client relations is to be able to answer the questions that give you the whole picture of your client, not just the singular legal profile.

GETTING TO KNOW YOU—THE INTAKE FORM

A good starting point for getting to know a client is the client intake form. This form should be completed by or for every new client. The information requested should go beyond phone number and billing address. However, it should never ask anything that is not directly relevant to your representing the client or that may be deemed discriminatory, such as, "What is your religion?" An example of one client intake form is shown on pages 52, 53.

Avoid thinking that you will take a shortcut and get the answers to the questions posed in the previous section by putting them on a client in-take form. Asking those questions in written form will offend many clients. Even if they answered the questions on a form, you would know only about your client rather than know your client. Acquiring the information conversationally is far superior because the information is not the goal you are seeking. Getting to know your client is.

A critical piece of information often overlooked is the name of the client's secretary or administrative assistant. Not only is it nice to know this information since she or he is the gatekeeper to access your client, it is essential to have good relations with that person. It is good practice to use that person's name and chat briefly with him or her each time you call or visit your client.

One way to manage client intake forms is to enter the information into a computer database. As you find out more about the client, you may change or supplement the initial information. Then, if you have a computer monitor on your desk, when the client calls you or you call the client, you can bring up the intake information screen to remind you of client-relations topics that you could work into your conversation.

As you get to know the client better, reliance on this intake form and computer screen should decrease. A lawyer who chiefly relies on the intake form for client information really can't have a personal connection

NEW MATTER IN-TAKE FORM

Client Name: _____   Client/Matter   # _____ - _____

Billing Name: _____   Date Opened: _____

Primary Phone: ( )_____ ( ) NEW CLIENT   ( ) EXISTING CLIENT

Alternate Phone: ( )_____ ( ) NEW MATTER   ( ) EXISTING MATTER

Fax: ( )_____

E-mail: ( )_____

Client Address   ( ) New Matter Address

_____

_____

_____

_____

City _____ State _____ Zip _____

Billing Address

_____

_____

_____

_____

City _____ State _____ Zip _____

Conflicts Check Completed—Sign and Date

     All Plaintiffs   _____

     All Defendants   _____

     All Third Parties _____

Note any conflict resolutions necessary or restrictions (if none, state): _____

_____

Statute of Limit.: _____ Fee Letter: _____ Retainer Amount: $ _____

Rate Code:	Fee Type:	Billing Att'y	Initials:	Rate:
___ Standard	___ Hourly	Orig. Att'y #1	_____	_____
___ Retainer	___ Contingent	Orig. Att'y #2	_____	_____
___ Special	___ Fixed $ _____	Responsible Att'y #1	_____	_____
___ Municipal		Responsible Att'y #2	_____	_____
___ Premium				

Billing Frequency Code   _____   Industry/Market Code: _____

Matter Type Code   _____   Office Code: _____

Fee Committee approval required for other than standard fee and standard hourly
    rate cases.

Signature of Fee Committee Member and date: _____

Description of Alternative fee arrangement: _____

Bill Format: Use current client format _____

Format A _____ Format B _____ Format C _____ Format D _____

Distribution

     Group Leader 1   ( )   File 2   ( )   Accounting 2 ( )

     Managing Partner 1 ( )   Others (List) _____

with the client. You don't need to refer to a database to have a conversation with your friends and you shouldn't with your clients. Shortly after being engaged by a new client, the lawyer should be able to throw away the intake-information crutch and converse with the client based on known interests and an internalized caring for the client.

LEARNING ABOUT THE BUSINESS

The more a lawyer knows about the client's business, the more the lawyer increases in value to the client. In many instances, the client is equipped to judge the lawyer's competence only by how familiar the lawyer is with what the client knows best—the client and the client's business.

Let's now focus on the client's business. Following are three examples showing three different franchise relationships, three different referrals, three different relationships among business principals and three different businesses.

Years ago, two people who were friends whom I did not know came to Pittsburgh, Pennsylvania, to scope out whether they wanted to start a franchise business with a national donut chain. They had never been to our area and were neophytes in business. They asked me to represent them on the recommendation of my sister, Sally, who knew them from their hometown in Rhode Island.

In another instance, two midwestern businessmen who worked in different states for a national lawn equipment manufacturer were put together by the manufacturer to start a lawn equipment franchise in Pittsburgh. They had only vague recollections of meeting one another at national sales meetings. The two visited Pittsburgh and met a banker who recommended that they engage me to represent them.

Finally, two brothers who were my friends since boyhood, decided to buy an automobile dealership in Pittsburgh. Though they were inclined to retain me, they first interviewed several firms. After making this more objective assessment and deciding that I stacked up well enough against the competition, they asked me to serve as their counsel.

What could I do to facilitate getting these businesses started? Obviously, I could apply my knowledge of franchise law—which, in truth, was precious little when I started to represent these folks. I could advise the out-of-town people on locations in the Pittsburgh area and that would be deeply appreciated, but perhaps better done by a commercial real estate agent. I saw that there was so much else to do, so much to learn, I had to prioritize.

My inclination as a lawyer was to start with the books, research franchise law, and search out franchise agreements in forms books. That is where I would be most comfortable, in a place where my newfound clients could not challenge me. In spite of this, I chose instead to find out all I could about the donut, lawn equipment, and automotive businesses.

I used several different study methods. I started by asking each of my clients hundreds of questions. This questioning by me about their businesses continued from our first meeting until I ceased to represent them years later when I left private practice for the corporate legal world. I also paid attention to and remembered the clients' answers. I integrated that business knowledge into all the advice I offered and drafting that I did.

Additionally, I sought out and received information about the businesses from the franchisers. Other knowledge about the fast food, lawn equipment, and car industries was obtained from a variety of public sources. Information sources such as the Internet, *The Wall Street Journal*, local newspapers, the clients' employees, civic organizations, chambers of commerce, and magazine articles provided valuable insights. This information is not tough to find or complex to understand. It truly will provide a valuable enhancement to your ability to serve your client and, therefore, to client relations.

When I closed those three franchise deals for my clients, the financing institutions' representatives commented that they had never had lawyers ask the kind of questions I asked. They also acknowledged that they had never made the number or kind of changes in their "standard" deal and loan documents that they made, but that they understood why these franchises needed the modifications we requested. They understood because we educated them about the nitty-gritty practicality of running the franchises. If we had taken them on exclusively in the legal language, statutory meaning or case precedent arenas, we would not have had the leverage necessary to gain the concessions. We obtained the necessary leverage by showing them that, with concessions such as the amount of cash reserves to be maintained, the franchise could be more successful in business, which, in turn, would mean less risk of failure and provide a greater return and opportunity to the franchiser and the lender.

The clients thanked me for helping them get started in business. Interestingly, their most profuse praise was for my knowledge of their business and the nature of their industry, not for guidance through the legal maze. This imbalance of kudos was overweight on the business side of the scales because they understood the conversation about business and knew that it took a personal effort on my part to learn about their businesses. I think they believed I already knew the law and this business education effort was especially and particularly for them. They were right about the business effort. If they had known how much law I had to learn also, they probably would not have hired me!

In social situations we react positively to people who express an interest in our personal and business interests. Likewise, clients usually embrace attorneys who converse with clients on the clients' home fields of personal and business concerns.

THE CLIENT AS CUSTOMER

Excellent salespeople know very well why you buy a product or service from them instead of another—it's the relationship they create.

The initial interest of a prospective purchaser may be because of a need for the product or service and even the reputation of a particular brand. However, most consumers now have inumerable choices of products and prices among competing suppliers. What causes them to choose one supplier over another when both are in the same price range? Oftentimes, the critical difference is the relationship with the salesperson. Further evidence of this is that the growth of Internet sales being held in check by face-to-face retail sales outlets. People just feel more comfortable talking with a person in the store or even on a toll-free 800 line than ordering from a computer screen with which they cannot establish any kind of a relationship.

SALES

That personal connection produces some psychological perception of assurance of quality and timely delivery. The personal relationship provides a sense of reduced risk to the consumer. How can this be when salespeople neither manufacture nor ship the product? The customer comes to believe that through trusting the salesperson, the salesperson will become the customer's agent, even though employed by the manufacturer or sales distribution point. The customer trusts the salesperson to ensure that what the customer expects from buying the product will occur.

An example of this is a car salesperson's reassurance, "I'll go to bat for you with the manager on price." The salesperson wants to create the psychological impression that he or she is taking your position on price in the discussion with the manager. Even if you have to pay more for the car than you offered, you still retain the image of the salesperson advocating your position to get the best price. This goes a long way toward bringing you back to that salesperson in the future.

This process is not unlike a potential client selecting a lawyer. The lawyer must convince the client that she or he will deliver what the client expects, whether it is to keep the client out of jail or to get the deal closed. If that confidence of trust is not almost immediately created in the client through references or the initial contact, the potential client is likely to select another counsel. This phenomenon is not hard to understand when you realize that there is no way the client can see the lawyer's legal competence demonstrated in a first meeting.

The customer also must be convinced that if a problem occurs after the sale, the salesperson will "fix" the problem without significant hassle or cost to the customer. According to a number of sources, this belief based on extensive warranties, enabled the Japanese automobile manufacturers to take much of the United States market from domestic manufacturers in the latter decades of the last century.

WARRANTY

When I was visiting an American manufacturer's car dealership, I overheard a customer say to the Service Manager, "Look, this problem according to you was no problem when the car was under warranty. Now that the warranty has expired, you say it is a dangerous situation that needs to be fixed right away. This just doesn't make sense." Lacking trust, the customer does not know if the car problem is dangerous or not. The customer does not know how to evaluate the severity of the problem. All the customer knows is that when the car was under warranty and the dealership was obliged to fix it at no cost to the customer, it was no problem. When the warranty expired, the dealership decided the same situation required immediate fixing at the customer's expense. The customer's trust factor and the dealer-customer relationship must have dropped to practically zero.

Lawyers do not give extensive written warranties as automobile manufacturers do. Some lawyer warranties are imposed after the fact by judges, juries, and disciplinary boards. Lawyers must be sensitive to a client's desire not to have such matters as shareholders' buy-out agreements or real estate deals go awry. If they go awry because of a drafting error, the client does not want excuses but expects the lawyer to fix it at no cost. This is an appropriate expectation because the trust the client had in the relationship and the reason for retaining the lawyer has been violated or unfulfilled. Some former clients in such situations are looking for compensation for the rupturing of the trust as much as for damages for the lost business opportunities. As lawyers, we know that we may not have been the cause of the situation going south. Unfortunately, the cause is irrelevant to the client and therefore we must resolve it to the satisfaction of the customer/client to preserve the client relationship.

All too frequently, a lawyer charges a client a substantial sum to correct mistakes in litigation and drafting that were created by the lawyer. Here, the lawyer-client trust and relationship will parallel that of the dealership-customer when "out-of-warranty repairs" to a document have to be done. Our lawyer attitude that it wasn't my fault often generates more than bad will . . . a disciplinary complaint.

SERVICE

The service sector is no different than manufacturing. A good number of years ago, right before Christmas, my wife, Mary, and I decided to take our children, Andy and Sarah, out for pizza so we could get a quick dinner and return to our holiday decorating activities. When we sat down, the server took our order promptly and returned shortly with our sodas (not unlike a lawyer accepting an initial work order from a new client and getting the engagement letter out). Then we waited and waited for the pizza to be served (not unlike lawyers failing to meet a deadline mutually set with clients).

Next, the server showed up with another round of sodas. When I protested that I had not ordered them, the server smiled and replied, "I know, but I guess I have to keep you folks occupied. Don't worry, no way am I going to charge you for these drinks—it's the kitchen's fault the pizza is taking so long; they had a lot of take-out orders." This smoothed feelings, added value and delighted the kids. The server's spontaneous concern for us overshadowed our being peeved about the tardiness of the pizza. Needless to say, this pizza shop became a favorite, and when we returned, the kids even hoped the pizza would be late.

Compare that to the way lawyers treat clients when lawyers fail to meet a performance date. Frequently, lawyers lack the courtesy to call the client to say the document will be a few days late and to ask the client's tolerance. How often have you, as a lawyer, undertaken a project and not discussed with a client when a draft of a will, brief, or contract could be expected? In most of these instances, the client's impression of a "reasonable delivery date" is much earlier than the lawyer's. The lawyer, if he or she knew the client, would realize this and set a mutually agreeable delivery date, just as astute salespeople and mail-order houses do.

An especially dangerous circumstance arises when a client says this does not have to be done right away—the "no-hurry job." That work always went to the bottom of my pile of things to do, and maybe it ends up in the same place in your pile. Even when it got to the top, some matter perceived by me to have greater urgency usually intervened, so the "no-hurry job" was again relegated to the bottom of the pile. Meanwhile, back at the client's ranch or other business, the client is wondering aloud to friends and anyone else who will listen, "Where is that work I asked my lawyer to do weeks or months ago?" Now the lawyer has irritated the client and has also substantially reduced the chances of converting the client's friends and acquaintances from potential to actual paying clients.

When the client hears no response from a lawyer, does the client call the lawyer to ask about the work? Sometimes. But more often than not, the client, lacking for a topic of conversation at the local hang out or at a place of worship, will tell all who will listen that he or she gave a matter to such and such a lawyer months ago and not only has the client not received the document but nothing has been heard from that lawyer—"and besides, the lawyer made me pay a retainer."

Now, the client has become disenchanted with the lawyer and consequently has also poisoned potential clients' thinking about the type of client relations this lawyer would create if a listener became an actual client. Rarely will anything that a lawyer says to or does with other potential clients overcome unsolicited comments from a present or former client.

Clients are turned on or off by things they understand. Delivery dates and fair, courteous treatment are just a few examples of things clients understand very well. And, these are frequently the very things lawyers neglect. Better that the lawyer and client should always agree on some specific time period or date. Words like "no hurry," "soon," and "rush" may have different meanings in different minds.

Compare the impact on the local hang out crowd or place-of-worship listeners if the client had said, "I gave a matter to such and such lawyer and told the lawyer I was in no hurry for it. Can you believe it, the lawyer called me two days later and said he would have it for me in another week. Before the week went by, I got the document. Unbelievable! I called about a question and the lawyer's secretary said she was sorry but the lawyer was tied up in a meeting, could anyone else help me? I told her no. She said she would have the lawyer call back. I expected a call back in a couple of days but, instead, I got it in a couple of hours! Even when my insurance agent is trying to sell me more coverage, she doesn't call back that fast!"

These client-comment ripple effects have a positive or negative impact on present and potential clients. They actually have more impact on the future of your practice than drafting a "perfect" agreement or prevailing in court. One way to assure that the lawyer and client start and stay on the same page is to use a Client Goals form as set forth on the following page.

CLIENT GOALS

In initial discussion, list what client says are client's goals and timetables for this matter and any cautions or disclaimers told to client (specify lawyer) in initial discussion:

_____

_____

_____

CLIENT MATTER PLAN

Action	Responsible Person(s)	Completion Date
_____	_____	_____
_____	_____	_____
_____	_____	_____
_____	_____	_____

AGREED AMENDMENTS TO PLAN:

Date	Action	Responsible Person	Completion Date
_____	_____	_____	_____
_____	_____	_____	_____
_____	_____	_____	_____

RECORDS:

Expansion 5 1/4	_____	Cross file under:	_____
Expansion 3 1/2	_____	Retention date:	_____
Flat	_____	Destruction date:	_____
Will	_____	Status:	_____
Original	_____	Location code:	_____
Subfile	_____	Computer directory:	_____

Key Words

_____   _____

_____   _____

_____   _____

_____   _____

Description of Matter:

_____

_____

_____

DISTRIBUTION:

Group Leader	1( )	Others (List)	_____
File	2( )		
Accounting	2( )		
Managing Partner	1( )		

NOT A BUZZWORD

Sometimes accumulating costs, adverse intermediate developments, or final results cause clients to truly regret they retained a particular lawyer. Psychologically, this is probably a form of "buyer's remorse." Lawyers may take preventive actions to minimize the chances of the client sinking into this state. The most effective actions are taken early in the lawyer-client relationship and involve something more than the client expects—a lawyer making an after hours phone report to the client at home or a response or document delivered sooner than promised. Clients also very much appreciate, during the course of the representation, the lawyer initiating a concerned conversation about mounting legal fees. Updating the client regularly maintains the client's good image of the lawyer.

Client satisfaction is not a buzzword; it is a guideline for successful law practice. If you take the time and make the effort to know your client and help shape client's expectations, you will be able to anticipate the positive or negative waves you cause by your action or inaction. Knowing this, you can ensure that your conduct will not rock your client's boat and will advance yours.

CHAPTER 7

CLIENT UNDERSTANDING

Eliciting compassionate client understanding from the client toward the lawyer is NOT what this chapter is about. Facilitating client understanding of what and how legal influences are impacting his or her situation is critical to forming an effective relationship with the client.

Many clients are quick to grasp the result of a regulation, law or verdict. Few are informed enough to understand what caused that result. Their focus—as it should be—is on living their lives or running their businesses.

Numerous clients don't understand that the law imposes restrictions on their commercial activities or ferments personal legal entanglements. The legal implications of the will, contract, insurance policy, and other documents are what the lawyer says they are because the language on the paper is obtuse to clients. Even when the client clearly understands that the signed document is legally binding, clients still don't know their legal obligations. Understanding the detail of the "facts" as the client has lived them becomes a barrier to the client even grasping the possibility that any finder of fact could possibly see the facts differently from the client's view.

Some lawyers fail to comprehend how anyone could not have these basic understandings and, at times, lawyers on both sides of an issue assign an ulterior motive to the client's lack of knowledge. This is as foolish and off-base as a space engineer thinking a lawyer is stupid or hiding something because the lawyer doesn't know how to build a rocket, which can rendezvous with a space station.

BURDEN IS ON LAWYER

The burden of bringing the client to an adequate level of understanding about the law and its impact sits squarely on the lawyer. This is a primary function of the attorney-client relationship. The client is counting on the lawyer to explain and make understandable the mysteries of the law. Most people do what they think is appropriate, so when "the law" dictates otherwise, they are mystified. No matter how elementary the concept, the lawyer owes the client an explanation of the legal details, why the law is the way it is, and how the law impacts the client's situation.

For many clients, the most valuable service a lawyer performs is educating the client on the law. Knowledge on the part of the client is also helpful to the lawyer. I have personally experienced clients who, having been "taught" the law, have made major contributions to constructing the theme of a litigation case and others who have provided a map through the maze of negotiating a contract.

To commence the legal education of the client, the lawyer must go to the client's level of understanding. Too frequently, the lawyer starts from the lawyer's level of understanding, instead of the client's. Both the lawyer and client then become frustrated, which has an adverse impact on their relationship. The client's initial level of understanding varies with the client and in the same client with the field of law. Real estate concepts are much more in the public domain than those governing the law of international trade. It follows that a typical client is likely to have a better understanding of a real estate transaction than one in international trade.

Figuring out the level of the client's understanding is no small challenge. Many people try to avoid the embarrassment of admitting they didn't or don't know what they are doing by nodding, smiling, and mumbling that they understand when they actually don't.

The lawyer should encourage the client to recite in the greatest detail at the command of the client, the current factual situation. Just because the client has had previous situations involving the same area of the law, such as engineers obtaining patents, you mustn't let the client think that this one is the same. As we lawyers know, no two factual situations are the same, even if governed by the same laws. The number of facts recited by the client that are relevant to the result the law dictates often provides a clue as to the level of the client's understanding. Then, the attorney should ask additional questions to bring out other facts critical to the legal outcome. Once you know the facts, ask the client what the client understands about the law as it applies to these facts. Only then do you have fairly accurate knowledge of your client's understanding of the law.

At this point, the lawyer's job is to educate the client about the law without blame, guilt, or ridicule. The very first step in this process is to avoid the teaching methods you experienced in law school. I'm amazed at the number of times that lawyers intentionally try and succeed in making their clients look dumb and feel small using law school teaching methods. Shame and humiliation have no place in any attorney-client relationship. Intimidation and alienation, which inevitably result from such behaviors, are to be avoided at all costs.

The object is to build a relationship on mutual trust between the client and lawyer. Lawyers communicating understanding observations and suggestions for resolution to clients are a good start. A genuine "we're in this together" attitude by the lawyer will advance the relationship. Just act and converse the way you do when you want to establish a new personal friendship. Your client will feel and appreciate it. Doing everything possible to establish a positive, open relationship with every client is the responsibility of every lawyer.

EDUCATING YOUR CLIENT

Once you determine the client's level of understanding, the process of educating your client should utilize the same techniques of the very best teacher you ever experienced. I bet that those techniques involved explaining the reason for learning the material, setting out the challenge sought, encouraging every small step of progress, and supporting the student in all circumstances. Eliminating the intimidation of the topic and the teacher is essential. This can be accomplished by admitting that you had difficulty understanding this law when first exposed in law school or when the legislature created it.

Throughout this education process, which continues until the matter is closed, the lawyer must constantly reinforce the student-client by giving credit for new understanding. Avoid guilt-provoking responses and lectures—like, "I told you so," or "This is simple stuff," or "What could you have been thinking when you did this,"—which are perceived as reflecting a lawyer's superiority complex. The key is to set your ego aside and build the client's. For a moment, reflect on the absolutely wonderful affect building your client's ego will have on the client's opinion of and relationship with you.

The object is to enlighten the client while, at the same time, bonding the client to you based on your caring and knowledge. "Exactly what is a tort?" A question such as this from a client does not merit the verbal citation of a bunch of cases, a recitation of the abstract legal theory, and a direction to go figure it out. Some may have experienced this methodology in law school and might be dying to victimize someone else with the approach, but it is inappropriate with clients. Also, giving the parental answer, because the court held or because it is in the formbook, is likewise insufficient. You must provide the reasoning for the law and support for understanding, if you are expecting to improve your relationship with your client.

The reasons for your recommendation and the law may be couched in business terms, which frequently make the consequences easier for the client to understand and to accept the legal result. In negotiating a collective bargaining agreement for an employer who recently became a client, I noted that the recognition clause required the employer to recognize the union as representing "all custodians." Even though the clause had been in the agency's certification of the union and in the contract for nine years, the employer was hiring regular part-time custodians who were not members of the union, were being paid less than union wages and were deemed ineligible for union benefits. The law states that regular part-time employees are covered by the recognition clause. I explained this to the employer who responded that didn't matter because it couldn't afford to pay part-timers the same wages and anyway the union representative knew this was going on and didn't object.

My campaign of enlightenment included facts that the governmental agency would enforce the recognition clause if one of the part-timers complained and that back pay and benefits would be owed to all part-timers with interest. I also taught the client that if the union agreed, we didn't have to pay part-timers the same wage rate as full-time employees, which was a revelation and relief to the employer. Next, I laid out the alternatives and quantified them by calculating the cost of each. I also laid out the operational consequences including improved productivity coming from refining the scheduling of custodians. This brought a new level of understanding to the client. Although it was going to cost somewhat more, the client quickly made a business decision that the least costly and risky (in that order) was to negotiate with the union about covering the part-time custodians in the collective bargaining agreement. And, we did.

DON'T BORE CLIENTS

When enlightening a client, the lawyer must make sure the communication content and delivery is interesting to the client. In the above illustration, the cost and risk factors made the discussion interesting to the client. Recall your lack of interest as a third year law student in hearing about some obscure IRS regulation and a recitation of appellate court decisions without having the experience to apply it to a factual situation you understood. Booooring!

One's interest in a conversation is directly proportional to one's understanding of the subject's relevance to the listener. If the lawyer is into demonstrating how much pure law the lawyer knows, the discussion is deadly dull to the client. You must tie every legal precept and factual example to the client's situation. Use illustrations and examples to build credibility with the client. Describe with examples that are within the experience of the listener. You may draw these teaching vehicles from your own experience, the media, cyber sources, or a guru's pronouncements. Great teachers make the subject come alive within the understanding of the student. That's what the lawyer must achieve for clients to understand and remember. The lawyer must create the connection between the law and what clients have actually experienced or can extrapolate with sufficient detail to understand the impact of the law on them.

My history as student and teacher, tells me that the lawyer's most credible examples for a client arise from the lawyer's personal legal experiences. However, there are many ways to supplement personal experience. Clients also react favorably to public information, such as a court ruling. A history teacher didn't have to survive the devastation of Pompeii to effectively teach about it. Citing a situation you have read or heard about is also effective. Less effective is using a hypothetical because the client can usually distinguish it from the client's situation. But, if the facts of the hypo are constructed so that they closely parallel the client's situation, it too is an effective teaching devise.

WATCH YOUR LANGUAGE

The lawyer isn't an academic scientist delivering a paper to peers in multi-syllable technical terminology. We are professionals attempting to bridge the gap between our knowledge of the law and the person's factual situation—an impossible task if the lawyer uses technical legal language. You can't be understood, if the listener doesn't have the background to attach meaning to the words you use. Hearing a conversation in Chinese will be of no interest or meaning if you don't understand the Chinese language. Technical legal language is more difficult for some than Chinese is.

Terms such as tort, consequential damages, potentially responsible party, and imputed liability are meaningful to lawyers, but not to some clients. A legal support staff person without any college training may well understand the meaning of some legal terms better than the lawyer for whom she or he works. It really is not a matter of how educated the client might be, as much as it is the client's experience that governs the level of understanding.

Since experience in life, not dictionary knowledge, is most determinative in a person's understanding, don't assume that a person with lots of education in a high corporate position necessarily knows the meaning of the words you are using. The corporate CEO, who comes from the service industry to a manufacturing company, may have no idea about the meaning of terms used in intellectual property and environmental law.

Part of our job as lawyers is to vicariously supply the missing experience to the client. The lawyer must study the law, the client, and the situations to grasp the best way to convey the missing link in a manner that will stick with the client. Only then is the lawyer prepared to communicate with the client in a way that the client will understand and appreciate. That achievement will solidify the client's relationship with the lawyer.

QUESTIONS REQUIRING
SPECIAL SKILLS AND ANSWERS

Clients are often most interested in questions which quantify recovery, loss, or risk. "How much is my case worth?" "What are the chances of me winning and how much will I get?" "How much will it cost me in legal fees to defend this claim and if I lose, what are the damages?" "Why are you suggesting I settle this case when I know I'm right?" These and similar questions require cautious answers for once the client hears the answer to this type of question, the client expects the lawyer's answer to become a reality.

Client inquiries of this type also pose major threats to the attorney-client relationship. If the lawyer responds that the client has a good case, that answer will be relied upon and thrown back in the attorney's face when it turns out otherwise—no matter what the cause for the changed situation. Trial lawyers suggesting that clients accept reasonable settlements are often accused by their clients of being afraid to try the case. Thus, conveying settlement possibilities requires a sensitive presentation so as not to create the wrong impression.

Getting clients to be realistic about the cost and outcome of their matters is dicey and requires special skills. Most clients have an honest and inaccurate impression of the merits and worth of their matter.

Whether they are a Pollyanna or pessimist, either is a challenge to the attorney's handling of the client. A lawyer could easily lose a client's confidence, if not the client, with a perfectly accurate answer to one of these questions. These questions can crop up at the initial meeting or during a later contact. Regardless of when they arise, the lawyer's concerns are the same.

Before attempting to answer, ask yourself if you have all of the facts. Especially in written opinions, it is important to recite the facts upon which you are basing your evaluation. Sometimes clients rely on their lawyers to assess the value of a business they want to sell. In suggesting a price the business might fetch, the lawyer may have no knowledge that the internal accounting procedures fail to comply with the generally accepted accounting principles that the prospective buyer will use in setting the price it is willing to pay. The lawyer's lack of this critical knowledge will sometimes be forgotten when the client concludes that the attorney didn't know what she or he was doing.

Secondly, double-check the applicable law. Whether you are an experienced lawyer or a novice one, the knowledge of the law is the most important contribution you make to any client. A major law firm constantly reassured me that under the circumstances, the state law limited the corporation's exposure in this industrial scaffold accident case to a maximum 25 percent of any liability assessed against all defendants. Relying on that representation, the corporation decided to sink much money into the defense of the claim. Years later at a mandatory mediation session just before trial, the plaintiff's counsel asserted that by statute the 25 percent limitation didn't apply to scaffolding accidents. Checking the books during the mediation, our counsel found that the plaintiff's position was correct. Besides the malpractice implications, the incident totally destroyed all client confidence in both the particular lawyer and the law firm. A lawyer rarely preserves or recovers a client relationship after communicating a blatantly incorrect reading of a clear statutory provision upon which a client relies.

The third piece of information needed is much harder to discern. The lawyer must gauge the resolve of the other side. Regardless of the merits, the other side may be totally committed to getting its day in court. In contracts and deals, some will have specific walk-away markers and others will get deal fever and be willing to compromise on their last and final offer. Knowing the personality and previous negotiating tactics of the lawyers on the other side isn't always helpful because their clients may insist on different outcomes than the lawyers normally prefer. Nonetheless, a client will be relying on its counsel to advise on the resolve of the opposition. This is an art, not a science. Rather than a line-in-the-sand answer, the lawyer is well advised to admit nothing is certain and propose reevaluation mileposts so that evolving information may be taken into account. Clients understand and accept this approach.

Your goals, of course, are to get an accurate picture for your evaluation, convince the client to see the same picture, and obtain client buy-in to your evaluation without the client losing confidence in your abilities as a lawyer. This is not easy to do. Effective techniques for handling the client include not summarily rejecting any position or perception of the client. Add facts and your expert opinion, which provide the means for clients to find their own way to your conclusion. If you achieve this convergence, when future circumstances cause the matter to go awry, it is those uncontrollable factors and not the unilateral evaluation you gave to the client, which will be blamed. The client is less likely to point a finger at a client-endorsed evaluation as the cause of the matter failing to reach the client's initial assessment of its potential.

Sometimes the lawyer on the other side comes to you with a proposal that you help with his or her client relations. Consider a lawyer saying to you that your offer of settlement is reasonable, but the issue can't be settled at that amount because the opposing party has an inflated opinion of the matter's value. This scenario arises because the opposing attorney did not do the job of converting the client's dream of the value to the realistic value. The opposing lawyer is asking you to jeopardize your relationship with your client by asking your client to pay for the opposing lawyer's failure to give an objective assessment of the value of the business, claim, or case. Often, both defense and plaintiffs lawyers unintentionally create this problem by bragging to their clients that they can get some grossly inflated or drastically undervalued deal, settlement, or verdict for their clients. My usual response is that this is the other lawyer's problem and I'm not going to recommend my client solve that lawyer's problem with my client's money.

Clients can be quite insistent that their lawyers give them answers to these questions, which depend upon several realities that aren't readily discernable. Suggested responses to these clients include: "It's too early to tell," "That would be nice if that happened, but it isn't likely," and "We could do that, but it would cost you more in legal fees than the potential recovery." These answers, coupled with an explanation as to why, usually will placate the client.

Successful teaching certainly requires a healthy portion of people skills. Every attorney has the capacity to refine and develop teaching skills. However, if you feel you are extremely weak in people skills and not particularly interested in making the commitments to improving them, you should consider joining your practice with lawyers who have such skills. This combination of lawyers with these different inclinations is, more often than not, a formula for a successful law practice. If such a firm or association doesn't interest you, maybe you'd enjoy a permanent research position, a government job, or filling a slot in a think tank.

A better-informed client acquires a greater appreciation of the value of the lawyer's advice and actions. The counselor providing information, not by arguing or using traditional persuasive approaches, pursues this objective most effectively. After your relationship is firmly established, the client will more readily accept your announcements and pronouncements. Don't try shortcuts. This more time-consuming informing or teaching process is building the relationship and trust with the client.

SUMMARY

The point of this chapter is to emphasize the importance of assuring your client that he or she understands the situation and what you are doing about it. Extra caution must be exercised when evaluating costs, losses, and recoveries. If these lawyer supplied figures are too far from reality, it will damage your relationship with your clients. To avoid that circumstance, I urge you to use your best skills to very gently teach your client a very realistic view of the value and risks of his or her legal matter. The outcome of the matter and your relationship with your client depends upon your ability to achieve a shared realistic perception.

CHAPTER 8

INVOLVING THE CLIENT IN THE DECISION-MAKING PROCESS

If one is part of the decision-making process, it is far less likely that the involved person will second-guess the decision made than the person who did not participate in the decision-making process. Why? Because the person is fully informed, "invests" some ego in the decision and accepts responsibility for the outcome, whatever it may be.

It follows that if a client participates actively with the lawyer in the decision-making process about strategy on the client's legal matter, it is far less likely that the client will be dissatisfied regardless of the outcome. It is also unlikely that the participating client will bring a malpractice action. Even if a malpractice suit is brought, the client's participation in decision making significantly diminishes the client's chances of winning.

Team psychology in sports or legal projects spreads the result's joy and disappointment. Watch the reactions of benchwarmers on a football team when a starter returns to the sideline after making a good play. Their enthusiastic and genuine congratulatory antics stem from the part they played in practice. The obvious disappointment of a lost game can also be observed in the team member who didn't get in the game. I have experienced a like emotional connection with clients when they have participated in the fate of their legal matter.

We lawyers must learn how to think like our clients, rather than like their lawyer. This includes focusing on how a legal matter fits into an individual's life or a corporate client's business plan. The suggestions contained in this chapter are intended to facilitate breaking down the wall many lawyers construct between themselves and their clients.

"MY-CASE" SYNDROME

Ever heard yourself or other lawyers use these expressions? "I'll take your case." "I got the judge to grant my motion." "I'm going to depose every person I can think of on the other side." "My case is going to trial next week." "Your facts are bad."

Our very lawyer language suggests that we consciously exclude the client and other lawyers in our firm from any case we brought to the firm or on which we are working. (An exception is, even if an associate is working almost 100 percent of the case with a partner, then the case becomes partner Smith's case or shareholder Jones' case instead of the lawyer associate's case.)

The "my-case" syndrome may be caused in part by (1) the lawyer's ego, which operates without regard to the facts on the assumption that only "I" can do the best job on this without regard to the truth of who all is required to service the matter, and (2) the system of compensation that most law firms use to reward those who bring in business and/or work on matters.

When lawyers take exclusive possession and sole proprietary interest in a client's matter, it takes on an existence of its own, separate from the client. This process of cutting out the true owner, the client, has the same psychological effect as foreclosing on the property of a delinquent mortgagee or executing on a judgment. In fact, the lawyer's grabbing possession of a case is more analogous to the bully's grabbing sole possession of the baseball on the sandlot because there is no formalized process of review, as in the instances of foreclosure or executing on a judgment.

Client resentment must naturally flow from lawyers stealing the right to make decisions from clients. If your spouse or significant other makes a decision on a matter you deem important without involving you, your likely reaction is to be upset or resentful. If the result of the decision is bad, this feeling is magnified in retrospect. Your client's feeling is the same when the lawyer makes a critical decision without the client's input. Unilateral decisions affecting another adult are sources of conflict in all aspects of life. The lawyer-client relationship is no different.

Many frequent users of legal services are troubled, panicked, and angry when they lose control of "their" case. In fact, a first-time or occasional user of legal services may be even more disturbed since he or she has never previously experienced the loss-of-control feeling in business or personal matters.

Even if the lawyer is victorious at trial or achieves everything the client sought in a business deal, the client may be resentful. The root of that resentment is not the result, but the process in which that the client was denied the chance to feel he or she contributed to the victory. One client antidote to this resentment is for the client to conclude that the lawyer's service was irrelevant to the victory since the client's prior actions were vindicated. In such instances, the fees charged become primary because that is the only aspect of the process in which the lawyer is permitting the client to participate—the paying part. People just cannot feel a sense of responsibility for success or failure if they have not been involved contributors. It is even worse when clients have been involved and the selfish lawyer gives no recognition or credit.

Separate and apart from all these client-relations reasons for actively soliciting the client's participation, the Model Rules mandate unequivocally that lawyers accept the client's authority to make decisions about the matter and to keep the client informed concerning those decisions. Yet the Model Rules are only the starting point for lawyers to create and develop relationships with clients. For lawyers to maximize their effectiveness for clients and to earn the clients' respect, they must do much more than the Model Rules specify.

In the remaining portion of this chapter, I'll suggest a number of ideas for your consideration to break down the "my-case" syndrome.

USING PRONOUNS APPROPRIATELY

To break the "my-case" syndrome, proper use of pronouns is of prime importance. Consistently strive in all oral and written communications to and with clients to replace "I" and "my" with "we," and substitute "our" for "your."

Instead of "I need to consider the implication of these new facts," it becomes "we need to consider the implication of these new facts." Similarly, "the IRS's position is that your forms were not filed on time," becomes "the IRS's position is that our forms were not filed on time" (regardless of the fact that the lawyer was not aware of or involved with the filing of the forms).

The use of the appropriate pronouns for a joint lawyer-client relationship will go a long way toward replacing the "my-case" syndrome with the "our-case" lawyer-client relationship. It will also convey and reinforce that the client is an important participant. Communications alone will result in greater client satisfaction.

Coincidentally, this team approach will also reduce stress on the lawyer. Team decisions optimize opportunities to have all of the relevant information before committing to a course of action. They lessen the chances that the course will have to be changed mid-stream. When the lawyer does everything possible to arrive at the team's destination, and it turns out to be an undesirable one, at least the lawyer does not bear the burden of having selected the destination.

THE ALPHA OF CLIENT INVOLVEMENT

The initial face-to-face meeting between the client and lawyer usually sets the expectations and tone for the lawyer-client relationship for the course of that particular case or matter. The relationships may change from case to case and during the same matter, even between the same lawyer and the same client. Likewise, the client's relationship with one lawyer may be entirely different than the client's relationship with another lawyer in the same firm.

Even if the lawyer-client relationship has not been what it should have been in the past, it may be altered on any new matter, or even during the same matter. The lawyer bears the responsibility for the client relationship regardless of the personality of the client. So, regardless of how difficult a client may be, the lawyer must be constantly proactive in shaping and reconstituting the lawyer-client relationship.

The client has selected the lawyer. From that very act, the client has demonstrated a willingness to pay the lawyer for advice, representation, and a relationship. The lawyer may reject the client's offer to retain his or her services. However, after the engagement, if the foundation of the relationship does not develop at the initial meeting and become stronger over time, the lawyer is responsible in 99 percent of the cases. To put the blame for a poor lawyer-client relationship on the client is a lawyer copout. If the lawyer agrees to represent the client, the lawyer must be sure that the relationship thrives within legal and ethical boundaries.

The client is in large part willing to pay the lawyer's fees in order to have a professional relationship with the lawyer. The client could probably obtain the objective reading of the law from any number of sources that now include thousands, including ones on the Internet. The client has chosen you not because you are the sole source of the needed technical legal knowledge, but because, for whatever rational or irrational motivation, the client desires to have a professional relationship with you—a client-lawyer relationship. The shift in perception from lawyers thinking they have been chosen to work on a legal matter to being selected as one party to a professional relationship is helpful for reorienting lawyer's attitudes about law practice.

Before asking the client to tell you about the situation, it is a good idea to discuss with the client the principle of attorney-client privilege. You might expound on that by stating that a lawyer can be most helpful to a client when the lawyer knows the worst about the facts. Explain that belated surprise about new facts involving any portion of the matter is the most devastating thing that could happen at trial or during final business negotiations. Assure the client that the attorney-client privilege extends to all those in your office as well as yourself. This assurance of confidentiality usually puts the client-lawyer relationship on a special and unique basis instantly.

THE INITIAL MEETING—THE FOUNDATION OF THE RELATIONSHIP

A couple of things should never be done in an initial meeting, or ever, with a client. We will discuss them before we explore what should be done.

First, it does no good to guilt-trip the client by saying that if he or she had come to you before, the client would not be in all this trouble. Frequently, lawyers who are replacing another lawyer on a matter enjoy expounding on the failures and shortcomings of the previous lawyer. What lawyers who do this don't realize is that no matter how dissatisfied the client is with the previous representative, such comments are slamming the client for bad judgment in choosing the first lawyer.

Most lawyers who use this approach are trying to obtain a superior-inferior relationship with the client and also to position themselves as blameless in case the situation becomes worse. Regardless of how pleasurable or protective to the lawyer it might be to guilt-trip the client or bash the previous lawyer, this paternalistic, judgmental, less-than-civil approach obviously is not the way to build a good working relationship between adults or attorney and a child client.

Second, telling the client how busy you are and how many other matters you have to handle will not build the confidence of the client. The initial meeting with the client provides the lawyer with the perfect audience for boasting; however, to boast about how busy one is will only worry the client about whether you will devote sufficient time and effort to the client's business to render effective representation. Instilling doubt in the client that the lawyer will not meet scheduled milestones is not an objective of client relations. It sets up the client conclusion that the first time the lawyer is late on a deadline—no matter how minor—it is because the attorney was working on some other client's business. Sometimes, resulting resentments hatch malpractice claims, even when the other client's matters had nothing to do with the delayed performance.

Now let's examine some things that should occur between lawyer and client early in the relationship.

The initial meeting with the client is critical to setting the substance and tone for the entire relationship. The most crucial aspect of that relationship is full, free and open two-way communication. The client-to-lawyer communication portion is paramount. Permit the client to tell every detail, even irrelevant ones, and to express feelings. Ask questions to gain relevant information about facts, feelings and goals. This is necessary information to serving the client well and will show you are interested. Take notes to demonstrate that what the client is saying is important to you and so you can remember what the client said. But, don't be so wrapped up in taking notes that it distracts you from listening to the client as a person or detracts from showing empathy for the client's situation. Discuss some of the general aspects of the law so the client is reassured that he or she has retained a lawyer knowledgeable about the relevant field of law.

Ask what goals the client wishes to accomplish jointly with you, as his or her lawyer. What does the client want from your representation on this matter? Make a list of mutual client-attorney goals. Read it back to the client. Ask the client whether any other items should be included on the list.

Some clients need assistance in thinking through their real goals. They also may need help clarifying what they can realistically expect from the legal intervention and their lawyer. You should use all of the information acquired from clients about what is to be accomplished to assist in joint goal setting (or refinement) and the clients' expectations of their lawyer. If the lawyer permits the client to leave the initial meeting with expectations soaring well above reality, the lawyer will eventually pay dearly.

The success and strength of a lawyer's relationship is largely governed by acquiring relevant facts and personal information and then using them effectively to guide the client while building the relationship. If the client does not articulate the expectations, the lawyer, in the interest of developing a fruitful relationship, must politely probe to marshal the materials necessary to construct the desired mutually advantageous relationship. The foundation of the "advantageous relationship" has to be that the client and attorney are working together to achieve common, realistic goals.

In addition to goals, the lawyer should learn, at a minimum, enough information to answer the following questions by the end of the initial meeting with the client:

1. What does the client subjectively expect from the lawyer?
2. How much time, effort, and money is the client willing to commit to this matter?

Each client brings unique expectations based on prior experiences with lawyers or the lack of them. If lawyers are going to meet those expectations, they must be known. These not only encompass goals, but other things like the frequency, nature and mode of communications. Some clients will invest large sums of money in a legal pursuit but not the time required to research a deal or prepare for trial. Others have limited funds to expend or think a matter is only worth a limited investment of money. The lawyer needs to know the extent of a client's commitment on all aspects required to see a matter through to a conclusion. This is necessary because that information will determine what course-of-action options are available for the lawyer to recommend to the client. It is also an obligation of the lawyer to educate the client about the real-world quantity of client time and money that will be required to best pursue the matter. Further, the attorney must be forthright in explaining when such expenditures are likely to be futile.

Being judgmental about the client's goals will accomplish nothing. For instance, saying that no one has ever won a case like this will do more to undermine the client's confidence in you than convince the client that the situation faced has little prospect of successful resolution. If you feel the client's goals are totally unrealistic and that you won't be able to convince the client over time to modify them, you will probably be better off declining to undertake the representation. Under these circumstances, it is highly unlikely that you will able to achieve the client's desired result, you won't develop a satisfactory relationship with the client, and the client will most likely make comments disparaging your efforts.

You don't want to be dubbed ineffective, even if the client pays your invoices in full.

Failure to develop a satisfactory client relationship—regardless of cause—will, in the long run, do your practice more harm than good. It will be detrimental because you will not be building toward repeat business and the client is very likely to "bad-mouth" you to others which adversely affects existing clients and prospects for new business.

ESTABLISHING A TIMETABLE

Develop a mutually acceptable timetable with the client for at least the initial actions to be taken in the matter. This timetable should set out what will be done, by whom (including the client), and when it will be completed. A simple example of a timetable is the drafting of an estate plan. It might appear as follows:

October 2: Lawyer first meets with Client.

October 5: Client gathers and mails asset inventory and insurance policies to Lawyer.

October 15: Lawyer mails draft of estate plan to Client.

October 20: Client reviews document and raises questions or make any changes to draft and sends them to Lawyer for legal analysis. If none, the client will notify lawyer that there are no changes or questions.

October 25: Client scheduled to meet with Lawyer in law firm conference room at 2 p.m. to execute estate plan.

An alternative to this specific date timetable is one that clearly ties the lawyer's performance to when the client performs. Such a timetable could appear as follows:

October 2: Lawyer first meets with Client.

October 5: Client gathers and mails asset inventory and insurance policies to Lawyer.

Ten Days after receiving complete materials from Client: Lawyer mails draft of estate plan to Client.

Five Days after receiving draft of estate play from Lawyer: Client reviews and raises questions or makes any changes to draft and sends them to Lawyer for legal analysis—if none, the Client will notify Lawyer that there are no changes or questions.

Within Two Days of receiving Client's comments on estate plan draft: Lawyer will schedule and notify Client of appointment time and date to execute the estate plan.

Obviously, in setting such a timetable one would substitute the client's name for "Client" and the lawyer's name for "Lawyer." Additionally, if it is appropriate to have an associate, legal assistant, or legal secretary involved, that person's name should be in the timetable. Be sure you introduce the client to everyone else whose name is in the timetable before the client leaves the office from the initial meeting.

By constructing a timetable, the client becomes a part of what is going to be done, deciding who will do it and when it is going to be completed. The client is also assured that even though there is not a daily communication from the lawyer, the lawyer and the firm have certain responsibilities and that the client can judge whether they are met. The timetable also has the advantage of providing the client with an early understanding that if the client does not provide information in a timely fashion, the lawyer can't be blamed for failing to meet the subsequent deadline.

TALKING MONEY WITH THE CLIENT

No matter how uncomfortable or painful, a full explanation of all fees and charges must be given to the client in the initial interview. If possible, quote for a specific fee, otherwise give estimates and ranges of total fees and costs. If totals are too uncertain to estimate or the matter is complex, tell the client a ballpark-number for the entire matter and the approximate cost of the first several steps that must be taken to achieve the agreed upon goals.

This is critical, not only to establish an essential element of the lawyer-client relationship, but also to give the client an idea of the cost of accomplishing the goals set forth. When the approximate cost is factored in, the client may choose to change those goals.

A good practice is to go over the fee structure, expense charges, and billing practice and payment expectations. Always ask if the client has any questions. Clients need to be put at ease or at least on notice about fees. You might offer some comment about the cost of quality. Remember, most first-time individual users of legal services are familiar only with the TV, newspaper or phone-book advertising for cheap divorces and lawyer pitches that promise, "You don't pay unless I get you money!" Explain the economic premise on which your practice and fees are based.

Many lawyers and firms do not show, or have a great reluctance to share, information concerning the cost of doing business with others. This is so even with people with whom we practice—for instance, partners generally don't let associates know the financial status of the practice, though the health of the practice is dependent on associates. There is an even greater reticence to letting a client know that X percent of the hourly rate paid or total revenue is consumed by salaries, computers, research services, insurance, rent and other expenses. Yet, the individual client has no concept of the cost of practicing. And, corporate clients which request deep discounts in rates often have no way to know that the lawyer's refusal to accept the work at the discount requested is driven by the reality that it would cause an actual loss.

You may want to give some clients a brief economic primer on the economics of your practice. This helps change the individual's perception that every dollar of gross revenue—the rate at which the client pays fees—goes directly to the lawyer's personal bank account. Similarly, such a discussion provides a corporate client an understanding that, like it, profit must be generated for specific business to be desired and accepted. When discounting fees for a corporation, the economic discussion will provide an excellent opportunity to emphasize the extreme importance of the projected high volume of work to entice you to accept the discounted fee rate.

Careful consideration must be given as to the whether such a discussion of the economics of practice will help or harm the lawyer's relationship with the client. For instance, it will be difficult to convince a client in the retail grocery business where profits are usually one to three percent that the lawyer can't tolerate a discount in fees, which "drops" profits below 15 or 20 percent.

Many who engage in such a discussion fail to make clear, where it is so, that the partners are whole or largely compensated from what is dubbed profit. Since such a practice of paying executives from profit instead of accounting for all corporate salaries in pre-profit expenses is foreign to a large majority of clients, it is worth explaining. Also, lawyers must be extraordinarily careful about the words and phrasing of any economic discussion. The same words, such as profit or adequate compensation, mean different things to an individual client and to a corporate officer. Nonetheless, such a discourse is worth considering.

Either after the oral explanation of fees and payment obligations or in a follow-up letter, the client should be asked to sign a written engagement letter that contains a fee agreement. Under no circumstances should the client be put in the position of feeling pressured to sign the agreement. In most cases, it is best to orally review the terms of the engagement letter and fee agreement with the client. If the engagement letter is typed at the time of the initial meeting, suggest that the client take it, read it, call if there are any questions, and only then sign and return it. If it is to be printed and sent later, go over what will be in the letter and urge the client to call you to discuss it before signing and returning the engagement letter.

Be sure it is clearly communicated in writing—and the client acknowledges understanding—that you are retained as the client's lawyer only after you receive the signed engagement letter and any retainer you may require. This process protects you from misunderstood cocktail conversation and people who come in or call to lawyer-shop, to compare price, or to casually tell you about a matter; say that they will get back to you if they want to proceed, fail to do so, and then later accuse you of missing a statute-of-limitations or response deadline.

If the firm or lawyer routinely requests a signed engagement letter and fee agreement with every client and every matter, then it could easily defend against such an accusation by demonstrating that no fee agreement was signed and so no lawyer-client relationship was established. Many fee agreements specifically provide that the lawyer has not been engaged until the client pays a retainer and executes and returns the fee agreement. While this practice may seem cold or harsh, it has proven to be beneficial to clients and lawyers in the development of their relationship.

Note that the absence of a written fee arrangement does not mean there is no representation relationship. Some case law implies a relationship even when none has been established in writing. Thus, a lawyer's standard practice of written agreements can also help to overcome this presumption and avoid this problem.

It is prudent practice to send a letter to anyone who discusses a legal issue with you—even in the most casual circumstances—confirming that you have not been retained and explaining how to retain you if the potential client desires to do so. Then an engagement letter and fee agreement should be drafted and signed. In smaller matters, a letter incorporating the essence of the engagement and the fees to be charged will suffice. The letter on pages 82–83 is an example of a basic engagement letter.

If it is decided at the first client meeting that an initial letter is to be sent on the client's behalf or any organizational work by a secretary or paralegal will be done on the file, ideally either the draft of the letter or the instructions for the organizational work should be dictated in the presence of the client at that initial meeting. In this fashion, the client witnesses and understands that you are already working on the matter. If, however, you discern some doubt that the client will retain you, do not commence any work on the case.

If the fee agreement is not returned within an agreed upon timeframe, then either don't start work or stop all work on the matter. Immediately notify the potential client in writing that because the engagement letter and fee agreement were not signed and returned, you have stopped work and are returning any materials the potential client gave you. Add that you regret the potential client has apparently decided on a different

Date

Potential Client
100 Main Street
Hometown, U.S.A. 11223
Subject: XYZ Matter

Dear Potential Client:

The Rules of Professional Conduct applicable to attorneys require that we inform you in writing of the basis or rate of our fees for professional services. Accordingly, we would like to confirm the understanding reached regarding the professional services you have retained our firm to perform on behalf of _____ in connection with the _____ matter[s], and the fees for such services.

You should understand that outcomes in legal matters are never certain. Therefore, while we cannot guarantee a result, we will seek to obtain the best result for you based on the facts as they develop and applicable law.

Fees for our services are based on the actual time incurred by each lawyer, legal assistant, or other support personnel working on your case multiplied by each person's respective hourly billing rate prevailing at the time. Fractions of hours are computed in periods of not less than one-tenth (1/10) of an hour. Currently, the hourly billing rate for lawyers ranges from $_____ through $_____ per hour and the hourly billing rate for legal assistants ranges from $_____ through $_____ per hour. My billing rate currently is $_____ per hour. Hourly rates are subject to change from time to time upon notice to you.

We will also charge you for all disbursements made on your behalf including copying charges, use of word processing equipment, long-distance telephone charges, telefax charges, filing fees, travel mileage, airline tickets, parking, certain meals and lodging, messenger services, courier packages, and our legal research computer service, if needed. A copy of the current ranges of some disbursement rates is attached. They are also subject to change depending upon costs incurred.

We are requesting an initial retainer of $_____ in order to consummate our retention and to begin our work on your behalf. This payment is due immediately. We will be officially engaged when we receive the retainer payment with a copy of this letter signed by you.

The retainer will serve as a source of payment of our statements. All fees and disbursements will be offset against this retainer amount. Any unused portion of the retainer will be returned to you upon completion of our representation. If the retainer is not enough to pay the fees and disbursements billed, we will expect prompt payment of the additional amount, and we may also request an additional retainer for continued services. Bills for our services and disbursements are sent on a monthly basis. Payment is due upon receipt of each bill.

Potential Client
Date
Page 2

It is difficult to precisely anticipate the amount of our time that will be required for this engagement and the amount of fees and disbursements that will be incurred. At any time during the course of our engagement, we welcome the opportunity to discuss with you the fees and expenses incurred or to be incurred and will try to minimize such amounts. Sometimes this will require the reassessment of your strategic goals and tactical methods. We are always prepared to reevaluate approaches, whether it be for cost reasons or otherwise.

Please be aware that you have the right to terminate our services at any time after consulting with us. In such an event, you will be required to pay in full our fees and disbursements incurred as of the termination date. This agreement also creates the right for us to terminate our services to you for any reason, including the failure to timely pay our statements in full as submitted, the failure to replenish the retainer if requested, or if in our sole discretion we determine that to continue our services would be unethical or impractical.

Should you decide to retain our firm for additional services not specified in this letter, we will be pleased to provide such services under such terms as you and we may agree upon.

If the foregoing terms and conditions accurately summarize and confirm your understanding of our attorney-client engagement, please indicate your approval and acceptance by dating, signing, and returning this letter, together with your initial retainer check made payable to this firm. Enclosed for your records is a copy of this letter.

We look forward to serving you and working with you on this matter.

Very truly yours,

Lawyer

Enclosures

Accepted and agreed to:

By: _____

Date: _____, 20___

course of action than what was discussed in your office and that you hope the client will decide to use your services at some point in the future.

This process may have to be modified to comply with all state and model ethical requirements, but you must clearly negate any possible inference of a lawyer-client relationship where there is none after an initial telephone or face-to-face discussion of a specific legal problem.

EXTRAS

A nice touch after the client has actually retained you is to give him or her an empty file folder, labeled with the name of the client and matter, in which the client is instructed to keep all correspondence and other documents pertaining to this matter. The file should be a distinctive color with the lawyer's law firm's name, address, e-mail, and phone number on the outside.

On the inside flap may be printed a complete list of all of the services that the law firm offers and repeat the name of the firm, address, e-mail and phone number of all offices. The file folder should contain the law firm's current brochure. The individual lawyer's business card should also be inside, but removable. The lawyer might give the client another business card for the client's purse or wallet. Thus, the client leaves the initial meeting with more information on the lawyer, law firm and its services. All of this information assists in building the relationship and cross marketing of other services.

Immediately following the initial meeting with the client, dictate a letter to the client that reflects a summary of the meeting just concluded. Extract the information for the letter from the information you recorded on your legal pad. This should include the timetable for performance and the mutually agreed goals. The letter should be framed with initial and concluding paragraphs that reflect (1) your gratitude at being retained to represent the client in this matter and (2) your enthusiastic commitment to represent the client.

INVOLVEMENT DURING THE PENDENCY OF A MATTER

After the initial communication, practicing lawyers have all been frustrated by "urgent" messages from clients that turn out to be unimportant, by clients posing naive questions, and by clients requiring unnecessary meetings to be added to your already overburdened calendar. It took me a long time to learn not to resent returning "urgent" phone calls that are not urgent, answering "dumb" questions, and scheduling seemingly "unnecessary" handholding meetings. The client will perceive any resentment or reluctant attitude. Instead, be thankful that the client wants your advice on something urgent and important to the client and desires to use and develop the relationship with you. The magnitude and substance of the contact are unimportant compared to the fact that the client wants contact with you.

Next stop and ask yourself where you have previously fallen down in the development of client relationships. How can you satisfy this particular client's need for the relationship with you as a lawyer in the future? The client may be seeking an avenue to develop the long-term relationship, rather than only seeking the answer to a technical legal question. Focus on the relationship, not the matter.

THE KEY TO YOUR FUTURE

Many lawyers resent the time they must spend "hand-holding" with a client. The urge is to get back to "work" researching, doing deals, writing, or trying cases. If, as I believe, the relationship with the lawyer and not the legal work brings the client back, few things could be more important than "hand-holding."

The doctor with a superior bedside manner will almost always have more patients than the physician lacking in such skills. Barbers and hair stylists build their trade on the relationships they establish with their customers, rather than purely on skill cutting and styling hair.

Clients of lawyers have a strong desire for relationships with the lawyers they hire. Lawyers who want to build a practice must respond accordingly. We attorneys must elevate the importance of the relationship to the same top shelf on which the client places it. Take every opportunity to spend time and effort developing the client's image of that unique human connection known as the lawyer-client relationship.

We must reflect, study, understand, and implement practices that satisfy the client's need for the client-lawyer relationship. This should be in the forefront of the lawyer's mind in everything he or she does with and for the client. For it is on the quality of the relationship that the client makes decisions critical to the lawyer's future.

SEND COPIES; GIVE UPDATES

It should go without saying, clients must receive not only a copy of every pertinent communication the lawyer sends out, but also a copy of every communication the lawyer receives concerning the matter or case.

However, it is astounding how many lawyers fail to fully execute on this basic tenet of client relations. These copies need to be sent to the client promptly with a record of their being sent kept in the client's file at the law firm. Clients really do read these communications and are very concerned about them. If they call with a question or comment, be patient and give a full explanation no matter how busy you are or how naive the question.

This copy requirement of good client communications inherently carries with it the mandate that the lawyer write in language understood by a layperson. If the correspondence received and forwarded is written in legalese, most clients will appreciate a note translating the essence of the document. Paralegals or experienced legal secretaries should be able to compose the large majority of these letters. However, guard against writing that explanatory note in a condescending style. Using phrases like "It appears that our opponent is taking the position that . . ." is far superior to "In case you don't understand. . . ."

The client should also receive regular status reports on what is happening with a case. These may be routinely produced by legal assistants or, in smaller offices, experienced legal secretaries. They need not be done monthly, but the frequency should be clearly understood in the initial meeting and confirmed in the letter summarizing that meeting. Then procedures must be implemented in the law office to guarantee these reports are sent to the clients on time. Legal and administrative assistants or secretaries are much better suited to assure the execution of this function than lawyers.

Additionally, the client should have a written communication summarizing any phone conversation of importance concerning the matter being handled by the lawyer. This is especially important if the client was not privy to the call. On more significant and urgent matters, the lawyer should call the client to report before dictating the written record.

The substantive material of these written and telephone reports is important, but even more important is using them as a vehicle to build a strong relationship with the client through increased client contact and involvement. They reassure the client that the lawyer is working on the matter and, interestingly, force the lawyer to pay attention to and work on the matter.

Inadvertently, I discovered that e-mail communications were causing me to fail to fully communicate with my clients. I shoot off e-mail to an opposing counsel, or received them, and failed to copy the client. As e-mail communications increased, the frequency of this oversight grew. One reason for the oversight is lawyers' reliance on secretaries or administrative assistants to be sure the client is always copied on all correspondence. When a lawyer types an e-mail, the mind-set is dictation, which leaves the details such as copies to others.

Regardless of the reason, the client must receive a copy of relevant e-mails sent and received. Sometimes putting a colored "sticky" on the computer on which you have written "Copy the client" helps establish the habit.

While thinking about e-mails, I want to remind you to have a hard copy of your e-mail correspondence with your client and between you and opposing counsel placed in the client's matter file. I was working on a number of large matters shooting an unknown number of e-mails to the client requesting information, giving advice and obtaining involvement in the decisions. Additionally, I was exchanging e-mails with opposing counsel—sometimes at a rapid fire pace—on very crucial aspects of matters. It hit me one day that I was deleting these messages and thus there was no record of the communication in our client file. This was an easy way to create disputes with opposing counsel and possibly with your client. Plus, there was no documented record as to what you advised.

To solve the problem I had created, I told my administrative assistant, that I'd be sending her blind copies electronically and that she should print a hardcopy and file it in the matter's correspondence subfile. This is now working well. I hate to think what might have happened if a dispute had arisen between a client and me or with opposing counsel about the terms of a deal which were only documented in the permanently deleted e-mails!

Voicemails pose a similar problem. I forward key ones I receive to my assistant to be transcribed, and where appropriate sent to the client, then filed. Dictating a memo to the file with a copy to the client is the only way I've recorded the content of voicemails I've left. How you record voicemails isn't of import; that you do it is.

The lawyer should request client input with respect to the strategy and direction of the matter. A lawyer has an obligation to describe the impact of the law on the facts that have been communicated, investigated, or formally discovered. Then the client needs to be a full partner in deciding what to do. Alternative courses of action, including the cost of each, need to be laid on the table, preferably in writing, by the lawyer for discussion with the client.

Posing several options for the client to consider is not difficult because the competent lawyer should be considering a number of different approaches to resolve the client's problem anyway. Asking the client, "What do you want to do?" will not be viewed as the lawyer's uncertainty of action, but rather an involvement of the client in deciding his or her future as it may be influenced by the outcome of that particular legal event. If the client declines your invitation to participate in decision making, as some clients do, take firm control by giving clear recommendations. Then get the client to agree to or alter the approach before pursuing it. If the client wants time to consider, give it. But, give it with a deadline, for some prefer to ignore difficult decisions hoping the situation will resolve itself. And sometimes it does, but as the client's lawyer, you can't count on it.

If the course of action costs money, even with participation, clients may still tell others, "My lawyer made me do it." At least, the clients themselves will know they made the decision and your relationship with that client will be preserved.

Never assume that the client does not care. Some clients deal with their lawyers as with their doctors: "Just Fix It". This does not mean that they don't care about their injury or disease. It may mean they just don't know what to do because they don't understand either their predicament or their options. Recent medical studies have proven that patients who take more control of their physical condition by meaning-fully participating in medical decisions heal better and faster.

The same holds for the cure of legal maladies. So, it becomes an essential part of the lawyer's job to get and keep the client involved. It may seem curious to some that when lawyers take steps to assure that clients maintain control and substantially determine the course of a matter, even if not the outcome, that the relationship with lawyers improves. When lawyers take the cooperative rather than the paternalis-tic approach with clients, the clients increase their reliance on lawyers. This seems like paradox. Those who have experienced the joy of being on an effective team in athletics, war, or work, will recognize that that it is a fundamental truth rather than a paradox.

It is imperative that the client remains involved with the legal process through the conclusion of the reason the client consulted with the lawyer in the first place. In many cases, the strength of the lawyer-client relation-ship is directly related to the degree the lawyer has allowed, enabled, or required the client's participation in the client's own legal affairs.

REVIEWING AND REVISING GOALS

At critical junctures in the case, such as after discovery is closed in liti-gation or after due diligence in a corporate acquisition, the lawyer and the client should review the goals set forth by the client in the initial meeting. If the facts appear to be changing from what was understood or anticipated at the first meeting, the lawyer must work with the client to reconsider and possibly change the goal, rather than the lawyer doing so unilaterally.

Obviously, the lawyer has the opportunity and obligation to influence the client's decision-making process considerably by the description and interpretation of the law and the impact of the discovered facts. Some clients may be embarrassed by the revelation that the facts, for whatever reason, are different than those conveyed to the lawyer at the first meeting. The lawyer must tell the client that this is not the first time a person has not been fully informed about what is going on in the client's life or business. This also provides an opportunity to point out what lawyers know well—that every situation is viewed differently—not necessarily disingenuously—by every person who examines it. Making this point often keeps the parties negotiating on a deal or changes a client's decision to go to trial. Proper handling by the lawyer enables the client to adjust goals with reality without feeling embarrassed or stupid.

Do not lose sight of the fact that based upon later-discovered evidence, favorable rulings, due diligence or recent court rulings, goals may be expanded, as well as contracted. If the facts, court order, or new statute reveal that a client is in a better position than originally anticipated, the client and lawyer should set their sights and goals higher.

If the lawyer discovers that an initial or revised timetable agreed upon will not be met, an immediate communication to the client is required. No matter how busy or how deeply immersed in other endeavors the client is, the client will almost certainly recall when a lawyer is to have accomplished a task. Not being informed of a significant change will certainly generate disappointment in the lawyer's performance.

Timetables need to be set initially to enable the lawyer to meet the work and time deadlines that they contain. While not telling the client, the lawyer must take into consideration the lawyer's entire workload, not just what has to be done for this client on this matter. A timetable creates expectations in clients. Therefore, the relationship between the lawyer and the client will be damaged if the client has to call the lawyer and say, "You were supposed to have completed the draft of my contract by last Thursday. Where is it?" Far better, the lawyer calls the client prior to the deadline and explains the delay and obtains an agreement on a new specific time for completion. While the client may not like the postponement, at least the client knows that he or she has not been ignored or forgotten.

The timetable has another beneficial effect. If the client knows when to expect that the lawyer will complete a phase of a project, the client will be less likely to call the lawyer's office asking when it will be completed. If you are like most lawyers, you will appreciate not having your work interrupted to answer such questions, and the timetable will facilitate the completion of the client's work sooner, and probably cheaper, by eliminating some unnecessary phone calls.

Inevitably a timetable creates reciprocal obligation on the lawyer. Do not agree to a schedule to complete work that you know you can't meet. You should regard a time commitment to a client as being as compulsory as one set by a judge or the expiration date of an option set in a contract. All the client cares about is that you do what you say you will do when you say you will do it. The reason you did or did not meet the mutually set deadline is irrelevant to the client.

Using a fax machine, e-mail, overnight postal service, commercial delivery service, or a messenger service often helps to develop the lawyer-client relationship. Recall the old movies where both important and ordinary people received telegrams containing either tragic or ecstatic news. It was delivered by the Western Union messenger on a bike. Modern-day electronic and personal communications services can provide clear evidence that the lawyer thinks the client and the client's matter are of great import.

Do not lose sight of the fact that your use of these services must be judicious so that the client does not conclude that you are unnecessarily expending funds frivolously. Use the expedited non-electronic services only for those items that will be viewed as important by the client. The remainder should be sent via regular mail. Routinely faxing a document and then following it with a copy delivered by overnight or messenger service, except when an original is required, is excessive. Such duplication of copies is viewed by most as just plain unnecessary, expensive, and sometimes confusing. The client does not need two copies of the document, especially at premium delivery rates.

As the lawyer works on any client matter, the constant question to be asked is, "Is there any other way I can involve the client at this step of the procedure?" If the answer is yes, the time and effort expended in that pursuit will contribute significantly to both the immediate and the long-term lawyer-client relationship. If the answer is no, then the client should always be kept informed about the services the lawyer is performing. Such information always needs to be conveyed in some form before the client receives the bill detailing the services.

THE OMEGA OF CLIENT INVOLVEMENT

Do not be misled by the title of this section. Client involvement never ends. However, what we are focusing on is the client's involvement in one particular matter.

Communicating the results of your efforts as a lawyer is a given, regardless of whether you are working in tax, real estate, litigation, corporate, or any other field of law. The real client relations skill is the wording of the communication and the method by which that result is communicated. Except for the initial client contact, this is probably the single most important contact the lawyer has with the client.

The lawyer's attitude about the appropriate timing for communicating an outcome is most often tied to the nature of the result. How anxious I am to let my client know that WE won the case! A telephone call, an e-mail, a fax, a face-to-face meeting, or an immediate overnight mailing of the result—none are quick enough. When the judge, the law, the facts, the witnesses, or any other factor that lawyers can create is or becomes the reason or excuse for an undesirable result, lawyers are much more reticent about communicating with the client.

In one instance I delayed about a day and a half before letting the client know that we had lost a labor arbitration matter to the union representing his corporation's employees. Before I called, I received an angry call from the client stating that the janitors and other employees were being stirred up because the union told them that the union had won the case against him, the employer. My client told me he had gotten into shouting matches with the employees saying that the case had not yet been decided and that the union was trying to lead them astray again. He was absolutely convinced that the decision had not come down and told the employees, "If anything like that had happened, Attorney Ewalt would have called me immediately." When I told the client that the information the union and employees were parading around the workplace was correct and I made some lame excuse about not contacting him, I got what I deserved. The details of the remainder of the conversation are not printable.

It was fortunate that the client's anger was expressed over the telephone rather than in person because the client laid me out one side and up the other. Had it been in person and had the client had an instrument—sharp or dull would have made no difference to him—I would have been physically filleted. I had compounded the loss by not conveying it, which embarrassed the client in front of his employees. The client was acting upon the candid prompt communications relationship he believed he had with his lawyer and defended me erroneously. The client was rightfully embarrassed. His anger grew from his disappointment in me, and the breakdown in our communications relationship, as well as the embarrassment in him. And now he was going to be forced to eat crow in front of all those employees from whom he always demanded honesty and respect. There was no question that I was the proximate cause of his embarrassment, not the arbitration's loss. However, the embarrassment and anger were far more devastating than the loss, both to the client and to me.

How do you deal with a client in that situation? There are no easy answers. I admitted that I was wrong, apologized for the embarrassment that I caused, agreed that his feelings about doing verbal and physical violence to me were justified, expressed the hope that he would forgive me and pledged not to let the situation occur again.

The client chose to continue our lawyer-client relationship. I am certain that my apology was not the basis of his choice. Rather, I think the client chose to continue to retain me based on the strength we had built into our relationship prior to the incident. The client's knowledge of my respect for him, more than a mere professional relationship, had much more to do with the continuation of our lawyer-client relationship than the sincerity of my apology (but that helped!).

Hopefully, you haven't caused the turmoil I did with our client. This unfortunate incident teaches the value of communicating promptly with your client whether the news is good or terrible.

The most effective way to communicate a good or bad result to a client is to meet face to face. That type of meeting will provide a free flow of communication. No other medium—except perhaps video conferencing—enables facial expressions and body language to be transmitted and read. When setting up the face-to-face meeting over the telephone, do not keep the client in suspense. Tell the client that you want to meet to discuss the result, which you should summarize very briefly. The client may decide there is no necessity for a meeting. If that happens, you should tell the client that you will immediately mail the document that incorporates the result or a memo you will dictate about an undocumented occurrence, that if the client has questions later to please call, that you will be glad to answer any questions and that you would be more than willing to meet with the client concerning the result after the client reviews your transmission. If the client has not called a few days after receipt of the written result, you should telephone to inquire whether there are any questions or concerns about the result or the consequences.

The tool of following up with a telephone conversation is a particularly effective one. In our family, our children had a series of childhood illnesses and accidents that required the attention of a doctor. Several of the doctors, after treatment had been prescribed, started, or completed, called a day or two later to inquire as to the child's progress. Both my wife and I have been most impressed with this procedure. It really didn't matter to us whether the call was motivated by a jury verdict that found some doctor somewhere guilty of malpractice because he or she failed to check the progress of the patient or whether the doctors were genuinely concerned about the health of our patient-child and the effectiveness of treatment. We were grateful. Our impression was that the doctor did more than what was required, more than what was expected, and that this doctor cared about something that we cared very dearly about, our children.

The follow-up call has another benefit. It provides a wonderful opportunity to ask if the client needs your assistance on implementing the decision. In the case of litigation, this may be whether to appeal; in a failed deal it may be to construct a plan to find another deal and in a successful real estate purchase it could be help on a subdivision plan approval. It is often overlooked when an estate plan is executed, that it isn't worth the paper it's written on unless the implementation, such as funding the trust, is completed. These and many other items can be covered in the follow-up call. The most important benefit is that the client knows the lawyer cares about something that is important to the client.

We lawyers should take heed and learn this lesson quickly and well. People care deeply about their businesses, their reputations, their inventions, their litigation, and their estates. Part of our job as lawyers is to learn to care as much and also reflect that we care.

GIVE THE DETAILS

Whether the client and the lawyer discuss the outcome of the matter face to face, on the telephone, or in writing, at a minimum, the following elements should be included:

POINT-BY-POINT REVIEW OF THE DOCUMENT

Explain each point. Provide an opportunity for the client to ask questions at the end of the explanation of each point. Be sure the client has a clear understanding of the individual points and the overall import and consequences of the result.

COST TO VALUE COMPARISON

Prepare and show a cost comparison to illustrate the value you have created by representing the client. For instance, in litigation, compare the demands or offers with the final settlement or verdict. When dealing with a corporate acquisition, illustrate the differences between the initially proposed warranties and representations and what you were able to negotiate into the Agreement of Sale. If dealing with a collective bargaining agreement, list the initial demands and the final agreement and then list economic gains (if representing a union), or savings (if representing an employer). These side-by-side comparisons will conclusively demonstrate the value you have provided to the client through your services. No matter how obvious, do not assume the client knows the value of your services—show the client.

At times this may be a difficult exercise. For instance, I tried a case in which a lawyer for an automobile dealer sued one of our clients in an attempt to collect $6,500 for repairing certain trucks that our client had purchased from the dealer and had taken back to be fixed. Our client refused to pay the $6,500 on the grounds the trucks had been defective when purchased. Our client had been willing to walk away and cause no trouble providing that the dealer wrote off the $6,500 for repairs. But the dealer sued. We were instructed to go after the dealer for all of the other warranty work that the client had done with his own truck-terminal mechanic and for the loss of income that had resulted from the times our client could not haul coal because the trucks were down. We filed a number of counterclaims, including breach of warranty, of merchantability and fitness and consequential damage claims. We calculated our client's damages at $189,000.

I vividly remember the conference in the judge's chambers after the judge found that we owed $6,500 but the plaintiff owed our client $156,000. The plaintiff's lawyer who initially filed a relatively small collection suit was pleading with the judge, "All my client wanted to do was collect a few thousand dollars and now we are faced with hundreds of thousands in liability."

Even my creativity could not have come up with an effective way to communicate the value of that lawyer's representation to the plaintiff truck dealer. I suppose the opposing lawyer's only hope was that the lawyer had explained the risks of litigation to the dealer before filing the complaint and again the risks of the counterclaim we filed and that the dealer had been involved in or made the decision to proceed in spite of the risks.

Cost to value comparisons with emphasis on the value are usually quite helpful to cementing good client relations.

GOAL TO RESULT COMPARISON

When the outcome becomes known, lawyers should compare the goals set or revised by the client. During this discussion of goals and achievements, it is important to acknowledge both the client's positive contributions to the result and the points at which the client directed a change in goals or a change in the course of the representation whether to reduce the cost or for another reason. Illustrations of involvement are critical so that the client may share in the responsibility for the outcome whether it be good, bad, or indifferent.

MINIMIZING LOSS/MAXIMIZING WIN

The lawyer and client should discuss whether there is anything else that may be done after the decision or deal to minimize the impact of an adverse decision or to maximize a victory. For example, tax counseling may be appropriate both in victory and defeat. An employer's or union's strict enforcement of a new term or condition of employment could result in turning victory into defeat. Maximizing a victory may require a victor to be extraordinarily gracious to a loser. In many instances we are talking about people's lives, their economic futures and their personal self-respect. Legal matters, be they lawsuits or negotiations, should not be intended to destroy the opponent as a person or a business. Objective counseling and follow-up by the lawyer may actually save the day even after the client perceives the sun has set. Hopefully, many nonlitigation situations will end with a win-win result. Even those may be improved by a little planning for the future.

After the client meeting is held to discuss results and the follow-up communication on matters of great import, it is helpful to conduct a matter exit interview. This interview might be conducted over lunch or cocktails. Or, it could be a subsequent no charge visit by the lawyer to the client's place of business or home. The exit interview should undertake to cover at least the following topics:

- What did you like as a client about how we handled your matter?
- Where did we fall down and not meet your expectations?
- What was your reaction to the individuals on our staff, to each of our lawyers, to our receptionist, to my secretary, to our legal assistants?
- How would you rate our overall efforts?
- How could we have done a better job for you?

One of the highest compliments an individual can pay another is to ask for advice. Here, the suggestion is that the lawyer turn the tables to ask the advice of the client about how the lawyer can better serve this client and other clients. The information obtained from this exit interview should be preserved, considered and, if valid, incorporated into the lawyer's and law firm's operational style.

The exit interview should be concluded with a sincere expression of gratitude for the client having chosen the lawyer and an expressed hope for continuing the relationship in the future. Sometimes these questions are being posed by the firm's marketing arm in survey form. If this is all the practice is willing to invest in follow-up client relations, do it. However, make no mistake, the survey is a poor substitute for a face-to-face meeting with the client.

MAKING THE RELATIONSHIP LAST

Client relations will be considerably advanced by the involvement of the client in the legal matter. The lawyer's proper use of the pronouns "we" and "our" to reflect the client involvement is only a start. Genuine, mutual, continuous concern and involvement of the client and the lawyer is critical for a successful and lasting relationship.

CHAPTER 9

BILLING: A VALUABLE COMMUNICATIONS TOOL

BILLS, BILLS, BILLS!

"In law nothing is certain but the expense."

Samuel Butler, English poet

"For Professional Services Rendered" reads the salutation to significant correspondence received by some clients. The contents of those communications have a profound impact on individual and corporate counsel clients, as well as the solo and law firm lawyers who are still billing in this fashion.

Bills to clients often control whether there is an understanding of the particular services performed. This understanding is the necessary step for the client to truly understand the value of the legal services received. If a person doesn't understand what he or she bought, there is no way clients can conclude they got their money's worth. For individual clients, the legal bill reflects a major investment in a service that frequently is not understood, even when all client goals have been met. In the client's mind, the amount of the invoice may not bear a relationship to the result obtained—another lawyer mystery. Billing formats must address the concerns of all clients.

For corporate counsel and other sophisticated consumers of legal services, a bill does even more. It shows (1) whether a budget is met,

(2) whether the matter requiring legal services was properly managed and (3) sometimes whether the recipient client will have a job or will even continue to exist. These issues have a direct impact on the ability of corporate counsel and other persons responsible for engaging the outside counsel, to execute their job duties and on the corporate perception of outside counsel. This perception ultimately determines the respect, position, compensation, and job security of corporate personnel. Thus, the bill for legal services is a very important document to all corporate clients.

For the solo or law firm performing services for a client, this billing communication is critical because it has a substantial impact on whether the individual client and the corporate client will perceive that they have received adequate value from the services performed compared to the amount charged. The client's conclusion as to how the received value justifies the amount invoiced is determined in part by the wording of the bill. When this perception of value is coupled with client relations, it becomes a crucial combination of factors affecting the client's decision to engage the same lawyer or law firm in the future.

Corporate counsel in large organizations annually review hundreds of legal bills and may authorize payment of millions of dollars in legal fees. These fees are paid to firms that vary in size from the solo practitioner to the largest law firms in the country. Corporate personnel gather a subjective sense of value even without formal objective measurements.

Although this chapter is primarily intended to be of assistance to outside counsel representing the smallest to the largest corporations, the principles set out in this chapter also apply to individual clients. The discussion that follows is relevant to all legal specialties.

THE PURPOSE OF THE BILL

When asked what the purpose of the bill from a law firm is, some clients respond, "to break the bank." Some corporate counsel react with a caustic comment about raiding the corporate treasury or fracturing the legal budget. Proper billing and active client relations minimize provoking these reactions.

Other clients say that the bill's purpose is to inform them what is owed. If that is the purpose, bills reading "for professional services rendered: $3,536.23" are perfectly adequate. Such a bottom-line bill would also serve internal corporate purposes of knowing whether the legal fees being paid were within the legal fee budget. Corporate budget-managing responsibilities could be fulfilled by totaling the legal fees in any particular time period and then projecting the expenditures into the future. For the individual client, this summary bill serves as a check against the total fee estimate by the lawyer or fee expectation set in the client's mind.

But such bills should be totally unacceptable to all lawyers and clients, especially to corporate clients. Why? Bills from outside counsel should serve as a corporate management tool to review the service performed on each particular matter, to assess the value of the service, and to evaluate outside counsel.

When a corporation's line and staff management ask corporate counsel whether the corporation received value for the services rendered by outside counsel or where legal fees may be cut, the bill must provide an analytical means to make such an evaluation data, which will support corporate counsel's responses. If the bill is general, it does not support the response and is a detriment to both outside counsel and corporate managers and executives.

The remainder of this chapter is directed toward making bills for legal services and disbursements a better communications vehicle for the individual client, a more effective management tool for corporate counsel, and a better client-relations document for all lawyers.

WHAT THE DETAILED BILL REVEALS

WHAT WAS DONE?

The bill should permit the client to readily know what counsel has done. Merely stating that the time billed was a result of "professional services rendered" leaves the client feeling that it is paying for the proverbial "pig in a poke."

It should not be a particular burden to specify that the time billed was for trial, witness preparation, drafting a particular document or some other specific activity. If research is listed, a bill should reflect the topic of the research. If a charge for deposition is billed, it should reflect who was deposed as well as which attorney took or defended the deposition.

The more detailed the invoice, the more effective the bill. Detail will enable clients to be better contributors in determining the strategy of a case. It will also enable the lawyers and clients to better control the legal fee budget. When the details of what was done are known, effective evaluation may be made as to whether to reassign tasks up or down the firm's rate hierarchy of timekeepers, take additional depositions, file summary judgment, appeal a particular procedural ruling or settle because legal costs are becoming too high.

Billing counsel's role is to assist corporate counsel and individual clients in this analysis by calibrating what it costs to have particular services performed. Discerning what it costs to file a brief is nearly impossible in the typical computer-generated bill. Little bits of applicable time may be scattered among a variety of other activities and among numerous billing persons over a period of several weeks. A client would have to search throughout one or more bills, dissect time entries, and add fees and costs to arrive at a cost for a brief.

Lawyers and law firms can facilitate any client's assembly of such information by summarizing or organizing the charges for each task, such as researching, writing, and filing a brief. This may be done by coding computer entries and sorting by activity. Most computerized billing systems are capable of sorting by activity just as they sort chronologically. The aggregated cost of each task to date may also be computed. The type of billing format being described often is called task-based billing. The American Bar Association has developed an excellent numerical system for standardizing the classification of tasks and portions of tasks. It is easily installed in a computerized billing system.

Some law firms may be reluctant to convert to task-based billing because the additional step of coding recorded time requires an additional administrative task, the difficulty in modifying computer programs to sort time by task, and the embarrassment about how much it costs to produce the brief. But, task-based billing is more rational to the client, keeps the partners of a firm aware of costs so that they can better supervise and evaluate associates and paralegals more effectively and provides added managerial value to both outside and corporate counsel through the billing process.

The lack of understanding between the individual client and lawyer and the absence of teamwork between corporate and outside counsel are frequent complaints. This should be a concern of the practicing bar. Detailing bills assist in overcoming these shortcomings that all too often develop into client misunderstandings.

WHEN WAS IT DONE?

It is critical that corporate counsel know when outside counsel performed the invoiced services. A significant portion of an evaluation of outside counsel is whether rigorous representation of the corporate interest has been undertaken. Balancing the other side of that issue is the concern that outside counsel might be "churning" the case with ineffective and unnecessary actions that run up the bill.

Knowing the dates outside counsel have performed services provides a way to track the timing of outside counsel's efforts and to evaluate whether counsel have been diligent. It also provides a means to relate total cost to elapsed time from start to finish on a matter. If similar real estate deals take one outside counsel the same billable hours but twice as much elapsed time to close as another outside counsel, the lawyer who took longer has not benefited the corporation and its interests because of the delay.

This conclusion holds even if the lawyer who took longer to close the deal charged less. Whether the corporation (or an individual) is buying or selling real estate, once that decision has been made, an expeditious preparation for closing is most often in the best interests of the client. On legal services billed by the hour rather than flat or contingent fees, the more elapsed time almost always means a higher bill. Many times this higher cost is without any relationship to improved quality or result.

When examining a legal bill that describes not only what was done but when it was done, one may assess the momentum of a case. Momentum provides a measure of how important a matter is to outside counsel and how well the client's interests are being served by retaining that particular counsel. A sense of urgency for closure on every matter, unless overridden by client direction with specific tactical rationale, is in the client's best interest.

These concerns and similar rationale also apply to individual clients. Frequently, as a result of a lack of understanding of the number of steps and the time it takes to complete each, individuals get the sense that a lawyer is dragging out or ignoring a matter. Individual consumers of legal services, have a more difficult time with such things due to their lack of experience with the legal process. Most individual clients don't have a history of dealing with the same lawyer, as many businesses do, which means that confidence that their legal affairs are being handled promptly and properly is fragile. Bills that show the date services were rendered should confirm earlier progress reports to the individual and corporate client that the lawyer has regularly paid attention to the client's legal affairs.

Finally, some corporations account for legal fees on an accrued accounting basis, as opposed to a cash one. This means that the legal department and controller charge the fees incurred, whether billed or not, to the corporate fiscal or tax year in which the legal services were performed. Obviously, having the date on which the person did the work on the bill greatly facilitates assigning the expense to the appropriate tax and corporate years.

WHO DID IT?

Who is doing what job is also an important element of detail on a legal bill. If a high-priced senior partner continues to bill time on matters that could be performed by a first-year associate, it is difficult to conclude that the client is receiving the best value for investment of funds in that law firm. On the other hand, if a senior partner sends the first-year associate to an important conference with a judge on a critical trial matter, it is not likely that the client would want to continue using that particular law firm.

When I was corporate counsel, we received a bill from a law firm indicating that a substantial amount of time was spent for a senior associate to file some routine papers with the Clerk of Courts. I asked the partner responsible for the matter why a legal assistant or even a secretary did not file those documents. The partner replied that the firm always has associates file with the Clerk of Courts to be sure that it is done properly. Clearly, legal assistants and support staff were being underutilized and lacked appropriate training. Better value for the client would come from a legal organization willing to have a trained support staff do the secretarial work rather than an associate.

On another bill, it was noted that a senior partner spent several hours "checking citations." As corporate counsel, I told the senior partner that the charge was not appropriate because that function could easily and competently have been performed by a paralegal. The partner proudly stated that his firm did not use paralegals and, moreover, that his firm didn't affiliate with local firms that use paralegals. When the partner graciously offered to reduce the charges for the hours spent by a lawyer for work I felt should have been performed by a paralegal, the corporation accepted the reduction. In spite of the reduction, the firm's stature with the corporation did not rise.

The reduction of the lawyer's hourly charges in that circumstance corrected the immediate imbalance between the charges and the value received. The proud announcement that the firm "didn't use paralegals" had undermined client confidence that the firm's philosophy of practice meshed with the corporate client's and mine. I resolved that if the firm did not hire paralegals, the next case in the firm's city would go to a different law firm, one that used paralegals. Parenthetically, the next case, as well as all those that followed, went to a different firm.

Who did it, as reflected on the bills, does have a positive or negative impact on client relations.

HOW WAS IT DONE?

Detailed billing should also reflect how each task of the job was performed. This means that the client should be able to evaluate the staffing of a matter on a task-by-task basis.

Corporate personnel who review detailed bills from law firms across the country are able to quickly spot the philosophy and approach to cases by particular law firms. Some firms approach a case by assigning a covey of lawyers. The bills reflect a myriad of conferences among partners and associates to ponder every decision, regardless of its import. It's easy to figure that this is a much more expensive way to resolve an issue than to have an efficiently functioning team consisting of a senior partner, associates of appropriate levels, paralegals or legal assistants, and other staff. The efficient team approach should facilitate the least expensive method to achieve a quality result in a timely fashion.

Even when the bill indicates that the senior partner performed work on the matter, corporate counsel must ask, "What is the partner in charge of the client bringing to the party?" If that partner is being used only for client contact and bill review, the services of that lawyer are probably of little or no added value to the individual or corporate client and therefore a waste of money. In most such instances, charges for these value-lacking tasks are driven by outdated law practice procedures, law firm compensation systems, and individual lawyer control issues rather than a desire to enhance value to the client.

Solo practitioners and small firms are finally being recognized by some corporations as being efficient and effective competitors to large firms. As a rule of thumb, smaller organizations are driven to greater efficiency by not having as many people who can accept delegated tasks. Technology has now equalized the smaller legal services organization's ability to fight or lead the "papering-to-death" wars. This equalization has most dramatically been observed in plaintiff's counsel in class actions and mass tort cases.

The client's interests are best served by decisive people and lean staffing on each phase of every matter whether handled by the solo lawyer or the large law firm. The bill must reflect who met with whom and what they did so that the knowledgeable and neophyte client alike may determine how the job was performed.

COMPARATIVE COST SHOPPING

With appropriate detailed billing, corporate counsel and other frequent consumers of legal services can do some comparative shopping. Rather than being frightening to the law firm currently representing the client, this should be viewed by the firm as a challenging opportunity to prove the firm is delivering value. After all, this detailed billing provides the incumbent lawyer(s) with the optimal means to best the competition on the playing field of value.

When analyzing bills, the client must be certain that the cost comparison does not compare apples with oranges. One must compare the type of legal work, quality of representation, size of the firm, reputation of the individual lawyers, and geographic area. Once it is determined that the level of legal expertise and kind of service required for a particular matter and the factors mentioned above are approximately equal, only then may the client rationally apply a cost comparison factor in choosing an outside lawyer.

The total cost of a legal job can best be controlled by comparing staffing, not by comparing hourly rates. All practitioners in private firms know that even if an associate's hourly rate is half that of an experienced lawyer, the total charge for a particular function may be significantly lower if a more senior, higher-priced lawyer performs it. It may take the senior lawyer less than half the time of the less experienced associate, which translates to a lower total charge. Caution must be exercised not to carry this concept to an extreme. For instance, I am aware of a client who insists a specific partner do everything and prohibits any billing by anyone else. This is foolish for it doesn't require a lawyer charging partners' rates to organize files. But this is what the client wants, that is what the client gets and that is for what the client uneconomically pays.

Excluding flat fee matters, the total amount charged to the client is a function of two salient factors—time and hourly rate. One cannot estimate or control total cost by ignoring one of the factors, the time it takes to complete the task. Clients who choose law firms solely on hourly rates may be paying far too much because they have not received efficient staffing or effective representation.

For instance, when a client (corporate or individual) receives an hourly bill from a law firm for an appellate brief, the reaction to the bill will be driven by the total cost, not the hourly rate. If the total appears extremely high, it can be checked against the comparator's charges. Comparing hourly rates of other legal services providers is a part of the analysis, but when used in isolation it may be misleading. When that total bill (time × hourly rates) is measured against other bills received for different appellate briefs from different firms, the client may determine whether the initial reaction or shock to the total amount was justified. Many corporate counsel offices now scrutinize legal bills carefully to ascertain the relative value of services received for costs. Many more will be doing so in the future.

If the bill turns out to be perceived as or is actually excessive, corporate counsel owes it to both the corporation and the lawyer or law firm involved to call the outside lawyer and tell him or her that it was an unreasonable charge as compared to other firms' charges. Most lawyers have no idea how much the competition is charging for similar representation tasks. Most are willing to meet the competition price. While it doesn't make sense for a client or lawyer to destroy an attorney/client relationship over one bill, that does occur.

Unfortunately, even if the partner immediately reduces the questioned bill, it is not likely to restore the client's confidence in the law firm's ability to provide value through its representation. In fact, it may make corporate counsel suspicious that a gouging or mismanagement factor might have been present when the original bill was written. Once the trust regarding billing is destroyed, the entire lawyer-client relationship is placed in jeopardy.

Thus, the detailed billing gives clients an opportunity to comparatively shop within certain boundaries and it opens opportunities for corporate counsel to provide greater value to the corporation and does likewise for the individual client. Bills are fundamental to maintaining good client relations.

Reducing legal fees while maintaining quality representation is a real and meaningful contribution corporate counsel may make directly to the bottom corporate fiscal line. Similarly, an individual may strive to conserve personal assets by reducing the cost of quality legal representation. In both instances, lawyers interested in their future have the same interest as their clients, to add value at a cost perceived to be reasonable.

COST MANAGEMENT

The examples cited provide self-evident methods of cost management. Knowing what is being done, who is doing it, when it is being done, and how it is being done provide effective ways to evaluate and manage costs of legal services.

Overall cost is the issue, but effective evaluation and control cannot be achieved without knowing the cost of each process that makes up the overall cost. The macro evaluation is appropriate but the micro approach to controlling lawyer actions and, consequently, charges determines the result of the macro cost. This is an effective operating and analysis process both for clients and within law practices.

When you buy a car, you wouldn't buy from one dealer instead of another because the cost was lower without knowing whether the options on the vehicle were the same. Similarly, a client should not presume that the same service or value is received when buying legal services without comparing the content as well as the cost of individual processes.

One might justifiably argue that a client cannot learn any of those things from detailed billing. All the client really knows is what the bill states. One does not know what was actually done or how long it actually took. That is technically true. However, the bill usually reflects the time actually expended on a project. The client should and will decide— rightly or wrongly—whether the total amount for services performed justify the charge.

The bill still may not reflect the reality of what was done. If a client has any suspicion that the bill does not reflect actual time spent and precise expenses incurred, that client would be wise to get a different lawyer, unless a satisfactory explanation is promptly forthcoming. It is part of the lawyer's job to assure that no such doubts are born in the client. Internal supervision of the work and a careful review of the bill before it is sent are key responsibilities of the responsible partner.

These detailed bills may give clients the means to weed out ineffi-cient law firms and lawyers. They also provide an obvious but rarely used cost-control device that may be used to enhance management within the law firm and corporate client. For instance, if a partner thinks too much time has been spent on a task, the partner, associate, or para-legal who recorded that time should be confronted. If there is no satis-factory explanation, time should be "written off" the bill. If there is no improvement in efficiency by the time recorder in the future, the recorder's future with that law office should also be "written off".

Whether these methods save an individual client a few dollars or improve operating profits, the legal profession should embrace them. Until the total amount billed for a legal matter is aligned with the value the client placed on the legal service and relationship with the lawyer, our profession will perpetuate the decline of its reputation and that of individual lawyers.

REQUIREMENTS FOR AN EFFECTIVE LEGAL BILL

The legal bills of most firms provide corporate clients and many indi-vidual clients with the type of information specified above. However, the number of legal bills still being issued that do not meet the mini-mum informational criteria is amazing.

Corporate counsel and individual clients should never forget that they are the consumers and may specify both the information required on the bill and also the format in which the bill is presented. Astute law firms representing institutional clients and sophisticated individuals may even want to involve high volume clients in designing their own bills.

When designing bill formats, decide with the client what functions the legal bills are to serve. If the client desires only to know the total amount of the bill, retained outside counsel may submit the bills in whatever form they choose, for the total is always clearly discernible. On the other hand, if the client decides to use the bill for specific management functions, the frequency and content of the bill must be specified. This is not an unusual or particularly onerous request by a client.

The best way for clients to clarify what is desired on a bill is for the lawyer to send a letter specifying the type of information to be contained in the bill. Law firms should also give an example of their standard format to the client:

Date	Timekeeper	Service	Hours	Charge
4/03	JGH	Research issue of minority shareholder rights	4.7	$470.00
4/07	PDQ	Called client to discuss summary judgment strategy	0.3	45.00
4/07	PDQ	Long-distance phone call to opposing counsel, discuss settlement possibilities	—	7.87
4/07	PDQ	Discussion with opposing counsel re scheduling court argument and settlement	1.1	165.00
4/08	GUY	Deposition of Sam Teflon in Podunk, USA	7.8	780.00

Some computer programs limit or specify billing formats. Occasionally law firms cannot conveniently provide this information in the exact format set forth above or in a particular format specified by a client. Format exceptions may be made by corporate counsel as long as all of the information desired is shown on the bill and it is an easily understood format. The more business a client does with a lawyer or firm, the more format tailoring the client may require and the more a law organization will be inclined to customize a bill. By way of example, defense firms exclusively representing insurance carriers produce invoices in whatever changing formats their then current insurance corporation contact requests.

When clients specify the information required in a bill, but the bills lawyers send do not contain that information, further action must be taken promptly by the client and lawyer in charge of providing service to the client. The client's needs for tracking expenditures in legal bills are every bit as important for client relations purposes as knowing what is happening in the matter.

If the bills are not modified to corporate client specifications, the client should pay the bill the first time and send an accompanying letter (with a copy to the contact lawyer) that reiterates the client's billing requirements. The letter should clearly state that if the next bill does not comply, it will not be paid. The next time, return the noncomplying bill with a note that review of the bill for possible approval for payment will not occur until the bill is submitted in the format requested. This usually brings compliance. In most cases, it is absolutely amazing how quickly previously insurmountable computer and administrative problems for getting the requested billing format are overcome.

Corporations, and most individuals paying for legal services on an hourly basis, should specify that they want to be billed monthly for all matters being billed on an hourly rate basis. In this manner, the client maintains better budget monitoring, cost control, and management of the matter. Budget limits on legal expenditures usually cannot be met by just stopping work in the last month of the fiscal year to meet a budget figure. The corporate client needs a much earlier warning to appropriately adjust the legal fees budget. Monthly billings are a way to provide that notice that will provide the necessary time in the fiscal year to make the necessary adjustments to the budget or the approach to the legal matter.

When I worked in a corporate law department, it absolutely astounded me when a very senior partner of a major law firm told me the firm could not bill more frequently than quarterly because of its computer set-up and the detailed review the contact-billing lawyer gave each bill. This was not only contrary to the corporate client's requirements, it was contrary to the law firm's best interest because of the detrimental cash flow that quarterly billing generated as compared to monthly billing.

I explained the economics of the situation and the benefits to both of monthly billing to the senior partner in charge. He responded that he knew the disadvantages to both the client and law firm, understood my concern, but could still only provide a quarterly bill; however, he agreed to give me a monthly oral estimate based on the time expended as it was reflected in the computer printouts! I exclaimed that if he had the monthly computer records he could get me a monthly bill. An irrational response came over the phone. We soon ceased dealing with that lawyer and firm, because they conclusively proved that they were not client-oriented, adept at practical problem-solving, or that they were even rational. Yes, billing truly is important to clients.

CLIENT RELATIONS THROUGH BILLING

Law firms should proactively demonstrate to clients and prospective clients how their bills assist clients in managing their legal fees. This is attractive to both individual and corporate clients. Solos and small firms that specialize in particular types of matters can become very competitive with large law firms by using this client relations technique.

Think for a moment about how a computer software company attempts to sell a new program. Its salespeople will show how you can manage a business better by flashing a series of computer screen applications or printouts before the prospective buyer. There is no reason to restrict this selling technique to computer software firms. Lawyers may also benefit from that type of approach, providing they have excellent billing quality to sell.

Showing corporate counsel or executives how greater managerial control could be exercised over all the law firms it uses through detailed billing may be enough to convince counsel to retain you. Demonstrating an understanding of individual and corporate financial management requirements and a willingness to assist in meeting them is regularly much more impressive to prospective and existing clients than multicolored law firm brochures.

With relatively little additional effort, law firms, large and small, can easily show clients how to use the information on legal bills to assist in the clients' corporate or personal monetary management responsibilities. Clients will favor the solo lawyer or law firm that effectively assists them in understanding the services and fees charged, for it provides the client an understandable means of control. Solo lawyers and law firms also should ask if the client needs any information other than what is shown on their bills. Solos and firms should also inquire as to how they may aid in the administrative aspects of the corporate counsel's job or the individual's tax or accounting needs by amending billing formats.

While most would not classify a bill as a client-relations tool, what law says it shouldn't be used as one? Meaningful, detailed billing can be a valuable management tool for corporate counsel and an enlightening, reassuring document for individual clients. Therefore, it provides a significant opportunity for solos, small firms, and law firms of national scope to enhance client relations.

MUTUALLY BENEFICIAL BILLS

When a vehicle such as detailed task-based billing provides a win-win opportunity for the client and the lawyer, both should enthusiastically embrace it. Even if one party has to drag the other kicking and screaming to adopt meaningful, detailed, and timely billing, it is worth it. When such a system is implemented, both should be quite satisfied with the resulting added control over fees and the legal matter.

Admittedly, detailed, task-based billing may cost a bit to institute and may force certain changes in timekeeping and billing practices. But, when analyzed, this minimal monetary investment and behavior modification in timekeeping and billing provides excellent leverage for increased returns.

Some lawyers claim that loading the bill with detailed information only enables the client to micro-manage and to argue about whether a phone call had to be made and question why writing a short letter took so long. I think that is probably so, especially for individual clients involved in highly emotional, personal matters such as divorce, custody and contested estate distributions. If a client is inclined to "Monday Morning Quarterback," it is not likely that this habit will be intercepted by providing less information to the client. Eventually, the lawyer is likely to produce the detailed time records to such a client in an effort to explain a vague bill, anyway.

Further, the genesis of the problem may be the client's emotional state, the downturn of the client's economic affairs, or the client not obtaining the result desired. Lawyers may not be able to do anything about these causes. If the second guessing stems from the clients not understanding the basis on which they were being billed or the necessity of the time committed to the matter, lawyers do have substantial influence on correcting what they should have prevented through a retention agreement covering services and fees and continually updating the client on the status of the matter.

Regardless of the cause of the client micro-managing or questioning, the lawyer is better off having sent a detailed bill. If the client eventually files an ethical complaint or lawsuit against the lawyer, the fact that the client had detailed information about the services and fees for each billed time unit takes away the "I didn't know" assertion and should be helpful in obtaining a favorable outcome for the lawyer. And, if the invoice complies with the fee agreement, it should be even easier to find that the client's complaints lack merit.

SUMMARY

Whether detailed billing is computerized or typed manually, there appears to be almost all upsides. It will give corporate counsel assistance in managing and participating in cases. Individual clients will feel more confident that they understand what their money is buying. Lawyers will be better able to more accurately supervise and evaluate timekeepers within their law firms, the quality of their services and the appropriateness of their charges. By so doing, lawyers will increase client confidence that value is being received for the fees paid. This, in turn, will advance the lawyer-client trust and relationship.

Like computer software sales pitches, if the lawyer sells the client on the concept that he or she can help the client control legal costs through billing, it gives that lawyer an advantage over the competition. The advantage is borne from the client's understanding that the lawyer is offering to help the client on more than the substance of the immediate legal matter at hand. In effect, the lawyer is offering to assist in increasing corporate profits or controlling an individual's expenditures through better-managed legal fees. Clients understanding this will view it as an excellent building block for establishing or further developing a mutually beneficial lawyer-client relationship.

CHAPTER 10

UNCERTAINTY—
FOR LAWYER AND CLIENT

Uncertainty is the bane of human existence. If there is a single thing that is uniformly disconcerting to humans, it is uncertainty.

We do almost anything to attain certainty. We want certainty in the weather, so we travel thousands of miles to assure that we have sun for swimming or snow for skiing. We buy insurance to attain financial certainty for our families and us during our life and after we die. When we pass a police officer while going over the speed limit, uncertain as to whether he or she will come after us, there is that sinking feeling until we are sure that she hasn't activated the flashing lights or his car has not sped forward in pursuit. We would like to be certain that our children's future will be fine and the lack of that certainty concerns us. If we or ones we care about feel ill but the doctor does not know what's wrong, often that's worse than a specific diagnosis because we think that whatever is wrong is worse than what it actually turns out to be.

The main reason people hire professionals, whether a lawyer, a doctor, or an accountant, is to attain greater certainty. Client relations are significantly enhanced when the lawyer delivers certainty to the client and the client recognizes it as such. Let's examine several lawyer-client situations involving uncertainty.

THE OUTCOME OF THE MATTER

The lawyer deals with the uncertainty of the outcome of the matter in a different fashion than the client does.

Economically, there are different investments. While most lawyers are concerned about the client and the client's matter, the outcome of it really affects the lawyer more in terms of his or her self-image as an attorney and professional reputation. Often, the lawyer is paid regardless of the outcome. The main exception is contingency cases, but even then, the out-of-pocket expenses are usually reimbursed by the client. Thus, the adverse economic impact on the attorney is minimal when compared to the client's fiscal risk.

Clients have an entirely different view of the uncertainty of the outcome of their matters. They may be uncertain in a criminal case whether they will be sentenced to imprisonment or death. They are uncertain during incompetency proceedings as to whether their freedom or that of a close relative will be taken away. In contract and inheritance cases, the uncertainty sometimes is whether money representing a lifetime of work will be delivered to a particular party while minimizing taxes. In pending custody cases, the emotions of children's visitation rights determinations [and one's identity as a fit parent or guardian] are uncertain for the client. Financial cases involving taxes and mortgages may place the client's very home in an uncertain status. In business, uncertainty about patents, copyrights, and contracts makes the status of one's income uncertain. For professionals, uncertainty of malpractice charges is of great concern. In rape and sexual harassment cases, the uncertainty of one's dignity and subsequent reputation is a worrisome matter for clients, regardless of the facts and verdict. Employment law cases breed uncertainty for the economic future of employees and, more often than realized, to the employer.

The point is, regardless of the type of case or matter, the client has much more at risk from the uncertainty of the matter's outcome than the lawyer does. To succeed at client relations, the lawyer must recognize and deal with the difference in the intensity of the client's feelings generated by a variety of uncertainties.

Sensitivity to client uncertainty will assist the lawyer in using supportive language in describing the client's prior actions and how they affect the case. Patient, empathetic listening to the client at all stages of the proceeding will go a long way toward cementing an excellent lawyer-client relationship. This is not to say that the attorney should offer unfounded assurances of certainty. Rather, the counseling skill is bringing the client to accept the emerging certainly, whether it is desired or not.

THE LEGAL SYSTEM

The legal system itself presents uncertainties to the lawyer and client. For the lawyer, those uncertainties are chiefly intellectual and professional. The attorney understands far better than the client that a statute or holding can be applied in more than one manner. The same goes for interpretation of contract or estate plan language. The litigator likewise is well aware that a judge's ruling and a jury's verdict are unpredictable. Lawyers' knowledge of these uncertainties comes from the lawyers' training and experience with our legal system.

For the client, uncertainties include legal procedure: "What happened in that argument?" "Why do I have to give a deposition? I'm suing him." "I don't know what this means." The substance of the legal system also brings uncertainty to the client's world. "What does the law say?" "How does that apply in my case?" "How can it be that I have done this all my business career and now they say it's illegal?" These are just a few of the uncertainties that clients often experience as a result of being unacquainted with the procedure and substance of our legal system.

Movies and television programs that depict courtroom scenes foster disconcerting uncertainty to clients about to go to trial. They remember cross-examinations at trial and have seen a plaintiff or defendant "lose" his or her entire case under intense cross-examination. The client wonders, "Will I be prepared and if I am prepared, how can I hold my own against the opposing lawyer?" That the lawyer will be trying to trick them on every question is another common perception that strikes fear into clients. Some media have also characterized lawyers as sly, tricky, and never straight forward. These depictions cause clients to worry about whether in real life they have retained a hero, villain or incompetent.

While the lack of understanding of how and why the legal system arrives at decisions is often very scary to clients, it is an accepted fact of life to lawyers. Because the result is not always rational, however, attorneys may be unable to adequately explain it to a client; this too increases uncertainty.

Educating away the mystery of the legal system is certain to endear lawyers to their clients. Sending clients to court to see proceedings before their trial, mock cross-examinations that are tougher than what they will endure at trial, and telegraphing what might be expected in negotiations in a judge's chambers will reduce client uncertainty and increase lawyer value.

By taking time to explain the procedure and substance of the legal system, the lawyers receive the added benefit of establishing their competence in the eyes of the client. Redirection of the fear factor created by lawyer horror stories goes a long way toward reducing one of the areas of client's uncertainty. That also improves clients' relations with those attorneys who have this talent.

WHAT'S HAPPENING?

Whether the legal proceeding is transactional or trial, the lawyer knows the process and why it takes so long to arrive at its conclusion. The client may never have experienced a legal encounter and is usually uncertain about what is happening and how long it will take.

If the lawyer forgets to call when promised after a milestone in the matter, the client is worried, stressed, and uncertain about what is happening. For the client, this is an extraordinarily important matter and uncertainty as to why it would take all this time to resolve is natural. The client receives no phone call and no letter. The client converts that lack of communication into a feeling that something must be wrong. As seen by the client, the client's position is so obviously correct that the matter should have been resolved quickly. Often uncertainty convinces the client that something is dreadfully amiss and the client assumes the lawyer can't even bear to call about it.

Other clients assume that no communication means the lawyer is not working on the matter. Or worse yet, that the lawyer has forgotten about the client.

In many instances, the lawyer knows what is happening and that the lapsed time is normal or insignificant, in a legal sense. The amount of knowledge of what's happening puts the client and lawyer on entirely different informational plains and consequently distant emotional planets. This state of affairs is a prime environment for major misunderstandings and non-factual accusations.

Besides meeting the requirements of Model Rule 1.4, keeping clients fully informed on a timely basis will dissipate this uncertainty, protect against one of the most common malpractice complaints, and build positive client relations.

WHO'S ON FIRST?

The lawyer-partner who accepts a piece of legal work knows to whom she has delegated the work in the office. She knows the delegate's ability and personality. If the associate is properly reporting to her, the partner is well informed about the substantive quality of the work as well as the progress of it.

What about the client? When the client calls and the partner isn't in, the client speaks to the partner's secretary. Her secretary says that the partner will likely be calling in, and will deliver the message. In some instances, there is no commitment or assurance that the partner will return the call. Other times secretaries reply that the partner will call back. Secretaries who know their partners well don't make that representation unless the partner is compulsive about returning calls promptly.

The client then may ask the secretary if the "papers" are finished. The secretary may respond, "What papers?" The client describes the papers and the secretary responds, "No, I haven't typed them. Partner may have given that to someone else to do. Let me see who. I just can't remember right now. I'm sure it's being taken care of by one of our young associates." The client becomes really confused and worried now because the client's expectation is the partner is doing the work. A young associate, the client thinks, is too inexperienced and shouldn't be doing this important work for me. Besides, the client worries, "I don't even know who it is."

Who's on first? Even if there is no call from the client to the partner-lawyer, the client will discover that some associate is doing the work when different initials appear on the bill beside the time charged, and the client will become very uncertain of many more things. If the client doesn't know who is doing the work, whoever is on first and the partner-manager who put the associate on first will not score with the client.

Sometimes, clients think partners are cheating them when they discover that an associate they've never met or heard of is working on their matter. The client assumed he or she engaged the partner, and if the partner doesn't explain up front that others, whether they are associates, legal assistants or other partners, will be working on the client's matter a misunderstanding which undermines trust is likely to arise.

The standard explanation for involving other lawyers is couched in terms of saving the client money. That always should be coupled with a substantive reason. For instance, I've explained to clients that an associate is going to research the law because the associate is so much better with computer research than I. Similarly, I have admitted to clients that when I fill out government forms, I read too much into the questions and my answers are to questions not asked. Once the client hears that, there is immediate acceptance of my assigning such work to a legal assistant. Combining a practical reason with the economic one increases client certainty that the delegation of work is appropriate.

If another lawyer and/or legal assistant will be working on the case, the lawyer that the client initially contacted should introduce the legal team. By this I mean a face-to-face introduction at the initial client meeting at which each team member will speak with the client and give the client a business card. It is counterproductive for the partner to have others present but silent at a client meeting. The client comes away from such an encounter wondering why the firm should be paid for the mute participants. The partner should follow up by writing a letter to the client listing the "team" members and the team members' individual contact information.

In all events, the originating lawyer must assure the client that he or she would continue to personally monitor the work. Giving clients a written or oral scorecard with the players' names, positions, and numbers (hourly rates) will bench client uncertainty in this area.

HOW MUCH WILL IT COST?

Cost to the lawyer is almost irrelevant. The lawyer is trained and motivated to do the highest quality job without regard to cost. In fact, some argue that the cannons of ethics infer that this is the obligation of the attorney.

On the economic side of the practice, more hours and more cost are both financially and operationally advantageous for the lawyer, except in contingency and fixed fee compensation arrangements. Certainly, the lawyer does care about the cost, but it is not as relevant to the lawyer's usual motivation as is thoroughness of preparation and the result. Nevertheless, the lawyer must bear in mind the cost value ratio to the client for every step of the legal representation.

Uncertainty as to cost of services is frightening to every client. As corporate counsel responsible for managing a case, I asked outside counsel how much it would cost to go to trial because we received a substantial settlement offer. The estimate for trial from outside counsel was between $100,000 and $150,000. Based on that, coupled with other factors, we risked a much larger loss and went to trial thinking our recovery prospects justified the trial costs. Fortunately, we won, but the legal fees and costs of trial were in excess of $500,000. That law firm was not retained again, because the case could have settled for less than what we spent in fees and would have had a certain result. The firm's gross underestimate of fees caused the corporation to pay more than it would have cost to settle, plus we were at risk for damages in excess of $1 million during the trial.

For individual clients, often the biggest potential expense outside the purchase of their home may be from a critical legal matter. Some such circumstances are defending a defamation complaint, suing for divorce, and defending an uninsured tort. The problem is that there is no guarantee of any return or even the invested principal at the end of the lawyer's service to the client. As might be expected, that uncertainty is unnerving to clients.

It is unbelievable to workers earning $18 to $20 an hour and to executives earning $50,000 to $75,000 annually, how a lawyer could quote a rate approximately ten times the hourly rate earned by those individuals. Clients have asked, "At these rates, do you play major league baseball?" Most lawyers are not aware of the resentment this disparity creates in clients. It is like the resentment most fans have for overpaid athletes.

It is uncertain in many legal matters whether the client will have anything left at the end of the matter—even if he or she "wins" the case. Some clients are uncertain as to how to read a multi-page bill from a lawyer, although they generally understand the bottom line total very well. They frequently deem the total to be excessively large and unjustifiable. Clients don't understand why they are charged several hundred dollars for copying costs. They can barely fathom that there would be enough documents copied for all clients represented by the law practice, let alone in their case, to justify that kind of charge. The many hours required to write a ten-page motion and brief is not comprehensible to many clients.

And worst of all, some clients are uncertain whether it is proper to ask a lawyer a question about the law firm's bill. Lawyers must be certain their clients not only know but feel they may question a bill. Otherwise, the client will complain to others or, worse yet, to the bar association, another lawyer, or disciplinary board to get an answer.

Lawyers must allay client uncertainties, if clients don't do it for themselves. This means lawyers must raise and answer issues about costs, make accurate client-cost forecasts, discuss changes in the matter that arise and promptly modify budgets with client approval.

RISK ANALYSIS

A lawyer might properly and accurately inform a client, "I think we can win this. It'll cost about $7,000, maybe more. The chances of winning on our motion are about 50-50. You have a good case, but the law is confusing on this point and you never know about even a good motion before this particular judge. Once we submit it to the judge, we could know within six weeks to a couple of months, but it may be longer."

In many cases, the lawyer can be no more specific than the conversation just described. That is no help to the client and not a satisfactory lawyer communication to a client. Realize that the client, especially one who is not a regular consumer of legal services, is not likely to question or register dissatisfaction about the answer for the client isn't informed enough to raise such issues. It is a detrimental oversight in client relations for lawyers to fail to educate the client sufficiently so that the client is equipped to ask the difficult questions.

The client worries about, and frequently doesn't verbalize to the lawyer, the following and much more:

- My lawyer is uncertain whether we can win my case—doesn't he know the law?
- My lawyer is uncertain what it will cost—does she just make up how much she's going to charge me as she goes along?
- My lawyer is uncertain when we will find out about the result— doesn't he realize I need to know these things soon to make adjustments in my business?
- My lawyer is uncertain. I was uncertain before I hired my lawyer. What have I gained by hiring my lawyer?

REDUCING CLIENT UNCERTAINTY

I trust that you are at least somewhat persuaded that uncertainty is debilitating to the lawyer-client relationship. What should we do about client uncertainty? Simple: take every opportunity to reduce it in any way we can.

The client will deem any lawyer, who is able to significantly reduce or eliminate the client's uncertainty on some or all of the client's concerns, a valuable asset. Clients pay for certainty. Excellent lawyer-client relationships are built on the lawyer delivering certainty.

As an exercise, try the following:

1. List other examples of how you could reduce clients' uncertainty about the various matters you are handling.
2. Look through the examples of uncertainty that you have listed and the ones listed in this chapter.
3. List at least one way to reduce or eliminate each client uncertainty on both of our lists.

After completing the above exercise, try this action plan:

1. Call or see three clients a day for the next ten workdays with specific information that reduces or eliminates their uncertainty on one or more items.

2. Don't charge the clients anything for this reduction-in-uncertainty conversation, and let them know you're not charging them. I am almost certain that within four weeks of completing the ten-day work-action plan, you will more than cover the time expended with new work given to you by your existing clients. On a longer time line, you will also benefit through others whom they refer to you.

The simple truth is that as the lawyer reduces uncertainty, the client increases his or her confidence in and loyalty to the lawyer. That is building good client relations.

CHAPTER 11

COMPETENCY IN CLIENT RELATIONS

Before we can discuss competency in client relations skills, we must distill the essence of client relations. Most of commercial corporate America, Asia, and Europe have defined customer relations as *service quality.* I perceive nothing so unique in the practice of law that it would dictate a different definition for lawyer-client relations.

We lawyers could easily and happily argue for years about the essential elements of client relations and never come to a conclusion. The list below describes the characteristics of desirable relations with clients. It is not exclusive and you may wish to identify other characteristics. Use my list and your additions to objectively evaluate your client relations competency and performance.

CHARACTERISTICS OF EFFECTIVE CLIENT RELATIONS

Some characteristics of client relations, in no particular order, include:

- *Trust*—Confidence that the client's best interests are primary in everything the lawyer does on behalf of the client.
- *Judgment*—The client must respect your judgment. Such respect comes from the lawyer's reputation and the client's personal experience with the lawyer.

- *Sociability*—The client should like to be with the lawyer, even when (or especially when) the lawyer is delivering news about a bad legal outcome.
- *Counseling*—The lawyer's ability to listen and be responsive to the client's concerns is key to whether the lawyer can become a valued counselor.
- *Business Courtesies*—Small things like promptly returning phone calls and being on time for appointments mean a lot to a client.
- *Involvement of the Lawyer*—The lawyer must get to really understand and know the individual client and the commercial client's business as thoroughly as the best-prepared lawyer knows the facts of a case he or she is trying in court.
- *Involvement of the Client*—Involving the client in every step of decision making and sharing the stardom of victory or the disappointment of defeat will bond the client to the lawyer.

The above practices and others in this book should motivate the client to retain the lawyer for additional work, regardless of the outcome on one particular matter.

ASSESSING "TECHNICAL LEGAL COMPETENCE"

The absence of "legal competence" on the list of effective client relations characteristics in the previous section is notable. As one who has committed years of his life striving to gain and maintain technical legal competence, I must sadly admit that when it comes to client relations, technical legal competence means very little. Shocking? It is not really so bizarre when you analyze it from clients' points of view.

TRIAL PRACTICE

Think for a moment of the trials you have lost or settlement negotiation points you failed to gain from those lawyers with discernibly less legal competence. Because the opposition prevailed, surely your opponent's lack of technical legal competence did not assure that the opponents would keep their clients. Conversely, your loss of the case or the inability to close the settlement deal did not cost you a client every time it occurred. Why does this phenomenon occur again and again?

Perhaps, an example from my personal trial experience will shed some light. I was trying a case against a bombastic trial lawyer. While I am not a plodder at trial, neither am I a flamboyant courtroom show-man. In this instance, I was diligently working the witnesses to make a record that would prevail at trial and be upheld on appeal or if we lost at trial would provide grounds for reversal on appeal. During the trial as opposing counsel pranced about the courtroom, flailed his arms, and uttered platitudes that had no relevance to the case, my client leaned over to me and whispered, "What a terrific job that lawyer is doing!" My blood boiled! I benignly smiled, even though I had instan-taneously recognized my client's unstated, unfavorable comparison of my performance.

We won the case. We got a tremendous result. My client thanked me. Then, in the same breath, in the courthouse hall, my client again pro-nounced judgment that the opposing counsel was absolutely wonder-ful. Fortunately, I had the good sense not to tell my client my strongly held opinion about his total lack of judgment.

Why did this occur? I thought about it because over the years the client returned to me for many legal services instead of engaging that opposing counsel, as I had imagined he would during our courthouse conversation. The conclusion I came to was that even in trial of the client's own case, the client did not understand enough of the law and what was going on in the courtroom to identify technical legal compe-tence. It was our lawyer-client relationship that made the critical differ-ence to motivate the client to hire me again and again.

APPLICATION TO TRANSACTIONAL LAW

In transactional work, I have at times been matched against lawyers with much more knowledge of the law, deals, and experience in trans-actional law than I possessed. Obviously, on a pure scale of legal knowledge, which many erroneously make their exclusive definition of legal competence, I would come out a poor second. However, because I was involved with the client, I involved the client in decision making, and we possessed superior negotiating skills, we were able to close deals with a favorable agreement for many clients. The client, not I, tipped the scales in our favor.

While the opposition focused almost exclusively on legal concepts, we centered on the practical aspects of the transaction to select which legal guidelines needed to be emphasized and then drafted language to mold them to our practical advantage. Had I ignored the client as a resource, the outcome would have been far less favorable. In the process, each client and I came to better understand our respective contributions to the negotiation. This grew into mutual respect, appreciation, and trust between client and lawyer.

In every one of these circumstances, we maintained the client's loyalty and our client returned with more legal work. Skills such as listening, reflecting, and advocating the client's point of view, when mixed with full utilization of our negotiating ability, rather than the most extensive technical knowledge of the law, must have caused the client to return. Technical legal competence may not even have been a factor in the client's judgment of results obtained or the client's decision to retain us on subsequent matters.

Competency is much more than the Model Rule 1.1 elements of "knowledge, skill, thoroughness, and preparation." Understanding the facts, perceptions, and feelings of the client are necessary. Without this knowledge, lawyers cannot understand how clients think lawyers can make their situation better. In large part, competency in client relations is defined by each client's perceived needs. The perception of one client may be that the lawyer should be professorial and of another client that the lawyer should be a warm and fuzzy hand-holder. To be fully competent in client relations, lawyers must discern clients' expectations and do their best to meet or exceed those expectations.

This more detailed example will present the point with greater clarity. In negotiating a transactional deal that included a revolver loan from a bank, I objected to a provision that permitted the bank to take significant control of the management of my client's business under circumstances when account balances slipped below certain very high floors. My client didn't want this and the provision was far more invasive than I objectively considered reasonable. My opponent, an experienced banking lawyer, said no one had ever raised the objection to the provision before. He then cited some obscure banking code regulation as the reason the bank had to insist on the provision that my client and I deemed particularly onerous. That didn't stop me!

Frankly, I had never heard of the section of the banking regulation cited, didn't care about it, except as it affected my client and would never hear of it again. But, while sitting at the closing where this life-or-death loan for our client's business was being formalized, I questioned the bank's lawyer on how he was interpreting and applying the obscure code provision. Did I care how he was applying it? Sure, but more importantly I needed to know what the darn regulation said and how it was interpreted. The first time it raised its ugly head was at the closing and I didn't know anything about it.

After my counterpart described the section in excruciatingly deadly detail, I used my knowledge of the client's business to question its applicability in this circumstance. Although I didn't know of any, I raised the possibility that there were exceptions to this application of the regulation by stating, "You have to admit . . . " The opposing counsel, who was highly ethical and very knowledgeable in banking law, agreed that there were exceptions. He explained that some of the case law (none of which I knew), as interpreted by other federal districts, held that the regulation might not apply to our situation.

There! I had it! I opined that there was a good possibility that the local district judge would hold that it didn't apply, and if he did, the bank would have gained nothing by insisting that it be included. Why, I argued, would the bank take the risk that the court would find the provision inapplicable? As I got the bank's attorney to admit, this would be especially risky because other bank customers had not raised the issue and if the provision were found to be inapplicable, it would be a very undesirable result for the bank. I also convinced him and the bank executive who was present that the likelihood of the provision being put in play by this borrower was slight. I clearly indicated that if the bank did try to apply the clause, our client would be forced to mount an all-out court challenge to the provision's validity.

I used the opposing counsel's legal knowledge to create doubt and gain leverage for my client. I then used this leverage to negotiate a loan document provision in which the bank was far less intrusive in the management of the client's business. After we left the closing, the client complimented me on my "knowledge of the law" and stated that the change in the agreement that we had obtained would be critical to the success of the business.

The truth is that it wasn't my esoteric knowledge of little-known law at all that saved the day. It was negotiating skills, knowledge of the client's business and, most importantly, knowledge of the client's expectations. The client's enthusiastic endorsement of my representation again demonstrates that clients generally are unable to or do not identify technical legal competence. If they cannot identify this factor, they surely cannot base their choice of lawyers or a client relationship with a lawyer on it.

THE CLIENT AS JUDGE

My point is not to confess my lack of knowledge of the banking code, but rather to demonstrate that legal competence as perceived by the ultimate judge, your clients, may in fact be driven by something other than extensive, scholarly knowledge of every obscure provision of the law.

Do not mistake what I say. In the revolver loan situation, I wish I had had the detailed legal knowledge to raise a doubt on my own instead of having to obtain it through an honest, knowledgeable opposing counsel. If opposing counsel had been less forthright or just had not known that there were exceptions in the district court cases, the final loan document would not have been as favorable for my client. That would have resulted from my legal ignorance. Knowledge of technical legal substantive and procedural rules always gives the lawyer a better chance to control the outcome.

Still, while the outcome is important to the client, it is not nearly as important as the client's perception of the lawyer. Winning repeat legal business is a decision made on the client's perception, which may or may not coincide with fact. A client's perception—accurate or inaccurate— that you can best service the client's legal and other needs is the only universally critical element you need to obtain that repeat business.

The obscure banking code regulation to which I referred probably had a plus-minus affect on the monetary portion of the revolver loan deal of 5 percent or less. Nevertheless, it had become a matter of principle with my client. Truthfully, I never believed it was nearly as important in maintaining the client's freedom to manage his business as the client concluded. To us lawyers' egos, the point meant close to 80 percent of the deal because it was the only real point in dispute that our clients understood and on which they placed a high value. This then became the only stage on which we lawyers could strut our stuff: a stage that the clients could see.

As it turned out, because I read the banker as wanting to do the deal, I did not win the legal argument (due to lack of technical legal competence in obscure banking code regulations), but I obtained slightly better terms for my client and a much higher regard from my client. Because of my client's misperception of the importance of the clause, I became an object of praise.

I have been in other situations where the lawyer has focused so much on the language of a particular clause that he or she has threatened to block the deal. In some circumstances where the client succumbs to the theoretical catastrophic predictions of her or his own lawyer, a good deal has been scuttled. Thus, our profession's reputation as deal breakers grows. How foolish! No client appreciates that sort of legal representation.

Such lawyers have lost sight of the fact that their client is committed to closing the deal on a commercially viable basis, not on gaining the ultimate theoretical legal protection. Such a situation often occurs when lawyers perceive themselves as competing with opposing counsel to demonstrate who possesses superior legal knowledge. Other times attorneys put themselves in this undesirable position by regarding themselves as superior to their own clients and their client's business judgment.

I know the bank selected the same lawyer to represent it in future transactions. I can virtually assure that the selection was not made on the basis of the lawyer's demonstrated superior knowledge of some obscure banking code regulation. Rather, the selection was no doubt made because of the lawyer's demonstrated flexibility that closed a desirable loan deal. Similarly, my lack of the specific technical legal knowledge did not hinder our client from retaining me again and again. Strutting technical legal knowledge rarely is understood by the client and is even less frequently appreciated or effective. It should be obvious that the client never appreciates a lawyer's condescending listen-to-your-elders attitude about what the client should expect.

When the client recognizes from the lawyer's actions that the lawyer understands and is trying to achieve the client expectations, the client becomes convinced that the lawyer is competent. The client rarely distinguishes between competence in client relations and the extent of legal knowledge. If the client is pleased with the state of client relations with the lawyer, the client is almost always satisfied with the lawyer's representation on the substantive aspects of a legal matter. This certainly provides a roadmap for lawyers to best serve clients.

DEVELOPING CLIENT RELATIONS SKILLS

Negotiation skills, listening to the client, keeping the client's interest in the forefront of your thought process and demonstrably advancing the client's position are the true indicators of "legal competence."

Competency in substantive and procedural aspects of the law should be taken as a minimum requirement because the client has many choices of lawyers and law firms that are technically quite competent. Given minimum technical competence, the key to setting yourself apart from the crowd of lawyers in your practice area is to concentrate on refining the talents that will improve your ability to have first-rate relations with clients.

Whether you accept the above premise or only believe there might be some iota of truth in it, surely we can agree that client relations is one element required for the successful practice of law. You would not still be reading this book if you didn't agree.

Lawyers should be constantly developing their client relations skills and those of less experienced lawyers with whom they work. Let's examine whether you have been enhancing your own and your law firm's competency in client relations skills. Please answer the following questions:

1. When was the last time you attended a course or seminar on the following subjects:

Topic	Month and Year Attended
Substantive field of law	_____
Negotiation skills	_____
Practice-building methods	_____
Interpersonal business relations	_____
Oral communications	_____
Written client communications	_____
Project management	_____
Interpersonal relationships	_____
Corporate decision making	_____
Marketing and sales	_____
Counseling techniques	_____
Business etiquette and courtesies	_____
Creative thinking	_____
Industrial tradeshow	_____
Law practice management	_____

2. Review the above question a second time and indicate the last time anyone with whom you practice attended a course or seminar on the subjects. (For solos, as well as firms, include administrators and other nonlawyers—not that it replaces the need for lawyers to attend.)

3. What orientation have you given to new colleagues (associates, legal assistants, support staff, and lateral transfers) with respect to question 1 and client relations?

4. Other than admonishing your law firm partners-shareholders and associates to build good client relations, when and what have you done internally in your firm to identify and teach the skills required to create and maintain good client relations?

5. What support (other than an expense account) and follow-up have you given to implement any lecturing or preaching in the law firm about developing clients?

6. If, as a partner-shareholder, a client complains about another partner-shareholder or associate, do you handle the problem yourself or ask the person about whom the complaint is registered to rectify it with the client?

7. If you communicate with the client yourself, how does the client ever know that the problem was actually handled and gain confidence in the one about whom the complaint was originally registered? And, how does the offending lawyer learn methods of correcting client relations mistakes?

8. When was the last time you visited the clients most influential to the success of your practice on nonbillable time at their home or business just to learn about the business or the client's personal circumstances?

9. What is your strategic plan, which lists specific steps and completion dates, to further develop client relations for the next 24 months?

10. What, if anything, do you intend to do differently about increasing competency in client relations, what time and money you committing to implement what you intend to do, and when are you going to do it?

These questions are not intended to provide exclusive, specific evaluations of your client relations commitment and training, but rather to stimulate your thought process about what might assist in taking clients to the next higher level of commitment to you and your practice.

Many of the skills and seminars set forth in the first question are better taught by businesspersons, academics and consultants than by lawyers. There are a myriad of worthwhile offerings from universities, management associations, consultants, chamber of commerce programs and specialty seminar companies. Additionally, numerous video and audiotapes exist that aim to increase awareness and skills in these particular people-oriented areas. Good business sales videos, audiotapes and seminars are excellent sources for tips on how to develop strong business and professional relationships.

SUMMARY

The point of this chapter is certainly not to denigrate substantive legal competence. That is an absolute prerequisite for serving clients and having a rewarding legal career. Rather, the purpose is to demonstrate that substantive legal competence is only one arrow in the large quiver of what is required to be a competent, successful lawyer. Legal competence truly should be redefined to encompass competency in client relations, as well as the substantive legal skills. All of these are required to serve our clients and potential clients. Without satisfying clients' expectations, we are not serving them or our profession, and certainly are not practicing law successfully.

CHAPTER 12

TECHNOLOGY

Philosophically, the current debate in university circles is whether technology is an extension of process reflected in ancient cave paintings or a whole new discipline. That is, whether technology is another form of communications or an entirely different process. For our purposes, the resolution of this question is irrelevant because our concern is the message being conveyed and whether the technological advances can be used to better glue the client to the attorney.

There exist marvelous sources for useful information on technology. Some of those include one of the American Bar Association's magazines, *Law Practice Management*, which lists and evaluates new products, the ABA Law Practice Management Section TECHSHOW each spring, many of the ABA publications and numerous commercial information publications and outlets.

Internationally, much excellent work is being done in a good number of countries by superbly qualified authors. Some of this highly instructive material is available on the Internet. Practitioners in the United States would be well advised to examine international sources for useful client relations technology ideas.

This chapter could not and is not intended to provide the specific technology guidance available through those sources. Instead, the chapter is aimed at reminding and making the reader aware of some of the opportunities technology germinates for propagating and growing client relations.

Credit for much of the content of the chapter goes to our daughter, Sarah, who is a freelance graphic and Web designer. Among her many successful projects are law practice brochures and Web sites. She knows that I embrace technology and what it can do, but that I don't understand, nor do I care, how it gets done. Her insights, cautions, and practical experience have provided more accurate, current information than I had and refined my thoughts on using technology to better relate to clients. I write this for myself, and you, that as lawyers we do not need to know everything but should know when to seek competent advice. That is sometimes difficult for lawyers so used to providing helpful advice to others. The best practices do not hesitate to obtain the assistance of specialists who help them with client relations matters.

The differences between Sarah's sophisticated understanding of technology, artistic ability, and people orientation and my very limited ability in technology and art illustrate nicely a widespread phenomenon. For the most part, familiarity and comfort with technology and its use is stratified among the population like sedimentary rock formations. Generally, the persons in the older strata are not as well versed or comfortable with technology as those in the more recent ones. This pertains within the legal profession and among clients. In utilizing technological connections with clients, these layers of varying knowledge about technology and its effectiveness as a communication tool must be considered.

CHOOSING AMONG TECH OPTIONS

The array of high tech options on the market today for use in law practices is overwhelming. Just trying to make a decision among computer hardware options available from a single manufacturer is daunting. And, if only law practice could be as efficient as represented in the various magazine advertisements for software! Add to these decision factors, some old-fashioned notion that when spending the kind of money required for hardware and software that the purchased items should last five or ten years. This plethora of information, which should be used in decision making, makes technology decisions complex.

While there were some early pioneers in the American Bar Association's Law Practice Management Section lighting the way to the use of technology in law practices, this development was largely driven by corporate clients. The corporations adopted newer means of communication and demanded that the law firms they retained do the same. The spreading use of technology increased competition and consequently drove the prices down making technology affordable for every practice. Now, technology is necessary for survival of the largest to the smallest law practice.

Clients are generally ahead of lawyers in their utilization of new, more efficient techniques. Years ago I noticed clients using the big, thick, leather-bound planning books; then they migrated to handheld LCD calendar/planners. Now, we regularly see lawyers and clients alike poking at their hands with little sticks when agreeing to meet on a specified date in the future. Not long ago when a group descended on a conference room there was a race for the electrical outlets and phone line connections. Presently, we are seeing more handheld wireless computers with capacities that far exceed that of desktops made only a few years ago.

The common use of pagers, cell phones, Internet and Web sites by clients shout the message that they demand and lawyers need to be connected at all times. Indisputable evidence of this constant connectivity is found by casual observation of automobile drivers, people sunning, and grocery shoppers, as well as in the most remote hiking places, the finest restaurants, and in public restrooms. Since the customer [client] is always right, lawyers too need to equip themselves to satisfy the clients' demand for constant and speedy communication.

Determining what hardware and software a law practice should acquire to communicate with clients cannot be a unilateral decision. Law practices must take into account what the client is using to stay connected. How frequently you communicate with clients will also have an impact on the decision. How much information needs to be transferred is another consideration.

E-mail is wonderful. With .pdf (portable document format) files and scanners, other material such as surveys, engineering drawings, and copies of court decisions may be attached to your commentary. Bulky attachments may be condensed for fast, easy transmission. Links to your or another Web site can also be forwarded. Getting the client's input on a draft of a document or during kinetic negotiations is quickly accomplished by e-mail volleying that is efficient and effective. Handheld wireless computers, cell phones and the more primitive cyber cafes make catching up with a client for an update on the legal matter you are handling relatively easy, no matter where you are.

But just a minute, realize it isn't always best for client relations to communicate in this manner. Remember the actress's reaction in classic black-and-white movies when she received bad news from a "just the facts" telegram delivered by an uninvolved uniformed boy? For the same reasons, much confusion about the message and client resentment toward the lawyer could be generated by an email stating, "Attached is the court's decision," when the decision is a stinging rebuke of the client's claim or defense. Even if the client reads the decision, there is a good likelihood that the implications won't be fully understood. Such a situation demands some explanation that would be best discussed in an in-person or over-the-phone conversation, difficult as it might be for the lawyer. In this way, the client isn't left like the actress to deal with confusion of the content or the emotional side of the news alone.

One of the great banes of law firms is the storage of information and finding what the client or the lawyer wants to see as soon as the client wants to see it. Years ago, law firms discovered they didn't need to store files for closed matters or little used ones for current matters on the premises of their high-rent offices. Boxing and sending such material to an offsite storage facility maintained by the firm or an independent business is commonplace. Technology has now advanced to the point that material can be digitalized and stored for instant cyber-access. The best part is that there are high tech firms that perform such services cheaper and better than any-size law firm can do itself. Retrieval of such digitalized information can be instantaneous, which will certainly meet any client's or lawyer's expectation.

Clients are mighty impressed when during a telephone conversation they ask about a document and during that very discussion, their lawyer pulls it up electronically, instantly e-mails it to the client and discusses the document in the continued conversation. Both access and speed contribute significantly to the client's perception that the lawyer is super-organized and on top of the client's matter. Clients relate to and appreciate this hyperspeed service. Regardless of their technical sophistication, clients are likely to tell others about this. Yet, my sense is that only a small percentage of law practices are utilizing this technological advance and advantage.

As an aside, contracting with a firm for digital storage of data and files is yet another illustration that modern successful law practices are partnering with a variety of specialized suppliers and providers. These alliances are usually more beneficial and cost-efficient to the small- and medium-sized practices than to a national firm. A great source of information about such partnership opportunities, which have been pretested, is your business clients. An extra bonus of such an inquiry is that the business clients will appreciate the lawyer asking their advice.

Although it was more of a problem in the past, lawyers must be certain that the technology they select interfaces with what their clients are using. This means that it is able to receive from and send to all hardware and interface with Mac, Windows, and other software applications. In truth, the advances in software have all but eliminated this problem. Nevertheless, check the universality of everything before you buy for more than occasionally there still remain interface issues, as between Word and WordPerfect.

There are some technology salespeople who swear that the fax is becoming obsolete and all you need is a computer and scanner. This has not been the experience in law practices or with clients. First, faxes are so easy and convenient to use, especially for larger documents, that clients and law firms prefer them. For the most part, faxes are faster, have greater accuracy and are more reliable than scanners. Even the long distance telephone charges haven't deterred the use of faxes. However, this is today and we all know that technology may change any reality tomorrow.

WEB SITES

It is a rare business that does not have a Web address. Web sites yield additional opportunities to communicate with clients and potential ones. They enlarge a lawyer's presence in a far larger domain than could be reached by personal contacts. Like all other client relations communications and means by which they are delivered, Web sites require careful planning and implementation.

Surely you have called up Web pages that you have found interesting and useful, and others that have caused you to promptly abort your visit. Web sites for law practices are usually oriented toward potential clients, but they must serve existing clients as well. Since the purpose for making a site available is different for these two groups, the site must be designed carefully. It is certainly a challenge to augment the text of a law practice Web site by incorporating graphics and pictures which will hold the viewer's interest while remaining professional in appearance.

If you represent personal injury victims or automobile insurance carriers, I suspect graphic pictures of accidents and the resulting injuries on your Web page will catch the eye of most readers. The question is whether that is what you want the Web browser or client to remember. Far less dramatic Web content would be a list of recent jury verdicts obtained in personal injury cases. That relatively bland list may well do more to convince a person to retain the lawyer than the tabloid-type pictures of gore. We lawyers have opinions about such things, but often our viewpoint differs from the person surfing the Web for a lawyer. That is why whoever designs a Web site for a law practice must design from the outside in—from the users' points of view.

Lawyers generally can articulate what they wish to accomplish with a Web site and a professional Web site designer may be the best way to bring those ideas into reality. But, picking a Web site designer can be perplexing. One needs to examine the candidates' portfolios of work to determine if the lawyer likes the "feel" of the work, if it contains a variety of design styles, and if it reflects experience in different fields. This is important because your clients and potential clients have a myriad of backgrounds and work in a wide variety of industries. Your Web site should "speak" to all of these people. Thus, a designer with broad experience is more likely to be aware of the language that best communicates to a number of industries and individuals with diverse backgrounds.

Lawyers or law firm committees assigned the extra duty of engaging a Web site designer should find one whose tastes appear to compliment the image they have of their practice and one with whom the group can work well. Just as the lawyer's taste in décor selected for an office creates an impression with clients, so does the Web site. Some basic knowledge of the legal field is to the candidate's advantage for it helps to assure that the designer understands the essence of law practice. If the designer is a bit thin on or lacks design experience for the legal profession, that can be overcome if the designer expresses a desire and commitment to learn more about your practice. Whether the designer is experienced in law practice designs or not, lawyers must be committed to teaching the selected Web site designer about their practice, their strengths, their clients, and the type of people they hope to persuade to become clients.

Even if you are planning to do a Web site design in house, it is probably wise to interview professional Web designers for insightful ideas and experiences. If, after interviewing Web designers, the lawyer or committee decides the site can be "homemade," be sure that the standards and measures for effectiveness are the same as they would be if services of a Web site designer had been retained.

WEB SITE DESIGN BASICS

Regardless of who designs the Web site, here are the basic Web site concepts. First, the Web site should be intuitive. That means the person who chooses to go to the site should find that it is easy to navigate. This can be accomplished by a "clean space" facilitating the user finding what is sought quickly and without confusion. To optimize the value from your investment, the design of a Web site must ensure easy access from the different platforms and various Internet software browsers used by clients and Internet-surfers. Graphics used must complement, not steal the attention from content. A fast Web site helps. Users who have to wait for significant seconds for the site to load, probably won't wait.

The most difficult Web site question to resolve is how much substantive content and how many answers to legal questions should be provided. Lawyers' inclinations are not to give any information away because we want the user to become a client and pay for the information. At the same time, if the site doesn't communicate to people that you have the specific expertise they need, it is not likely that "hits" will retain you. Convincing people that a lawyer is capable of handling matters in particular areas of practice is best achieved by revealing some advice, as opposed to exclusively trumpeting the education, court admissions, bar memberships and articles authored.

Guidance about the depth of legal information may be gleaned from examining what a browser can get free from other competing legal services sites. Another gauge is how much you would tell a person about the law if she or he were interviewing you for possible retention. Investigate what information is available in the public domain—such as government regulations and statues. Taken together, all these may give you confidence to include more information on your site. In the end, lawyers have to be comfortable with the amount and detail of the information placed in the web site. While this information may be regarded as marketing, it applies to client relations because if the client looks at the practice's Web site before or after retaining the lawyer, the Web information may well form the foundation of the client relationship, set the expectations, or set up a conflict between advice or service received and the material on the Web site. Examine your Web site to be sure you meet all the claims and are in accord with the legal information provided.

Another very important function of a Web site is to provide clients and potential clients a means of confirming recommendations of others to hire a particular lawyer. The user must be able to gather meaningful information about the lawyer who has been recommended. This means that the function of the site is much more than just a new kind of yellow pages. Information about each lawyer's education, experience, and area of practice will be of assistance to the person seeking reassurance that the lawyer recommended is qualified.

Adding pictures and biographies of the lawyers in the organization is a nice feature. Sometimes, listing information about lawyers' families or hobbies helps the client round out an impression of the lawyers. The client (or potential client) can use a Web site with these features to get a "feeling" about the lawyer. This breeds confidence and trust. In smaller offices, this more personal touch can be extended to all timekeepers, and even all staff, so that the Web user feels she or he knows all of the persons involved with providing legal services.

For sure, all sites should contain information that is of practical value to the client. Making it easier for the client to contact and visit you is a must. For instance, all contact information—office telephone numbers, fax numbers, e-mail addresses, postal addresses, cell phone numbers—all should be easy to find. Putting the general office contact information on every page facilitates their use. Directions to the law office and where to park are usually much appreciated, as is a link to a map.

Marketing experts may be able to better advise about the amount and type of content that should be loaded into a site. It is important to get it right to maximize the number of users and their positive reaction to your Web site. An additional source for information about the design of a Web site is to assemble the intended users—clients and potential clients—to get their opinion. A win-win arrangement with your clients is to invite them to a meeting with you and your Web site designer to obtain their advice and then take them to dinner. If you want reactions of those who have no connection to you or the law practice, you may have to pay a focus group. In both cases, the additional viewpoints are intended to provide advice that will increase the value of your Web site.

A final word on law practice Web sites. Be sure to have prominent disclaimers of any attorney-client relationship and negate the possibility that anything on the site could be construed as giving legal advice. Many sites have such a disclaimer on the first and/or last page. That may not be enough. A client user could only focus on information set out on interior pages that may be in conflict with the advice being given by the lawyer. If the Web site is an interactive one, be sure to indicate that the lawyers' responses (or the automatically generated ones) are based on the facts provided by the user, who must consult with a lawyer to obtain legal advice. The safer way is to have such disclaimers on every page of the Web site, whether interactive or not.

It may seem incongruous to write about how not to have a client in a book about client relations, but you only want to have client relations with those whom you choose. Further, you need to assure that an existing client doesn't use information from the Web site inappropriately as legal advice.

The potential conflicts between marketing and client service information on law practices' Web sites must be considered and addressed in order to assure information on the site is not misunderstood or misused. Otherwise, clients may be disappointed or the site may inadvertently create a malpractice claim.

FUNCTIONAL ENHANCEMENTS TO CLIENT RELATIONS

We know that technology enables us to communicate more rapidly. We know that technology opens "cyber-markets" for new clients. We know that technology provides additional means of connectivity between attorney and client. What we don't know for sure is how effectively all of this technology functions to enhance client relations. After all, attorney-client relations is an actual experience between real people, not simply some wired or wireless, faceless connection.

E-mail communications about a specific topic among a small number of people have been shown to be an effective means of communication. The more puzzling question is how well e-mail works for mass communications. Many law firms are considering changing or have changed the distribution of their newsletter from hardcopy to an electronic transmission. The question arises whether this change has any affect on the effectiveness of the communication. While e-mailing the newsletter may be easier and cheaper, it isn't worth the savings of effort and cost if it is read less or fails to generate at least the same amount of legal work from the recipients.

I suspect that the most accurate answer to this question of effectiveness is that we just don't know. Rational speculation might lead one to conclude that the change of delivery system would be neutral: those who didn't read the hardcopy won't read the electronic copy and those who read it in one format will read in another. On the other hand, in spite of efforts for the last twenty years, electronic newspapers have made no significant inroad on the circulation of hardcopy newspapers. Also, some of the television news cable networks are now trending a declining viewer share. These facts raise interesting issues for law practices distributing newsletters.

I think that more people probably read hard copy newsletters from law practices than e-mailed ones. People are more adept at glancing at hard copy headlines and determining what they want to read than scrolling down an electronic newsletter. But then again, the reader preferences may split along those demographic strata discussed at the beginning of this chapter.

This much is certain: electronic layout and formatting is very different from that used in effective hardcopy. Commercial magazines have learned their lesson when their "e-magazines" failed when editors for it were transferred from the hard copy side. The "e-publications" became more viable when people with "e-talents" were hired to manage and edit them. The lesson for lawyers is that if they choose to communicate with clients through an electronic newsletter, they would be well advised to engage someone who thoroughly understands the medium.

EXTRANETS

A solid technological advance in client relations permits clients to access information on their matters through a private, secure connection utilizing a client name and confidential password. This helps the lawyer too, for the lawyer doesn't have to be interrupted by the client for a status report. These often called "extranets" can also reduce costs to a client and free administrative time for the practice, if the client agrees to substitute electronic access for hardcopies of letters, filings and memoranda. Remember, access doesn't equal understanding. The lawyer will still want to converse with the client to be sure the client understands the impact of the electronic information on the client's situation.

A creative use of technology is to make client profiles accessible to all attorneys in your practice. Such information for a corporate client may include the scope of responsibility for key contacts, the contact's hobbies, any pet peeves of the contact, the name of the contact's secretary and who really makes the decisions on the matter. This information facilitates another attorney covering for the attorney primarily responsible for the client or matter by providing information that becomes the basis for instant client rapport.

The advantage for lawyers on each new phase of evolving technology and its use to improve the client's image of lawyers is limited only by one's lack of knowledge about technology and one's perceived horizon of the use to which such technology can be utilized in client relations.

NOT THE BE ALL AND END ALL

Some are so enthralled with technology they think and talk as though it were the be-all and end-all . . . it isn't. Technology definitely has its limits in client relations.

The security of electronic communications is one of the top concerns of both lawyers and clients. We know about encryption of information and secure sites for credit card transaction. We also have read of the breakdown of super-secure systems in commercial credit card operations. Rationally, the chance of breaking through a law firm's properly constructed firewall built to protect the privacy of their client's files may well be far less than the risk of having a break-in to a hardcopy file storage facility. Yet, many people just don't have the gut confidence that cyberspace is as safe as a locked physical storage space.

You must ask your client and get agreement in writing with all necessary protections before your law practice converts the client to a paperless environment. If you fail to do this, even when nothing untoward happens electronically, the client, who psychologically is unable to conclude there is sufficient cyber security to provide a satisfactory comfort level, will regard the attorney practicing cyberlaw as reckless.

There is much less chance that any computer communication will be regarded as personal by the client, even if the client is the sole recipient. Technology, even with its script signatures, will never be as personal as a visit, a telephone call or a handwritten note. Think of how you regard an e-greeting on your computer as compared to receiving a greeting card in your mailbox. The lawyer must make a judgment as to which communications are more appropriately delivered the "old-fashioned" way. Communicating sympathy, concern, joy, anger, outrage, and other emotions by e-mail is difficult, for your choices to convey such complex feelings, even to those you know well, only extend to the selection of typed words and symbols and the order in which you place them. Gone are the opportunities for tears, long pauses, laughter, tone of voice, high-fives, and spontaneous comments to assist you in fully communicating your intended message. Determine in each circumstance which means of communication with your client is most appropriate.

The communications link to the client that is most effective varies with the nature of the communication. E-mail can certainly be used for everything from relaying routine information to joshing a client. As the seriousness of the content of the communication increases—that is, as the prospect of positive or negative impact escalates—the appropriateness of e-mail decreases proportionately. In these circumstances, a visit or phone call provide a better means of communication.

Remember too that individuals with computers in their homes still expect a more personal communication from their lawyers than people in business settings. This holds even if the lawyer handles both business and personal matters for the client. There is just an expectation that communications in and to a person's home will be more personal than those to the same person's business.

If the appropriate means of communication is unavailable or, if by using the appropriate method, there would be an unacceptable delay before you could connect with the client, communicate by any means possible. Then, follow that with a communication in the proper format. Both communications should include an apology for being unable to use the appropriate means to relay the message initially.

One little test to determine the appropriate means of communication is: considering the subject of the communication and the client's state of mind when the client will receive this communication, will the client feel that I, the client's lawyer, really care about the client, as a person? If the answer is no or I'm not sure, use a more personal means to convey the message.

TECH SUMMARY

Lawyers have two major areas of opportunities to use technology to augment their client relations efforts. First, they must constantly take the initiative to find and utilize new technology to communicate with and serve the client better. This may mean an investment in an interactive Web site and the education of clients as to how to use it. Second, if clients want e-services and e-communications, lawyers will have to provide what the clients want. This means that lawyers should have a continuing dialog with clients about what technology they are using and what e-capabilities they expect their lawyers to use.

Technology provides tools to enhance client communications and relations. It cannot replace face-to-face discussions, telephone calls or handwritten notes. Use every technologically advanced hardware device and software program to enhance client relations . . . but don't misuse them . . . and bear in mind the difference.

CHAPTER 13

ENTREPRENEUSES AND ENTREPRENEURS (NEWLY LICENSED AND "BREAK-OFF" LAWYERS)

CONCEPT AND DEFINITION

Entrepreneuse! I never heard of such a person. The dictionary informs that this is a female entrepreneur. I really don't differentiate. The characteristics required of a businessperson to succeed are the same regardless of sex. They are all entrepreneurs to me. Certainly, the challenges of the female entrepreneur differ from the male, as do those for persons who are minorities, others who move into a new community to practice, and those practicing in the neighborhood in which they were raised. Differences are easy to point out, but I'm struck by the common client relations factors, which have such an impact on the outcomes for the lawyer entrepreneur.

The entrepreneur is a special subset of practicing lawyer. *Entrepreneur* is defined in dictionaries as a person who organizes and manages an enterprise, usually with substantial initiative and risk. Enterprise turns out to be characterized as an endeavor requiring boldness, energy, and adventurous spirit. This hardly sounds like the staid established or large law firm. Although this could be someone in a medium or larger firm, I wish to focus this chapter on the small practice, usually solo or a firm of three lawyers or less.

Often these practitioners are newly licensed or have broken off from a larger firm. Others are those lawyers who have reached a mandatory retirement age or chose to "move on" after a reassessment of their life's priorities. And, tens of thousands of lawyers just simply choose to practice in a smaller organization because it produces a higher level of satisfaction from greater opportunity for personal freedom.

These are lawyers who by choice or circumstance are practicing on the edge. The struggles to serve clients in a quality fashion and become or continue to be economically viable are daily in the enterprise. These entrepreneurs are required to conduct the business of law practice in this manner in addition to meeting the rigors of practicing law.

Entrepreneurial practices don't enjoy the luxury of a marketing director, information systems expert, or, in most cases, even an administrator. Such folks have to become experts and decision makers in all these and a myriad of other business topics just to economically survive to practice law. Entrepreneurial practice is drastically different from the young associate or partner in an established firm where the responsibilities are more limited and the support is vastly greater.

Amazingly, most who take this difficult, self-motivated journey say that they gain an extraordinarily high level of satisfaction from practicing law. When our daughter, Sarah, was about two years old, she started replying "I'll do it myself!" when I asked if she wanted help. In her work as a freelance graphic designer, she is still doing it herself and getting a great deal of satisfaction from it. While doing it yourself involves great risk and many frustrations, the satisfaction obtained when successful cannot be exceeded in another law practice setting.

There are many roads by which individuals become lawyer-entrepreneurs. The newly licensed lawyer who, for whatever reason, couldn't get a job with a firm is one. When an individual or small group of lawyers tire of the big law firm atmosphere and spin off, or get spun off from the firm, are others. More lawyers who have enjoyed successful careers in a corporation or government setting are now setting up law practice enterprises.

The nature of an entrepreneur's practice is different from others. While there are many common client relations techniques that apply regardless of the size of the firm, there are also some special adjustments that the entrepreneur will want to consider in pursuing client relations. The rest of the chapter addresses client relations issues for entrepreneurs, but many of the points are fully applicable to every practice.

OTHER HELPFUL REFERENCES

Entrepreneurs—regardless of the length of time they have been practicing—would be well advised to buy and review Jay Foonberg's classic *How to Start and Build a Law Practice, 4th Edition* (ABA Law Practice Management Section, 2000). Jay's writing stimulates your thinking on how you can further develop your practice. His suggestions are stated in such a way that you can immediately recognize whether they are applicable to your practice.

Paul McLaughlin, in *Welcome to Reality, A New Lawyer's Guide To Success* (www.dogonit.ca), clearly lays out what one must do in the first two years of law practice to maximize the chances of success. This reference is understandable even for those who haven't yet practiced, is formatted in easy-to-read fashion, and is chock-full of practical advice and step-by-step implementation plans that are easy to follow. Paul's writing, the bullet points, illustrations, and advice combine to make this a "must have" reference for every new lawyer entrepreneur.

Chapter after chapter, fifty-five in all, of practical information for solos and firms can be found in the new edition of *Flying Solo, A Survival Guide for the Solo Lawyer, Third Edition*, Jeffrey R. Simmons, Editor (ABA Law Practice Management Section, 2001). The topics addressed by experienced practitioners cover all phases of practice, even how to collect fees billed to clients. Please note that the applicability of the good advice provided in the book is far broader than just for solos. This is an excellent, well-written reference for all lawyers to keep on their shelves. When they are faced with a management problem, a quick scan of the table of contents will usually guide the reader to pages containing effective resolutions or terrific opportunities. Many managing partners and administrators from firms of all sizes, as well as corporate and government supervising attorneys, will find this volume an invaluable resource.

All three of these recommended references cover a wide variety of topics. This book and chapter are more detailed and focused on developing fruitful client relations.

NEWLY LICENSED LAWYER AND CLIENT RELATIONS

A dilemma for many a new lawyer is how to deal with clients. Most law schools instruct primarily on the law, not clients. Even if one had the experience of clerking in a firm during law school or for a judge after law school, there is very little exposure to clients and how to deal with them. Prior business experience may help some, but the attorney-client relationship is somewhat different from other business relationships.

So how does a new lawyer handle clients? All too frequently the answer is by trial and error. To achieve client relations success by this method requires a very long and bumpy learning curve. Unfortunately, it also increases the risk of economic failure and malpractice charges.

There are two critical issues that warrant emphasis for new lawyers. In some ways they are different faces of the same coin. The client must be convinced that the new lawyer can handle the matter, and the new lawyer must do that convincing while not violating ethical obligations.

For most of the experiences and observations in this section, as well as some others elsewhere, I'm truly indebted to our son Andrew who bravely waded into the water of becoming an entrepreneur lawyer in Connecticut, where he and his wife moved after law school. He knew no one in the area and his law school didn't have more than one or two alums in the area. And, as he insightfully said to me in an early phone conversation when I asked how it was going, "Dad, I don't know how to practice law and I don't know how to run a business, but I have to do both." As much as I wanted to, giving long distance support proved difficult. With able assistance from his wife, Kim, who is a certified public accountant, and digging deep to find the "boldness, energy, and adventurous spirit" required to do things you've never done before—some that you never wanted to do—after two years, Andrew's practice started to develop. It can be done . . . but don't be fooled: It is very difficult.

ETHICS AND CLIENT RELATIONS

If you are new to law practice, worrying about paying your rent at the office and a mortgage on your house when a person knocks on your door and asks you to handle a legal matter, how can you possibly know enough law to accept it? Then again, how can you afford to reject the proposed retention? Think about it, the law school graduate who hangs out a shingle has never handled a single matter in any area of practice. How can the new lawyer represent that she is competent to undertake the matter?

Obviously, every practicing lawyer has had a first matter. Your passing the bar examination and being licensed to practice law entitles you to legitimately claim a certain level of competence, regardless of your grades in law school.

Model Rule 1.1 lists some elements of basic competency including knowledge, skill, thoroughness, and preparation. This standard may be fairly easy to meet if you are an associate in a large firm, performing a limited role, and are under the supervision of an experienced partner. However, when you are an entrepreneur, you are being asked to be responsible for the entirety of the client's matter, instead of doing the research or drafting something to be reviewed by an experienced lawyer or sitting second chair in a deposition. This places a much greater burden on the new lawyer entrepreneur. Be aware of your obligations to the client and be sure you meet them.

KNOW YOUR LIMITS

Knowing your limits is the only concept you need to apply to assure you comply with this ethical obligation. But you must have a realistic view of your limits. I'm as concerned about new lawyers who immediately conclude that they can't handle a matter as I am about the ones who assume that they know it all.

The following is intended to provide some guidelines to assist you in defining your limits and ways to meet your ethical obligations to clients.

AREA OF LAW

First, ask yourself what area or areas of the law are involved in this matter. This is not as clear-cut as you might suppose. For instance, suppose a walk-in says to you in your initial meeting that she was an engineer with a company and on her own time developed a new process to manufacture more efficient carburetors, bought a patent-it-yourself software kit, obtained a patent, entered into a contract with a different company to produce the device, her employer discovered the patent, she was fired, and now the manufacturer is refusing to pay her any patent royalties and her former employer is suing her for the rights to the patent.

Like life, client's issues don't come in neat little factual packages all tied tightly with no loose ends, like some of the appellate cases you read in law school. The client probably perceives this is just a simple matter of defending a meritless lawsuit brought by her former employer and getting the manufacturer to pay her the royalties she thinks she's owed on the patent. But, right off the top, in assessing competencies needed to handle the matter, the new lawyer sees issues in the fields of litigation, intellectual property, contracts, and employment law. The more experienced counselor will also see the critical jurisdictional and procedural points, as well as other substantive issues.

All lawyers and especially new lawyers need to be sure that all the core competencies necessary to handle the matter are identified, then recall whether they had exposure to those competencies in law school. Finally, each will have to decide if the level of understanding they acquired from such exposure is sufficient. The grade received in law school is not enough; true present understanding of the basic issues is the standard.

If new lawyers decide that they can spot the basic issues applicable to the client's situation and know where and how to get those refined by further research, they are probably competent to handle the matter. But, the area of the law criterion is the start of the inquiry, not the conclusion.

COMPLEXITY

Another area to consider is the complexity of the matter. It makes eminently good sense for beginning lawyers to initially handle elementary matters and work their way up to more-complex ones. Follow that old saying, "You have to crawl before you can walk (or sprint or run a marathon)."

There are many issues. One of our obligations in client relations is to explain to the client what the maze of laws under which our society lives means to the client and how it applies to the client's situation. It is elementary that a situation involving many questions from a variety of legal fields is more difficult to understand and explain than one with fewer questions. Thus, if the new lawyer entrepreneur cannot succinctly explain to the client how all these issues interrelate, the matter shouldn't be accepted.

Even where there appears to be a single area of the law involved, the new lawyer entrepreneur must evaluate its complexity. For example, one of the first people to come to my son Andrew's office for a consultation was a person who needed help with an immigration issue. This is an area in which our entrepreneur wanted to practice and one in which there is plenty of help from many sources. Some of the most competent are the federal administrators and lawyers who I've found to be quite helpful. When the appointment was made, the potential client seemed promising as one of Andrew's first clients. But, when the initial conference concluded, it turned out that this wasn't a simple green card application. Among other things, the gentleman was in the United States illegally and was seeking political asylum. This was too complex for an entrepreneur with virtually no legal experience. Andrew declined to represent him.

The standard of what is too complex for an entrepreneurial lawyer is not absolute. It's a flexible bar whose height is determined by the individual lawyer. One may feel perfectly comfortable in the real estate field closing a residential deal. A closer look must be given before accepting a complex commercial real estate transaction involving a conservation easement, a fight over proportional ownership from an estate, and multiple condominium owners' interests.

Complexity of the issue does have an influence on the outcome of client relations and the competency of a lawyer as it is judged by our ethical standards. There is no shame in telling a potential client that the situation is too complex for your level of experience.

SIZE OF THE CASE: STAFFING

Many new entrepreneur lawyers wish for the one big case that will instantaneously create their reputation as a star and make them rich. As the old adage advises, "Be careful what you wish for—you may get it!"

We have an obligation to our clients to honestly tell them when we will not be able to handle their matter effectively. Your client will not have good relations with you if you give many assurances about your ability to handle a large matter, and then months down the road find you don't have sufficient or trained staff and are forced to tell the client you can't continue. Further, shorting yourself on the staff required for a matter creates a fertile bed for the seed of malpractice to grow.

The focus is not the dollar amount involved, but rather how many qualified people it will take to pursue the client's interest effectively and efficiently. Understaffing will inevitably result in the lawyer dodging communications with the client so as to avoid revealing that certain work hasn't yet been completed. This is just the opposite of the on-time or before-deadline performance we all strive to achieve to establish good client relations.

The rewards of entrepreneurship do not necessarily include "big is better." It is better for you and your client if you refer a matter too large for you to staff to a law firm able to adequately staff it. Or, as detailed later, you may choose, with your client's permission, to form an alliance and affiliate a larger firm on the matter.

FINANCIAL COMMITMENT—COSTS

Many newly licensed entrepreneurs don't know enough about the business side of practice to accurately gauge the financial commitment required to undertake clients' matters. It may sound great when a contact you have been cultivating at a bank or finance company calls and asks you to handle one hundred collection cases. What may escape your radar screen is that each of those cases requires cash for discovery costs and filing fees. This is also true for most contingent fee cases and some new entrepreneurs don't realize this until they are in a position of not being able to afford to take the next step for their client or toward collecting a potential fee.

Some lawyers don't have any way to obtain money to advance the necessary costs. Others take costs from their take-home pay or ask a rich uncle for a loan. Going back to the client months after the engagement to ask for money to file lawsuits, patents, or licenses isn't wise. The client's reaction will be, "Why wasn't I told I'd have to put up this money when we initially discussed the matter?" Or the client's thought might be, "This entrepreneur is a fly-by-night." Either way, and even if the client advances the needed funds, the client has lost a degree of trust and confidence in the lawyer. This adversely affects all other aspects of the professional relationship.

Be sure you have the means to finance all expected up-front client costs . . . you owe it to yourself.

DO NOT TAKE ON WHAT YOU CAN'T DO

The bottom line of all these guidelines is: "Don't take on what you can't do; it will be unethical and detrimental to your practice." This maxim hits the entrepreneur right between the eyes, for it often requires rejection of immediate income to avoid bad client relations. But it builds toward many superior client relationships and an excellent long-term professional reputation.

ALTERNATIVES

Don't be discouraged by all of the things that a newly licensed lawyer must consider before accepting a matter and client. Don't conclude that ethical and client relations considerations all but prevent the less experienced attorney from earning a living. Don't think you can't become an entrepreneur in law practice. Many, many others have, and you can, too.

The object of the advice given in this chapter thus far is to raise the level of awareness of what has to be considered to maximize the chances of good client relations before a lawyer undertakes a matter. Remember, as an entrepreneur who "organizes and manages an enterprise," you must be cognizant of both the pitfalls and the opportunities. Below are a couple of avenues to represent that client, while at the same time meeting your ethical and client relations obligations.

CONSIDER CO-COUNSELING

One way to overcome the lack of knowledge of an area of the law, the traps of complexity, the limitations of staff, and the insufficiency of your financial resources all at one time is to engage a competent co-counsel. With just one simple arrangement with an appropriate co-counsel, you can obtain all the experience necessary and satisfy your ethical obligations to represent almost any client on virtually any matter.

Most lawyers resist co-counseling because they fear the co-counsel will "steal" their clients. For the most part, this is an unreasoned fear. If you do what you should with client relations and in controlling the co-counsel, no ill will should seep from this arrangement.

Yes, you must very clearly lay out the role of co-counsel to both the client and co-counsel at the beginning. Yes, you must continue to play a major role in representing the client on the matter. And, most importantly, yes, you must spend more time and effort continually relating to your client when a co-counsel is involved in a matter.

These are relatively minor adjustments when measured against the alternative of not being in a position to be retained by a new client or being unqualified in experience, staff, or finances to undertake the larger, more complex matter.

The first thing the entrepreneur has to realize is that co-counseling doesn't necessarily mean that you involve the co-counsel in every aspect of the matter. As a newly licensed entrepreneur you are perfectly competent to handle some aspects of the most complex situation. You, as the lawyer to whom the client came, are in a position to keep those tasks, which your education and experience qualifies you to perform. You may retain only the portion of the work which interests you, if you choose. The remainder, assign to a co-counsel.

Some are reluctant to make such an assignment for fear that it will diminish their status with their client. Certainly there is some risk of that. However, if one develops and maintains the relationship with the client, status will not shrink. In fact, if properly presented, the reputation of the entrepreneur engaging co-counsel is likely to be enhanced. What better way for the client to become convinced that his lawyer has the client's best interest in mind than to augment the team with a more-experienced co-counsel arrangement that is also an economic detriment to you, the entrepreneur?

As a rule of thumb, if the entrepreneur needs to engage co-counsel for all aspects of the matter, it is better to refer the total engagement to another lawyer. Under these circumstances, it is in the client's best economic interest to have the entire matter handled by one competent lawyer. If the entrepreneur cannot add value by competently and efficiently performing a portion of the work, the work should be referred in its entirety rather than handled via a more expensive co-counseling arrangement.

Referral of the total matter does not necessarily mean a total loss of income to the referring lawyer. The Rules of Professional Conduct, Rule 1.5(e), contemplates a referral in which a lawyer can be paid even if the referring lawyer does no actual work. Check the Rule and commentary on it. Also review your state and local rules. If still in doubt, ask for an ethical opinion on your precise situation. Likewise, if the referring lawyer wishes to become educated about the field of law, that lawyer could easily shadow the lawyer to whom the work was referred and be copied on all documents. If it is the referring lawyer's choice to become educated, that lawyer should never charge any fees or expenses to the client just for the education. The client may appreciate being able to converse in general terms with the referring lawyer about the progress of the case. This time should be classified as nonbillable client relations time.

There are many divisions of labor that make good sense when working with more experienced co-counsel for the benefit of the client. For instance, in litigation it may be advantageous to do virtually all of the pre-trial prep, engage co-counsel to try the case, and the entrepreneur then sit second chair in the trial. Likewise, when drafting a complex contract or estate plan, it could be advantageous to have co-counsel review the entrepreneur's finished product before it is presented to the client. None of these activities would detract from the stature of the entrepreneur. Co-counsel can easily be rationalized to the client as calling in a specialist, a move acceptable to most clients and appreciated by many.

Phantom co-counsel is also a possibility in certain situations. Government lawyers, especially in the federal government, are trained to represent the interest of the public. When I was practicing with the National Labor Relations Board, I often helped counsel and nonlawyer representatives of unions and employers with interpretations of the law and understandings of the impact of the facts with which they were faced. They used this information to assist themselves in advising how to comply with the law and discussing the potential impact of a charge. This assistance is available from most governmental agency lawyers whether you are currently representing a client with a matter pending before the agency or not.

From a client relations standpoint, it often helps clients accept that they have little or no wiggle room if the entrepreneur's advice is confirmed by a government lawyer. Clients bringing a charge against their employer or another in a position of power are often afraid of the possible fallout. The entrepreneur may well be assisted in encouraging the client to follow through on a rightful allegation by taking the client to a meeting with a government lawyer who can assure the client of the protections provided by statute.

These no-cost phantom government lawyer options are intended to stimulate thinking on how entrepreneurs may easily obtain greater credibility with clients. These opportunities also provide solos and those with little or no experience in a field with a process to check their conclusions before advising clients. The entrepreneur who advises confidently and augments the advice with authority, governmental or otherwise, will strengthen the relationship with the client.

MENTORING

Lawyers generally, and male lawyers in particular, are loathe to ask for directions or help. Perhaps that's the reason mentoring opportunities are not more frequently available and utilized. How very unfortunate that is. Especially for the entrepreneur lawyer, a more advantageous arrangement than mentoring could hardly be imagined. Think about it! Mentoring provides a chance to acquire sage advice and help with no risk of losing the client and at no cost.

Many state and local associations have formal mentoring programs. Sometimes the mentor and mentee are in different locales so that there is little chance of the mentee losing the client's loyalty. There are also opportunities for informal mentoring. Many a respected practitioner is more than willing to assist a newly licensed one. Sometimes the experienced person will think to offer, but the entrepreneur shouldn't hesitate to ask if she or he could call upon a more experienced lawyer from time to time. Most often the answer is an enthusiastic, "Sure."

The Internet provides cyber-mentoring options. A very helpful source is the American Bar Association's Web site (*www.abanet.org*), which lists various discussion groups organized by field of law and size of firm. Other helpful online communities can be found in other bar associations, marketing groups, substantive law groups, and by browsing the Internet. For instance, I know of an organization that provides marketing services for a particular field of law. As an additional benefit, it hooks up all those purchasing the marketing service in a chat room so that practitioners may help one another with answers based on practical experience. It is my understanding from an entrepreneur that when he asks a question, he gets a number of prompt responses from across the country. The added confidence growing from confirmation of other practitioners aids him in his client relations efforts.

Entrepreneurs should actively seek mentoring on practice management matters, as well as on questions about substantive law. Excellent guidance can be obtained on diverse subjects like how to handle a difficult client, how to finance software, which timekeeping system works best for a small practice, and the best method to collect an unpaid legal fee bill. These very practical aspects of the business side of law practice can be the most difficult for the entrepreneur and most easily answered by mentors. Because solos to mid-sized firm practitioners are more likely to have dealt directly with these situations, mentors from that sector of the legal profession, not large firm mentors where administrators handle such matters, are likely to have more useable advice for the entrepreneur. Handling the business questions properly will have a greater effect on the entrepreneur's relationship with clients than the legal side. There is great practice development value in obtaining mentoring on such topics.

Humans learn most easily from others who are more experienced. That is how we all learned to speak. That is also how we can learn to practice law and relate to our clients better. To obtain this type of learning, entrepreneur lawyers must make conscious efforts to find mentors. Entrepreneurs don't have the option of having a mentor provided by the law firm. The additional insight gained from mentors benefits clients and their entrepreneur lawyer.

ETHICAL OBLIGATIONS AND CLIENT CREDIBILITY

No matter how glib, lawyers must eventually prove themselves to their clients on the playing field of substance. For the entrepreneur lawyer, this could appear to be insurmountable, no matter how much the books are studied. There is always a temptation to compromise quality of legal representation for the immediate dollar. That approach never pays long-term dividends with clients or to law practices.

One method for the entrepreneur lawyer to determine whether presently he or she possesses the education, training, experience, understanding of the application of the law, as well as the business assets, to handle the matter is to more objectively assess the realities. This assessment should be completed on every matter, at least mentally if not on paper, before agreeing to undertake it.

If it isn't objectively apparent that the entrepreneur lawyer can presently marshal the resources to represent the client on the matter and meet all ethical and client relations obligations, co-counseling and mentoring are very viable paths to satisfy all concerns. These routes yield valuable ancillary benefits to the entrepreneur lawyer as well. They give lawyers unique opportunities to learn to practice law or to gain experience in a legal field in which they have never before practiced.

Putting the client's best interest first may leave some short-term money on the table, but it will build a long-term relationship and good reputation that will pay much bigger dividends. Having good intentions to perform work that you don't know how to do or don't have the staff and financial assets to perform is unethical and will not sit well with the client. As Henry Ford once observed, "You can't build a reputation on what you were going to do."

The constant object is to build credibility with the client. To do that, lawyers must produce desirable results. This is especially important for newly licensed entrepreneurs for they may be under the greatest client scrutiny. Clients judge results based on amount of effort, ability to teach legal substance, and cost control, as well as legal outcomes. Credibility with the client is dependant upon the client coming to know that the lawyer is doing everything possible for the client. That can best be shown through developing relations with clients that build clients' confidence in lawyers.

BREAKING OFF FROM A FIRM

There must be numerous phrases superior to "breaking off" to describe lawyers who leave firms to set up an entrepreneurial law practice. "Break off" and "spin off" indicate it was the choice of those leaving to depart. In these days of bottom-line law practice, some don't make the choice, so "break off" can also mean involuntarily "separated," "broken off," or "spun off." For the purposes of this discussion, it doesn't matter how the individual lawyer or group got to be a "break off." The opportunities and challenges with clients are the same whether it was a result of a voluntary or involuntary action.

The advice I was given upon graduating from law school was to pick the firm in which I started my legal career very carefully, for I would be there 30 to 50 years. This is simply not true today. Yes, you should choose carefully, but not for that reason. Fundamental changes within and among firms and breaking off have become everyday occurrences. Most of the motivation for such moves stems from a desire for a different lifestyle, dissatisfaction with compensation on a comparative basis with others in the firm and outside, and conflicts of interest that prevent one's practice from evolving in a more satisfying direction.

Going forward, the most immediate and important concern for the break-off organization is clients. Potential entrepreneurs should take this consideration into account before they make a final decision to break off.

BREAK-OFF DECISION FACTORS

If you are considering breaking off from a firm the most important factor of the decision is whether a critical mass of business will follow you or your group. No matter how frustrated or dissatisfied you may be, if you break off without adequate legal business—which means clients— you only will have made your situation worse. Frankly, the answer to the essential business element in the break-off equation depends upon how well you have conducted client relations in the past. Truly, it is not the quality of the work you have done, but rather the relationship you have built with your clients that will determine whether your break off is successful.

It is far too late to schmooze the client at the time you decide to leave. Just as the smooth closing argument will not sway a jury that has observed an insincere attitude in a lawyer throughout a trial, a self-serving blitz of client relations activities coupled with a "please follow" pitch will not normally carry the day.

A lawyer doing all of the work of a corporate client—thanks to a relative who was a decision maker there—decided to leave a firm with a group of other lawyers. This lawyer paid little or no attention to client relations for the years he had been doing the corporation's work. He assumed that because of his connection, he'd always get the work. He constantly told other partners in the firm that he was the sole key to the firm getting this corporation's work. He left with the renegade group sure in his assumption that the corporate client would follow. He deluded himself on several fronts. The client didn't follow him to the break off. Because he neglected client relations, he had no other significant business from other clients. Consequently, he had to eat crow and plead to his former partners to take him back.

Besides paying attention to and constantly implementing a good client relations plan over the entire time one represents a client, you should, on a highly confidential basis, ask your clients if they will follow you. In such situations, it is essential to determine which are "your" clients. Your agreement with the firm may specify that all clients are the firm's clients. Asking your clients if they will follow is dangerous, especially if ultimately you decide not to break off. But, it may be necessary. Not surprisingly, if you have been doing what you should be doing in client relations, you will know and be confident of the answer to your question before you ask the client.

Before discussing an impending break-off move with clients, check and comply with the ABA Model Rules. The last thing a new break off and its clients need is a dispute or lawsuit over which organization has the legal right to the clients. Make no assumptions, do the research, and, if necessary, obtain an opinion from an ethics board or committee. Client relations will suffer terribly if clients are left in limbo or have to testify in a dispute resolution process between two law practices.

ENTICEMENTS TO GET CLIENTS TO FOLLOW

I repeat: Before you contact "your" clients about following you to the break off, you must take into account the ethical considerations. These pertain to contacting clients, removing files, the use of information obtained while at the firm, and other potential problems. Also, you should educate yourself on the practices within the local bar regarding these matters. Such customs may impose additional informal burdens that should be satisfied if the departing lawyer desires to maintain good standing in the local legal community.

Fee structure is indeed part of the client relations mix. Explaining to the client that the same legal skill level will be available after the break off, but at a lower hourly, percentage, or flat rate, should encourage a client to follow. A properly managed break-off practice will reduce administrative overhead and enable fees to be lowered without adversely affecting the lawyers' take-home pay.

A more convenient office location may also be attractive to clients. This is especially true if the new location is closer or provides free parking. One may also credibly point out that the client will rise on the totem pole of importance to the new break off organization. That usually results in greater attention being paid to the client by the lawyer. It always results in the client feeling good about being told how important the client is to the enterprise. A side effect of this feeling is that with the entrepreneur's modest effort the client becomes tied tighter to the break-off lawyer.

SOME GENUINE CLIENT CONCERNS

Genuine client concerns are basically the same as they have with a newly licensed attorney, even among those clients inclined to give their work to a break off of one or more experienced lawyers. Who is your backup if you get sick? This can be anticipated and should be dealt with in any enterprise, regardless of whether it is a break off or not. How are the two of us—the client and break-off lawyer—going to be as knowledgeable and able to respond to being papered to death by the large, powerful firm that opposes us? This can largely be overcome by pointing out that the most critical brick in the foundation of representing the client is your personal knowledge of the matter and the client's individual or business goals. Also, you should note that the development of technology has given smaller organizations the means to stand as an equal to large firms in paper wars.

Lower cost and greater client importance will usually counter these genuine concerns. Surprisingly to lawyers, some clients are more interested in who will be on staff in a break off than in which lawyer(s) will be available. This is a product of the client having as good or better day-to-day relationships with the staff than with the lawyer. By itself, the inquiry emphasizes the wisdom of significantly involving staff in your client relations efforts. In the break-off situation, this means to do everything you can to take your legal secretary and paralegal with you if they generate client attachment and loyalty. These staff members will contribute far more than technical skills to the enterprise. Taking staff also gives your clients a more concrete sense of familiarity and continuity.

Some clients worry about the loss of prestige of being represented by a well-known law firm. Don't even think about trying to convince the client that your little break off will be as well regarded. Although this may be a fact with respect to other counsel, in the bar associations and among judges, the client is thinking about the cocktail party and country club talk, not legal substance. Sometimes you can head off this client worry about image by promoting the lower fees and the more–nimble, smaller–organization paradigm.

AVOIDING SOME NEWLY LICENSED AND BREAK-OFF PITFALLS

Most of the booby traps for both newly licensed and break-off lawyers are similar. The chief difference is that the newly licensed lawyer just never knew about the pitfalls, and the break-off lawyer probably knew, but didn't think or have to do anything about them. All these pitfalls involve, in one fashion or another, the amount of time and effectiveness of effort on the business and client relations side of law practice.

The nitty-gritty of daily client activities and the practicality of getting closure on client projects demand time and attention to detail about which many lawyers know little. Listen to the newly licensed and break-off entrepreneurs talking to themselves:

"I never knew that client X called so much about nothing."

"I don't know how to do a chart on the computer for the upcoming settlement negotiation."

"How many copies of the brief do are we required to file?"

"What is the name of that person in the patent office that my former secretary said was so helpful?"

"How am I expected to find the time to figure out how to aggregate hours and expenses to get this billing out?"

"How many CLE credits do I need by the end of the year to keep my license?"

"I never knew there was this much junk mail to wade through every day!"

Obviously, the level of support in a larger organization is not available or affordable to the entrepreneur. Think about this and plan for the support necessary for you to perform at your optimum, even if you can't reach that support level immediately.

Newly licensed and break-off practices need all the referrals they can get. But you must be realistic. In neither case are you likely to be the recipient of referrals from large, well-known clients who want big, prestigious law firms' names on their work. If you are considering breaking off, calculate how much of your work comes from such clients, how much comes from intra-firm referrals, and how much is self-generated. Once you have made that assessment, you will have a better picture of potential business and what you need to do in your client relations program.

Even if you self-generate work from large clients in the larger law firm, you will want to be very conservative about projections of how much new referral work you will receive from those large clients. In many circumstances, there is just nothing you can do to counter the client phenomenon of not following a break off because the corporate decision maker wants to be able to hide behind a big name law firm if things don't go well. In fact, in some loan transactions and acquisitions and divestitures, banks or other financing entities, may require your client to retain and obtain an opinion from a big name firm. No matter how successful your client relations program or how strong your personal relations are with your large corporate client contact, you and your break off will not get work where prestigeous law firm names are required.

The point of this is to be realistic about your client base and what you will personally have to do when you are a newly licensed or break-off lawyer. If you aren't committed to these realities before you jump into the entrepreneur role, you are in for an unpleasant shock and major disappointment.

The critical realization for any entrepreneur is that entrepreneurs have to spend more client relations time to make the enterprise profitable and to assure their future success.

PEOPLE SKILLS

We're asked to evaluate candidates, associates, legal assistants, and staff on their people skills. But, what in the world are they? Human resources experts and linguists have constructed many definitions and lists of characteristics describing people skills. What I mean in this context simply is:

PEOPLE SKILLS = THE ABILITY TO GENERATE CLIENTS' TRUST.

The methods by which this trust is created vary very widely. Lawyers have various methods of gaining a client's trust. Everything from conversations on the golf course to an extraordinary intellectual ability serve to generate distinct conduits for the client's trust to flow to the lawyer. There is no exact formula for creating such a relationship through trust; perception of the client is everything and every client perceives differently.

For sure, politicians', singers', and actors' connections with their audience are not enough. It is not a connection with a group of people that is desirable between lawyer and client. Rather, the goal is an intensely personal connection. This regularly occurs when the lawyer projects genuine caring about the client's situation. Abstractly, the end for which we lawyers need to strive is that the client perceives that we are capable of and personally interested in helping the client adjust or confirm the present legal reality.

The follow-up question is, "How does a lawyer show a personal interest in the client and prospective client?" Nothing but trouble follows getting too personal with a client. But, asking about jobs, hobbies (not just golf), where they have or would like to vacation or travel, what their preference in music is, and what they do in their non-work time are all topics which demonstrate you are interested in clients beyond their ability to resolve your cash flow problems. Don't chime in with your preferences, unless you are asked. This is about listening to your client.

I was dumbfounded when in response to my inquiry a very distinguished, late middle-aged and portly client who held a high corporate position told me that he and his wife jumped on their motorcycle every weekend to attend bike rallies. I'm not into motorcycles, but when he described why he enjoyed this hobby so much, it gave me a much better insight into his personality and decision-making processes, which armed me to serve him better. Besides, it was just plain interesting to hear about a hobby that was unfamiliar to me. This conversation gave both the client and me a connector that wasn't related to his legal situation. The wonderful by-product of this human-interest conversation is that it measurably strengthened our attorney-client relationship.

Two other topics of conversation support lawyers in conveying that they do care about clients. Inquiries about the client's job or business are always appreciated and sometimes generate legal work. The other is a person's family. Even if a person is divorced, single, or widowed, the preceding or next younger generation is usually a topic that interests the client.

Everything to which you expose your client should contribute to the end of showing the client you are a multi-dimensional human being, are interested in him or her as a person, and want to earn the client's trust in you as a person. Trusting you as a lawyer will flow naturally from trusting you as a person.

THE INITIAL MEETING

This meeting is the crucial foundation to building client trust and confidence. It is a difficult time for newly licensed lawyers, for they realize they don't know very much and if they are confident about what they are saying, they shouldn't be. The trick is to overcome where the newly licensed lawyer is on a confidence scale and go to where the client expects the lawyer to be.

The first thing to do is to take control of the meeting. You ask the questions, very carefully listen, seek clarification to understand, and take notes. If you don't take control, you will end up trying to respond to a goodly number of questions to which you either won't understand or don't know the answer. The same thing applies to the break-off lawyer. Don't let the client focus the meeting on why you left your firm.

Instead, describe how well you are going to serve the client in your new setting and focus on encouraging the client to tell all that is known about the situation that brings the client to your office.

The problem is that some lawyers, especially newly licensed ones, don't know the detail of what they have to do. They panic or make something up when asked what the next steps will be. Assuming you have the ethically required level of competence to handle a matter, you need to project that you know what you are doing. This will give your client confidence. And, you can figure out specific details later!

However, if asked, tell the truth about your actual experience in the field. Neither underestimate nor overestimate your capability. Several times, I've had friends and potential clients ask about my experience in a specific area of law. I have responded quite honestly, "None." A number of the clients have said, "That's okay, what I want is your judgment, anyway." One particular potential client's comeback to my response was quite enlightening to me, "Well then, we can learn together, can't we?" The "we can learn together" response has become one I have adopted to use with clients when my experience meets the minimum requirements, but is very thin.

Finally, no matter how experienced, no lawyer has ever had a matter that is exactly like any matter previously handled. Facts, people, and conversations, perceptions, and motivations make each one unique. Therefore, from a client relations standpoint, representing a client in your first matter has to be approached the same way you'd approach your one-thousandth matter—as unique.

REFERRALS

Referrals . . . what are they? Pretty dumb question, isn't it? Everyone knows what a referral is: being engaged by someone for legal services based on the recommendation of another. The definitions of "refer" and "reference" primarily define this act as "to direct the attention or thoughts of" or "direction to some source of information." While accurate, these are actually very superficial.

For a lawyer receiving a referral, it means that the referring person is making a statement to another that you are capable of doing the legal work and will treat the person referred "right" in every way. This referral may be initiated by a person organization (bar association, labor union, or employer organization) that is not even personally known to you or you to them. In some way—by hearsay, personal knowledge, lists of best lawyers, advertising or otherwise—referrers have come to acquire sufficient confidence in you to stake their reputation on your ability to do the legal work, connect with the client, and bill reasonably.

This puts the entrepreneur in a special position. It is truly a privilege to receive a referral. Treat the referrer and referred client as special, too.

HOW IMPORTANT IS A REFERRAL?

Referrals are crucial to successful law practice, especially to a newly licensed or break-off lawyer. When the referred client walks in your door the first time, you have the highest chance of success to establish a solid attorney-client relationship with that person. Based on the referral, the client is expecting to have a wonderful relationship with the recommended lawyer. If the client didn't trust the referrer, the client wouldn't be in your office. That trust is immediately transferable to you, even before you meet or do anything for the client.

This feeling of trust jumpstarts your relationship with the client. In fact, instead of the initial meeting being one of starting to build client trust, it becomes one of further developing an existing level of trust. This trust is yours to further develop or to lose, not to start building from nothing.

Thus, referrals are "the best" for any practice, but especially entrepreneurial ones.

SOURCES OF REFERRALS

Your family is usually the first and easiest source from which to receive a referral. This is especially true of the relatives—usually your parents or spouse—who have assisted you financially in law school. You see, they have a financial stake in your success. When I started practicing, my mother recommended to everyone she knew that they should hire the best lawyer in the world, her son. And you know what, some of them hired me, even when they knew I couldn't possibly be the best lawyer in the world!

Recommendations from family members do have drawbacks. First, because of the person making the recommendation and the reasons the recommendation is being made, they lack the credibility some other independent sources impart on referrals. Second, often the lawyer isn't practicing in the area of law that the client requires—that won't worry a committed family member a bit in making the recommendation. Third, whether you live across town or across the country, the family member is likely to make the recommendation without ever considering that you may be "GU" (geographically undesirable), as teenagers used to say about some potential dates. Nonetheless, family recommendations are terrific.

Bar associations usually have programs for referring persons in need of legal assistance to lawyers. Even though most of these programs work on a lawyer self-identification/self-registration basis, they do start the attorney-client relationship with more credibility than without the associations' providing your name. The difficulty is that sometimes you must accept types of cases in which you have little interest at substantially reduced fees.

In certain jurisdictions and in some fields of law, bankruptcy and guardianship being two, judges make recommendations or appointments of lawyers. What ideal circumstances on which to establish attorney-client relations! Clients have a great deal of respect for judges and it appears to them that the judge is endorsing you and your abilities, even though the client may have been told that your name came up on a rotating list of lawyers. This type of referral is much more effective in client relations terms when the client is faced with a civil, rather than criminal, situation.

The greatest potential source of referrals is from other lawyers. Lawyers need to refer good legal work to other counsel because they don't practice in an area of law or they are conflicted out of a particular situation. Entrepreneurs will receive many more referrals from other lawyers if they know you personally or by a solid reputation. Opportunities exist to get to know other lawyers through bar association work, charitable organization service, sports leagues, and just hanging out where lawyers gather, whether it is at a country club or gym. Receiving a recommendation from a lawyer who is trusted by a client truly is a good foundation for your relationship with that client.

Professionals of all sorts are very credible sources of referrals. But, frequently the yield on professional sources is low and quite specialized as to the areas of practice. Therefore, the professionals you cultivate for referrals should be somewhat governed by the type of work that interests you.

For instance, a lawyer I know was interested in doing legal work for professional partnerships and corporations. He did the legal work for a physical therapy practice; they liked the work and enjoyed him on a personal level. The practice recommended him to other physical therapy groups. On the basis of their recommendations, a few years later, he became counsel for the statewide physical therapy association. While the association's legal work wasn't extensive and didn't pay a lot, more than any other lawyer in the state, he became the go-to lawyer when physical therapists needed legal help. Being counsel to an association is tantamount to a blanket recommendation from the association for referrals.

Other examples of specialized referral sources abound. Stockbrokers, life insurance agents, and financial planners are good sources for estate-planning clients. Real estate agents, financial institutions, and title companies refer much work to lawyers in real estate law. Engineers and their associations are sources for intellectual property work. Construction litigation representation is frequently needed by architects, construction companies, and builders' associations. Banks refer a wide variety of work including banking regulation, collections, business organization, documentation of loans, and employment law.

A referral from a professional or a professional association is a very valuable acquisition. But, if you want to develop a practice in construction litigation, it doesn't make much sense to invest time attempting to obtain such referrals with the local teachers' union. Referrals from professionals are restricted to much more specific fields of law than those from the general public.

Whatever the potential source of referrals to jumpstart your attorney-client relationship, several things are quite certain. First, you must be prepared to commit a great deal of effort developing and maintaining a referral source for a small percentage of return. Regardless, referrals are worthwhile. Don't be discouraged: It takes a long time, for some are consciously or unconsciously testing your credibility through your staying power. Second, you must, by any legitimate and ethical means, stay in constant contact with the potential referral sources whether they be people or organizations. Third, be yourself, for if you are putting on an act or exaggerating your capabilities, you may be referred clients with whom you will have to remain constantly on stage and will sooner or later disappoint. Fourth, client relations with an association is different from individuals, with the cardinal rule being not to get involved with the internal politics of the organization.

GOOD REFERRAL ETIQUETTE AND RIPPLE EFFECT

One method of getting your foot in the door with a potential referral source is to offer to be a second supplier. That is, if the source already has a relationship, offer to take an occasional matter when there is a scheduling or ethical conflict. Emphasize that you are not trying to replace the primary supplier of legal services. This eases the conscience of the potential referrer about the loyalty issue to the referrer's present preferred counsel. Even as a second supplier, you will start off further along the client relations road than when obtaining the client on your own.

Another is to offer to do one matter at a reduced rate, if the referrer is willing to "just try you." Both this and the second supplier approach work best with a contact within a corporation who wants to refer work to you, but is foreclosed by the boss or other considerations. By giving that person these means to overcome anticipated objections or inertia will encourage the contact to take additional steps to get you some legal work. The cost of legal services is an issue with all consumers, and the reduced rate alone may be persuasive.

Do not become a pest, for if you do, people will take evasive action to avoid you. When I was with the corporation and purchased millions of dollars of legal services annually, there were some outside counsel whose phone calls I didn't even return, for they always asked what legal work I could get them or when I was going to send them a new case. This avoidance often was not related to their ability as a lawyer, but to an encounter anticipated to be unpleasant. Sometimes when I'd ask lawyers how things were going, the reply would be something to the effect that they'd be better if I'd get them more work. Who wants to hear that? Not I!

There is a fine line between staying on a referrer's radar screen and becoming a pest. I can't draw that line in words, but it has more to do with tone and style than with words and actions. One thing for sure, you don't want to try to "guilt trip" the potential referrer to get business. It backfired on lawyers who tried it. The lawyer is supposed to be serving the referrer and referred clients, not the other way around.

Always thank potential and actual referrers. Thank them for taking the time to see you, to listen to the description of your services, for the referred who didn't call or retain you, and, of course, for new clients. One way to do this is to send the referrer a copy of a letter to the new client mentioning how grateful you are to the referrer. An enhancement to sending this copy to the referrer is to add a handwritten note to the referrer, reinforcing the expression of your thanks. If the referred clients tell you that you have done a very good job, ask them to tell or write the same thing to the referring lawyer. This will be appreciated by the referring lawyer and will elevate your status with the referrer.

Before leaving referrals, I must mention the highly valued client ripple effect from receiving referrals. If you do an excellent job for a client who has been referred, the chances of that referred client recommending you to another is much higher than a client who came to you on the client's own initiative. This is so because the client, having been referred by another, when coupled with a positive experience with you, confirms the client's judgment that you are indeed a good lawyer. This double confirmation instills much more confidence in the client to risk recommending you to yet another person or business. Besides, the client has an example of how to refer a person to a lawyer, which makes it easier to do.

Referrals are extremely useful to your practice, both for themselves and the positive consequential impact they have if you take the necessary steps to establish a strong relationship with the client and the referrer.

ADDED SERVICE

Every lawyer will benefit from providing extra service to clients. But for the entrepreneur, it is a necessity. Even if retaining a lawyer for the first time, the client will be able to identify and appreciate extra service. The added service of which I write usually costs the client nothing. It is a lawyer's investment in improving client relations. In other words, it is investing in your clients and consequently in yourself, your practice, and your future.

The most important element of extra service is to convey that you care about the client and the legal matter you are handling. Means of accomplishing this include monthly updates on the status of the legal work, a document showing how you have added value for the client, a phone call about an important development, or a heads up that the month's bill will be higher than usual. Detailed descriptions of added service opportunities are contained throughout this book.

As in most relationships, it is the little things that determine the attitude about the relationship. These positive little things must be done constantly and consistently over the entire length of the relationship. It takes a long time before you are likely to see any recognition or return on these little things. In spite of this, make added service a habit; it will serve you and your clients well.

FOLLOW-UP AS ADDED SERVICE

Follow-up in all of its manifestations is a necessity for a lawyer to be regarded as providing added service. If you ask for a glass of water in a restaurant and there is none forthcoming, it creates a far worse impression than if the server failed to offer bread before the order is taken. The difference is the water omission was a failure to follow up. Similarly, no matter how many added services you provide automatically, if your client asks you for something, be sure to do it and let the client know that it is done. "I forgot" is grossly inadequate in providing legal services and to creating a client relationship based on trusting the lawyer.

Every inquiry about your services warrants a follow-up response. Ethical restrictions prevent lawyers, in most circumstances, from making an unsolicited in-person pitch to a layperson for legal business. If you receive an inquiry, don't squander the opportunity to make a contact that has a good chance of being, at the very least, remembered. Many folks contact a lawyer and then decide to postpone engaging one. If you follow up with a personal, written thank you, you have taken the first added service step toward establishing a client relationship with that person.

Many inquire about legal services and get cold feet for the present, but life's circumstances have a way of evolving to cause the person or the business to later decide to retain a lawyer. The follow-up thanks for the initial inquiry increases the chance that you will be remembered when the potential client finally does decide to get a lawyer. This increased chance that you will be retained stems from the person understanding that you are willing to communicate even when you weren't retained. And the "feel good" part of that grows from the person's perception that you are interested in her or him as a person, as well as a client.

Letters following up potential client inquiries should contain a beginning thanking the person for considering you, a middle part referring to your experience and asking if you can add the person to your newsletter distribution list, and an ending which again expresses appreciation and a hope that the person will think of you for their legal service needs. As mentioned elsewhere, in such response letters, be sure to negate the creation of an attorney-client relationship unless and until a retention agreement is signed. As an enclosure to this letter, you should include your business card and, if you have them, a copy of your brochure or current newsletter.

We've all been told hundreds of times to return every phone call promptly. You should also take the opportunity to add service by initiating phone calls inquiring as to whether the person (client or potential client) has any questions since you last spoke. If you receive a telephone inquiry about your services, be sure to offer to send written material about your services. Written material may end up in a pile or file from which it will be pulled later. Also, give them your Web address and e-mail contact information. And always express appreciation. You really should feel appreciative. It is a privilege to be asked to help others who are perplexed by the law, or by anything else.

E-mail is far less personal—and therefore less effective when developing trusting client relations: a fact lost on many users. But it's still a necessary one. The client or potential client expects express follow-up if their communication medium was e-mail. Other than this caution, the advice about follow-up content remains the same as for other means of communication.

Try to get the name, address, telephone number, and e-mail address of every inquirer. If you are working with support staff, they can sometimes gather that information before they put the call through or bring someone to your office. Although some corporate and business clients are jaded, most other clients appreciate and think of it as an added service when they receive your newsletters, updated firm brochures, newspaper and magazine clippings about you—and even more so, clippings about them.

Web sites are now commonplace and almost all businesses are expected to have one. Be sure that all of those making an inquiry about your services and each of your clients are given your Web address (URL, on Uniform Resource Locator) in writing. Client reactions to Web sites and other free added-service information is interesting. The more useful the information provided, the more likely it is that potential clients will use and appreciate the site. This should mean a greater percentage of users will be converted into clients, and existing clients will realize that they have more legal work that they should have you do. The best type of formatting is often as a news story, not a dull recitation of statutes, regulations, and case holdings.

For sophisticated and longtime clients, newsletters are old hat. The entrepreneur should consider buying a newsletter service. There are some very good purveyors of newsletters pertaining to particular areas of practice, including general practice. The entrepreneur can personalize these canned newsletters with a different message each month. Sure, they cost money, but many are reasonably priced and more effective than homemade newsletters. Newsletters from services save the time of writing the copy and mailing. They also generally look better. Some use color or colorful article titles to stimulate the receiver to read. Clients view newsletters and other nonmandatory communications positively as added service and good follow-up.

Many times I've heard the older generation lament the passing of the house calls that used to be made by doctors. Most lawyers are oblivious to how much individuals and businesses appreciate the added service of lawyer house calls. Also ignored by entrepreneurs and other lawyers is the extraordinary degree to which a house call raises the status of the lawyer and the client's good feelings about the lawyer. Unlike accountants, who frequently go to the client, lawyers generally sit in their offices requiring clients to visit them. There is more on this subject elsewhere in this book, but suffice it to say, visits to clients are always deeply appreciated and usually result in a stronger relationship with the client, which leads to more legal business.

ADDED VALUE IS APPRECIATED

Clients and potential clients alike are appreciative of added service. They value it. It has value to the lawyer for it distinguishes her or him from the competition, especially if the lawyer is an entrepreneur. I have heard of clients passing on newsletters and referring others to law firm web sites. So, this added service opened doors to other client growth opportunities, as well as cementing the lawyer's relationship with the client.

In talking to potential clients, newly licensed lawyers should emphasize the added service they provide and their commitment to follow-up. Break-off lawyers need to figure out how they can supply more added services than their old firm and point out that increased level of service to clients and others.

The type and extent of added services you provide is limited only by your client relations intelligence and creativity. One thing for sure, if you provide it and, for whatever reason, you choose not to continue it, notify the people on your distribution list before you discontinue the service. Don't let them speculate about the reason the service stopped. Give a plausible explanation for discontinuing it, or they may think you have gone out of practice.

LOCATION

Unlike established law firms, entrepreneurs have much flexibility in choosing their office location. The old real estate maxim about the three key factors in establishing a premises value, "location, location, and location," applies, but for both the same and different reasons. Location projects something about the lawyer and the practice. The impression differs if you are located in a first-class high-rise or have your office in your home. Just as location has a significant impact on property value, so too it directly influences the type and number of opportunities for the entrepreneur's law practice.

The entrepreneur may choose to rent Class A office space, but there is no need to do so. However, the cheapest space in a run-down part of town should be avoided. There are plenty of choices in between. A funky locale may be quite neat for a high-tech practice, but it may not be comfortable for older clients seeking estate-planning advice. Give some thought to the type of clients you are trying to attract to build the most important fields of your practice, then decide on an office location within your budget.

It used to be that a downtown office, regardless of the size of the town, was necessary to attain client credibility in top-flight practices. Remember when even those firms with large suburban offices had downtown space? This isn't true anymore. Quality suburban space is fine for the same type of client as downtown space. Some suburban space costs as much or more than downtown space. If free client parking is provided with the suburban space, it may be more useful for client relations than downtown space, even if it costs a little more.

When considering where to locate your office, include what the client expects. A large corporate client located in a suburb may appreciate the convenience of a suburban office or may expect its lawyer to be located downtown with the rest of the high-profile law firms. On the other hand, when high-tech businesses are going strong, they favor firms, which have Silicon Valley offices, as opposed to those only located in San Francisco. This office location issue may be easily evaluated by asking your clients where they prefer the location of your office to be and why. If you locate somewhere other than where a client suggests, explain to that client why you couldn't locate where the client suggested.

Another strategy is locating an entrepreneurial law office where you are more likely to "bump into" potential clients and referrers. For intellectual property firms and ones interested in serving the start-up corporations, an office in a university area might be a good choice. That location could provide opportunities to introduce yourself to potential clients at lunch or in the elevator. There would also be less time wasted visiting your clients' offices or meeting one for lunch.

Sharing space with an established firm or lawyer is often an attractive option to the entrepreneur, especially for the newly licensed one. Subletting from a professional who is a potential referrer of legal business, such as an accountant, offers other interesting possibilities. Keep in mind that if the entrepreneur sublets from one accountant, no other accountant in town will refer any business to the entrepreneur. There are also office options in business suites, which may include support services and conference rooms. Generally, sharing space, subletting, or leasing a business suite is cheaper than setting up an independent office because sharing the cost of support personnel and common areas reduces the total outlay. Operating costs are often also reduced in such arrangements by the use of common equipment, such as copiers and fax machines.

Cost of an office is an important consideration for every law practice. However, it may be outweighed by the client and potential client considerations mentioned earlier. A balance must be struck between saving money and spending more money to better position the entrepreneur to attract more clients.

If the landlord of the sublet office is a lawyer, there are some additional advantages. Access to a staff trained in "how to do it," to reference materials such as books or the Internet, and a lawyer or experienced legal assistant with whom an entrepreneur may speak about the practicalities of law practice or some area of law are some of the items of extra value. Those coming directly from law school have had no experience in the degree to which law is collaborative, so they may not see the benefit, but it surely exists.

Caution must be exercised because, to some degree, clients, potential clients, and other lawyers will paint the entrepreneur with the same brush as the lawyer or firm from which the entrepreneur sublets. This impression extends not only to the reputation of the lessor, but also to the type of practice. For example, if you have a general practice and sublease from a firm that does exclusively criminal work, some may assume that you practice only criminal law. Similarly, if your lessor doesn't enjoy a fine reputation among lawyers because of cutting ethical corners, you may be assigned the same reputation without any basis in fact. Just consider this as one factor when deciding from whom to sublet—it may affect your ability to build your reputation with clients and referrers as being trustworthy.

We have already addressed locating for the convenience of the client. But, the entrepreneur must consider the convenience of other stakeholders in the practice as well. Think about yourself. Is the location convenient to you? The concern is not so much in miles from your home as it is for the time required to commute at the hours you usually go to and come home from the office. If you travel a lot you need to think about the time it takes to get to and from the airport as well as the automobile traffic patterns for other frequently traveled routes. Your staff may travel by mass transit, so the location of train stations, subway lines, or bus routes may enter the equation. Convenience to clients and staff may be enhanced dramatically by the availability of free parking. The trick is to take all of these things into account and balance them.

The better all of the above location considerations balance the needs of the stakeholders of the entrepreneur's practice and clients, the more effectively the entrepreneur may reduce the pressure of law practice and better serve clients.

WHO'S YOUR BACKUP?

When I was starting out, I had a potential client tell me that I was the most qualified labor attorney they interviewed and had the best fee arrangement, but they were too worried about my not having any backup to retain me. Despite telling them I hadn't been sick or missed a day of work for years, and that I had a partner who wasn't a labor law specialist but who was quite capable to cover for me in an emergency, I just couldn't allay their fears and wasn't retained.

For some clients, assurance that if anything happens to you that their legal business will continue to be handled with the same level of expertise is extremely important. A few clients panicked about this every time I'd be away on vacation, for I would not give them a vacation phone number. I always told them to call the office and the staff could track me down if necessary. In private practice, it was very rare for a call to come through while I was on vacation—clients just needed the comfort that they could reach me.

Today, the interruption of your vacation by phone, even cell phone, may be the least of your worries. Clients and your office want to be constantly tied to you by overnight delivery, e-mail, and fax. Their expectation is that you will use part of your vacation to review documents. Entrepreneurs especially need to prioritize between their vacation time, the needs of their clients, and an added-service feature in their client relations program. If you choose not to be in contact while on vacation, you need to make arrangements as to how your obligations to clients will be fulfilled.

You need a plan in case you become unable to practice law, either temporarily or permanently. Any number of things could incapacitate you, from mental illness from stress and pressure, a family crisis, or an automobile accident. Clients appreciate being told, without asking, how a small entrepreneur organization will respond if you are unavailable.

It is especially important for entrepreneurs to have such a plan for the clients and for the protection of the entrepreneur's economic future. There are some obvious options to consider. If you are subletting from a law firm, consider your landlord as backup. Another non-landlord lawyer in your building would allow convenient access to your clients' files. A lawyer you have met through the bar association whom you think would do a competent job and not steal your clients could be considered. Lawyer friends are usually willing to help whether they are your contemporaries or not. Years ago, my Uncle John Stewart regularly drove 50 miles one way to an ill lawyer's office for many months to cover for his friend who couldn't run his solo law practice as a result of a serious illness. People with this kind of commitment still exist.

Responses to potential and present clients about your backup need to be carefully considered. From a client relations objective, the object is to increase the level of trust your clients have in your sense of responsibility to them, not to assure the client you have made arrangements to hand off the client's work. Expressing how insightful and astute the client is to have this concern is a good start. Tell the client of your shared concern to have the legal work completed in a quality fashion and a timely manner. You may explain that you have made arrangements to cover this contingency. It is best to talk about the arrangements in generic terms while trying not to reveal the identity of the lawyer in another firm who would actually do the work. You may wish to change your selection later and shouldn't get the client locked in on a specified substitute.

Making prior arrangements to have your clients' work completed if you are unable to do it is a valuable added service for your client, as well as for you and your family.

BUILDING CLIENT RELATIONS BUDGETS

Every entrepreneur needs a budget to conduct a successful business. The days of buying a set of used law books and hanging out a shingle are long gone. Capital for computers, fax machines, and other equipment and software, along with adequate working capital for monthly operating costs such as rent, is essential. Whatever these costs, they should be minimized when a newly licensed break-off lawyer starts practice.

For newly licensed lawyers raised on the latest home computers and games, the tendency is to buy the very best hardware and software. This is a mistake, for neither the most expensive hardware or software can build your practice or guarantee you'll be in business a year from the day you hang out your shingle. Your limited assets will be utilized better by concentrating them on client relations. I don't mean you should minimize your other expenditures to the extent of damaging your ability to service clients' work. No, the object is to maximize assets available for getting and building a law practice without crippling the ability to do the work. This approach will reduce the prospects of incurring significant debt or increasing the debt already incurred going to law school. It also has the pleasant side effect of shortening the time between your door first opening for business and your first take-home pay. Finally, it puts the budget focus where you practice focus should be . . . on the client.

The entrepreneur should start building a budget by determining the funds needed to get clients and develop the relationship with them. All too frequently client relations costs are budgeted only after all other costs are allocated, assigning the meager remaining funds to this activity, which will ultimately determine the future of the law practice. That isn't rational.

Such client relations expenditures include funds for lunches, travel, newsletters, Web site, brochures, business cards, bar dues, organization dues (as the Chamber of Commerce or other community service organizations), charitable contributions and benefits, clubs (not necessarily country clubs—could be fishing, lunch, or chess clubs), and giving and taking seminars to build contacts and knowledge used in client relations efforts.

The entrepreneur's time is also an important asset. A portion of it must be budgeted for client relations activities. Starting out, the break-off lawyers should allocate a minimum of 20 percent of the time they are willing to spend on their practice to client relations or 10 percent more than they spent at their former firm, whichever is greater. Newly licensed lawyers must spend a much greater percentage of their time, 35 percent at least, building client relations. If new entrepreneurs don't have sufficient work to fill the remaining 65 percent of their work days, they'd do well to increase the client relations time. Even if their efforts aren't immediately successful, they will be learning about people and what lawyers must do to serve clients. Attracting clients is just the start of the time commitment needed. That marketing activity must continue while the client relations time with the clients who have been attracted to the practice continually increases.

Calculate the cost of the time budgeted for client relations so that you know the true cost of practicing law. Budgeting client development hours will also be useful as a self-check on whether you are meeting the weekly minimum time for finding and relating to clients. This is entirely separate and above the billable time required to service the clients' legal needs. The discipline for billables and nonbillables alike is hourly and daily, not monthly and annually. That discipline must include regular blocks of client relations time.

COST OF SERVICING CLIENTS

The newly licensed lawyer has no way of knowing and many break-off lawyers never paid attention, to the cost of servicing clients. Know it or not, provision for these costs must be made in your budget.

Once lawyers get clients, they need additional operating funds to conduct the clients' legal business. Obviously, support staff has to be paid. Additionally, such items as filing fees, postage, notary fees, overnight deliveries, investigators, and reimbursable travel expenses, all must be advanced by the entrepreneur. In some cases, a portion of these expenses may be prefinanced by agreement and with the client's retainer. If the retainer is to cover these items, put the retainer funds in your trust account, don't draw any out until the money is going to be immediately used for an expense or to reimburse a previously incurred expense. Carefully account for and document every penny. Understand, if the client doesn't prepay it, your practice will have to have cash available to procure the necessary services on behalf of the client. This is a more substantial amount than many anticipate.

Local law practice customs, clients on contingent fees and competition may foreclose the possibility of getting these expenses prepaid. Investigate and assure you have funds sufficient to serve your clients. Client relations are soured when lawyers go back to clients for unanticipated payments.

IT'S A LONG, LONG TIME—DON'T UNDERESTIMATE

Client development efforts don't pay off like the instant lottery. The current societal concepts of immediate gratification and return on investment are just not applicable to client relations payback. The entrepreneur must plan for a minimum of two years of hard, and often unrewarding, work about six days a week to provide enough time for focused, intense efforts to build a sustainable practice. Even then, there are no guarantees.

It is daunting when realistically budgeting the amount of money and time required to sustain that entrepreneurial effort for two years. Compounding the situation is that most financial institutions will not lend money to new entrepreneur lawyers. It may not seem so to the entrepreneur, but a nascent law practice is a totally unsecured, risky investment.

While your budget should project some income flow during the first two harrowing years, don't overestimate your ability to generate cash. This is especially true if you intend to restrict your practice to a certain type of legal work. No matter what your practice field preferences, you can maximize your opportunities to create cash flow by an enthusiastic willingness to accept any type of legal work during the practice's first two years and postpone specialization until later.

Knowing all of this, and accepting that more businesses and practices fail from an inadequate supply of operating capital, why take the chance of underestimating a budget of time and funds devoted to client relations? It seems to me that a liberal allocation of hours and money to clients—the lifeblood of the new and break-off practices—significantly increases the chances of entrepreneurs' success.

This recommendation directly contradicts the philosophy of buy "things" and appearances now on credit and pay later. Without clients there is no law practice. The best-practices approach for entrepreneurs is to invest to acquire and keep clients now so that you will have cash to pay yourself later.

TRY IT!

If you've always wanted to try entrepreneurship, or circumstances give you little other choice, try it. Don't be scared off by the content of this chapter or anything else. All I'm trying to do is alert you to some issues, which if addressed, will improve the entrepreneurial success rates for law practices.

Actually, I enthusiastically embrace the entrepreneurial approach to law practice. It is difficult, but I found it was the most personally satisfying way to practice law. The entrepreneur's thrill of getting a new client, of being entrusted with legal work that is vitally important to a client, or of taking home an increasing paycheck can not be duplicated in any other law practice setting. Being an entrepreneur in law practice is an exciting, unpredictable, but great adventure. You couldn't find a better opportunity to be stimulated and grow your personal skills. Most studies indicate that newly licensed law practice entrepreneurs make less money than lawyers in firms. Most catch up in pay and often surpass their law firm peers over the years. The break-off lawyers I know usually make no less than they made at their former firm and sometimes more right from the get-go.

The greatest reward for lawyer entrepreneurs is not monetary. It is the ego satisfaction of taking risks and converting them into a viable, client-oriented law practice.

CHAPTER 14

CORPORATE COUNSEL CLIENT RELATIONS

In this chapter we narrow the view of client relations to special aspects of the relationship between lawyers or law firms and their corporate clients.

Winning is not everything, but it is a whole lot of almost everything. Strange as it may seem, even when lawyers win a case they may still lose a corporate client. Many factors besides winning go into corporate decisions about which outside counsel to retain.

How many lawyers in private practice who represent corporations have ever thought through the process of how the corporation earns the money it pays out in legal fees? I venture to guess very few lawyers have much of an idea of the process, capital, and effort required to earn sufficient profit to pay the fees they charge corporations. Probably, not many lawyers have even been intrigued with or contemplated the question.

It is, however, a question that every lawyer who represents corporations should be able to answer for each corporation represented. The answer reflects whether the lawyer possesses an appropriate depth of knowledge of the corporate client's business. Discovering the answer will also instill a greater sensitivity as to why corporations are retaining less expensive firms, are hiring more corporate counsel, and are relying less and less on traditional outside law firms, especially those that do not grant special fee arrangements.

WHO IS THE LAWYER'S CORPORATE CLIENT?

Sure, on the documents and in the legal directory listing representative clients, it's Big Corporation, Inc. In spite of this, no corporation, even those created by documents drafted by the most skilled lawyers, ever retained a single lawyer. In truth, it is people working for that corporation who retain outside law firms and lawyers.

The next question is, which corporate people hire outside lawyers? In many instances, corporate lawyers retain outside counsel. Does this mean that the corporate lawyers are truly the outside counsel's client? The answer is "no." Even if the corporate lawyer is fully satisfied with the performance of outside counsel in terms of service, result, and cost, there are other corporate employees who participate in or control the decisions about outside counsel.

If the businessperson who employs the corporate counsel gets the impression that outside counsel is incompetent, charged too much, did not treat him or her with appropriate respect, or did not put forth sufficient effort on the matter, the outside law firm will most likely lose the client. The corporate counsel has the businessperson, the executive, or line manager as a client in the corporate chain. Consequently, the outside counsel has the same businessperson as a client even when the two have never met or communicated.

There are also other unseen corporate clients. The corporate Board of Directors, which sets the policy for the corporation and imposes spending limits and performance goals on executives, is also a client. Board members' opinions are often heavily influenced by their experience with their personal counsel or the corporate counsel for their own business or counsel whom they got to know while sitting on other boards.

Don't forget the shareholder as a client. Astute executives recognize that they must add value in the corporation for the shareholder. The adding-shareholder-value operating principle is not for the selfish aggrandizement of the executives. Many businesspeople have internalized a true desire to benefit their ultimate employer, the shareholder. If the actions and costs of outside counsel do not seem to those responsible businesspersons to assist in achieving the goal of adding shareholder value, the outside counsel will soon be wondering why he or she has lost a corporate client.

Some lawyers in private practice think they have a corner on the ethics market and that businesspeople and corporate counsel have obtained only an infinitesimal share of it. I must confess that as a private practitioner, I made the erroneous assumption that the ethical standards observed by corporate counsel were not as stringent as those of private practitioners. I was absolutely wrong. Based on my knowledge and observation of numerous businesspeople and corporate counsel, I've concluded that, for the most part, they have a highly developed sense of business and legal ethics. It matches, and in many cases exceeds, that observed in private and government legal practice.

Granted, corporate ethical concern has been imposed in some situations by government, talented plaintiffs' lawyers, judges, and juries. Regardless of the motivation, the fact is that ethics do guide many corporate behaviors. Some outside counsel make a fatal mistake of assuming and acting as though the executive has been attempting all along to skirt ethical and even legal standards. Imagine what you would think of another lawyer who was working with you on a case if even the suggestion were made that you could win by destroying evidence or forgetting about your officer of the court responsibilities? The relationship would be irreputively ruptured.

Any misguided lawyer who errs in the perception or assumption that the executives' or corporations' ethical standards are lower than they actually are will make a fatal client relations mistake. Moreover, the business executive may conclude that all outside counsel are likewise inclined. The damage will not be contained to the client relationship; the lawyer, law firm, and legal profession suffers generally.

Who is the corporate client? It consists of layers of diverse corporate employees and shareholders who, while having different interests, are united in a common desire for a good legal result at a reasonable cost. Although corporate counsel may interface with outside counsel on behalf of the entity, executives, who are not lawyers, ultimately make the big decisions. This means that to have excellent corporate client relations, outside counsel must be aware of, communicate with and satisfy all of these people and serve their interests, including the financial ones. This applies even if these persons are not in the lawyer's chain of communication.

CORPORATE GOALS AND LAWYER SERVICE QUALITY

CORPORATE GOALS AND CLIENT RELATIONS

A solid understanding of corporate business goals will improve corporate client relations for the following reasons:

1. The lawyer's value to the corporation will escalate;

2. The executives' appreciation of the lawyer will increase;

3. The communication will flow easier; and

4. The lawyer's heightened awareness will cause him or her to more closely align legal representation with what the executives expect, thereby improving service quality as judged by the only judge that matters, the client.

If the lawyer demonstrates knowledge of these goals and sensitivity to working toward achieving them to the executives, all of the above will raise the lawyer's status with decisionmakers within the corporation. When executives realize a lawyer, either within or outside the corporation, shares the executives' desire to meet corporate goals, the lawyer is accepted as a member of the corporate team.

Next, we'll look at particular corporate goals and how client relations are linked to each of them.

TO MAKE A PROFIT

To make a profit, in fact a double-digit profit, is a goal of almost every corporation. Some mistakenly perceive that the universal corporate goal is profit at any ethical or quality cost. History has proven that most companies with such an operating standard don't last. If they happen to last, they aren't respected and probably are not profitable in the long run. Lawyers, especially plaintiffs' class-action lawyers, have played a major role in assuring that corporations comply with ever-evolving standards acceptable to our society. Making a profit while complying with legal, ethical, and social responsibilities generates far more return to shareholders and employees over successive fiscal quarters. Big or small, those are the corporations that last and prosper.

Regardless of the business—manufacturing, sales, or service—lawyer fees are paid with dollars that otherwise would have been added to bottom-line profits. Thus, the lawyer may be viewed, because of the fees charged even for excellent representation, as being at odds with the businessperson's objective to maximize the return to the shareholders, or even more crassly, to increase the executive's incentive bonus.

If a lawyer wins a difficult case or strikes a great deal in a business transaction and then charges a fee perceived by corporate executives to be exorbitant, the corporate executives will resent the fee and oftentimes the lawyer who billed it. This is understandable. What some private practice lawyers fail to understand is that legal fees are always a cost and never a profit center. This resentment can exist even when the corporation gains far more value than it spent on legal fees.

Litigation settled at a reasonable number on the courthouse steps coupled with the lawyer charging the corporation twice the amount in fees as the cost of an excellent settlement causes the corporate executives to resent the fees. The executives and general counsel may well feel that the outside lawyer's responsibility was to get the matter settled earlier so that the amount of fees did not exceed the value of the settlement. If the lawyer who is asked to advise the corporation on the legality of an aspect of a prospective business deal gives an "on-this-hand-but-then-on-the-other-hand" answer from which the executive has no more guidance for a contemplated action than he or she had before counseling with the lawyer, the corporate executives will also resent the fees charged. Lawyers are paid by corporations to lend certainty to a situation at a reasonable cost.

Many other examples exist, but these should suffice to focus some attention on why many corporations are severely distressed about legal fees. The concern in each of these examples goes beyond fees. The issue is the cost of the service provided in relation to the perceived value returned. All of this is further considered by the executive in the context of the business value of the issue, measured in dollars or principle.

In many such cases, lawyers do not understand corporate resentment over fees because they believe they have done an excellent job of lawyering. And, perhaps they have—if lawyering is defined as researching and reciting the law and charging for all the hours expended on the effort.

To be valuable to the client, lawyers must solve a real problem or create a viable opportunity for the client that is worth much more to the client than the fees the client pays to the outside lawyer or salary and benefits paid to corporate counsel. Otherwise, lawyer-client relations are fractured because the lawyer has hindered or not advanced the corporate client's legitimate efforts to maximize profits. Alignment with the corporate client's perception of the best way to maximize profits and minimize legal fees is critical to positive corporate client relations.

NO SURPRISES

One reason investors buy blue-chip stocks is they are pretty sure there will be no surprises. Their expectation is that the stock will predictably appreciate in value while reasonable dividends are paid. In light of this observation, it should not be startling for lawyers to discover corporate executives also want the security of no surprises.

In the corporate world, predictability is prized, mistakes tolerated, and surprises abhorred. If a lawyer significantly underestimates the cost to litigate in the case management plan, it is a surprise. If a lawyer advises a business executive, the executive acts on that advice and the executive or the corporation is subsequently held liable for that action, it is a surprise. If that suit is lost after constant outside counsel predictions of victory, it is a bigger surprise. If the product warranties are improperly drafted and liability results, it is a surprise. If the corporation finds itself the losing party in a suit on a contract because of a lawyer's misinterpretation, it is a surprise. If the corporation is enjoined from marketing a product because of a patent infringement, it is a surprise. If a lawyer represents that the corporation has a good defense and then on the courthouse steps strongly advocates settlement, it is a big surprise. If a lawyer charges more than the perceived value of services, it is a surprise.

Each of these examples is a surprise because it has an adverse impact on the corporate profit forecast, causes monetary and other goals to be missed, and diverts management time and attention from primary business matters. Each of these surprises is delivered to the corporation by a lawyer, a corporate counsel, or an outside law firm. This makes the executive decisionmakers distrustful of lawyers.

If early in the process, the lawyer had told the executive that the corporate executive or even the lawyer made a mistake or misestimated the chances of prevailing, thus giving the executive sufficient lead time to build the adverse consequences into the business plan, the corporation might tolerate the mistake and the persons who made it. If the lawyer accurately predicted the fees in a matter, the outcome (there is not a quantum difference between predicting an accurate good or bad outcome), and the time frame in which the outcome will occur, the lawyer's ability to accurately predict will be prized.

A key to good corporate client relations is predictability, because that has a direct impact on the executive's ability to meet goals, bottom-line projections, and obligations.

POSITIONING FOR BETTER BUSINESS

In general, businesspeople spend more time strategically planning than lawyers do. They usually believe they know where their business is and where it is going. The lawyer who can deliver a more advantageous competitive position to a corporation than planned will be highly valued.

One obvious such circumstance occurs when a proposal to buy out a competitor dies and the lawyer creatively resurrects it. Something as simple as demonstrably saving a corporation legal fees puts the corporate client in a better business position because it has more cash for investments or profits. The latter can only occur if a budget for the case or matter is prepared and the lawyer delivers the result at an under-budget figure.

The critical element is assuring that the client understands how the lawyer has improved the corporate position. Let's take saving fees. Suppose the lawyer writes off some associate time. Then the lawyer sends the following bill to the corporation:

Date	Timekeeper	Hours	Rate	Charge
1/14	Partner A	1.0	$150	$150
1/15	Partner Z	1.5	$200	$300
	Total	2.5		$450

The above bill is not nearly as effective as sending a bill for the same services and write-offs that reads:

Date	Timekeeper	Hours	Rate	Charge
1/14	Partner A	1.0	$150	$150
1/14	Associate 1	3.0	$ 75	No Charge
1/15	Partner Z	1.5	$200	$300
	Total	4.5		$450

The corporate counsel, controllers, and the executives have no way to recognize that you are advantageously positioning the corporation, unless the invoice reflects the advantage. Showing the "No Charge" on the second sample bill is much more effective than just writing off the hours and deleting fees as done in the first bill. Just striking out the dollar charge and computing a new total may be even more effective.

Words of caution: If you cannot rationally quantify the competitive advantage, forget raising the subject with the executive. Corporations are run by MBAs, engineers, salespeople, financial folks, and other executives who have risen to the top because they can quantify and effectively improve the profits of the corporation by managing those quantities to an advantage. If it is not measurable (convertible to productivity, headcount, or dollar equivalents), it just does not exist for most executives.

For instance, a lawyer arguing that she or he saved the corporation millions by negotiating perfect representations and warranties article language in a divestiture agreement even if true, will probably not be heard because the company was never sued on the contract language. When businesspeople close a deal, in spite of the advice of their lawyer that there is substantial risk of future litigation, the businessperson's decision process quantifies the risk of not having ideal contractual language against the commercial opportunity to significantly improve the corporation in the marketplace. Maybe it is not an exact science, but using what the businessperson knows, he or she mentally quantified the legal risk and competitive advantage while the lawyer was measuring negotiated language against the perceived ideal academic contract.

An interesting phenomenon is that the more successful a lawyer has been in representing corporate causes, the less risk the businessperson will assign to the potential downsides raised by that lawyer. The calculation often made is that the lawyer won a tough case or negotiated a complex deal for the corporation before and the lawyer will do so again in spite of what he or she says about the possibility of an adverse result. For this reason, the lawyer with a long history of success must be brutally honest and convincing when informing a corporate client of the magnitude of a particular risk.

Questions from executives to lawyers like, "How often does that happen?" or "If they sue, what are our chances to win?" or "What'll it cost us?" are all eliciting information that helps the executive to quantify, not qualify, the risk. Lawyers attuned to client relations should anticipate such questions, prepare, and give the answer before the questions are asked.

A lawyer who insists on ideal contract language when compromise is needed to close a deal will soon be known as a deal breaker. At first the lawyer will be ignored, and then replaced. The marketplace is a competitive arena of give and take. The theoretically perfect one-sided, win-lose legal solution is not viable in that arena. The "perfect" legal solution and one-answer lawyer cannot survive. Such approaches rarely put the corporate client in a more competitive position. They normally only exist as a figment of the lawyer's mind.

Creative competitive positioning through well-crafted compromise is a powerful weapon in the lawyer's corporate client relations arsenal. This will be a good legal solution and the corporate executive will recognize the value of such a solution as measured in the marketplace. The worth of the lawyer who makes such a contribution is well recognized in corporate circles.

A failure of the lawyer to recognize the diverse considerations in the executives' risk analysis will and does strain lawyer to corporate client relations.

PUBLICITY . . . IT'S NOT GOOD

Some lawyers do almost anything to attract publicity. Ever wonder why those lawyers do not represent corporations? In many instances, it is because the lawyer does not reflect the public relations philosophy of the corporation.

In most corporations, the executive directly involved in a legal or other matter does not speak with the media. Corporate or public relations specialists handle those duties. The media contacts, credibility, and skill of these specialists dictate this division of duties. In addition, it is not favorable to the executive to be associated with any litigation, at least not until it is won.

Remember, people buy or do not buy stocks and products in part on image. "Psst—I heard of a hot stock" excites many an investor's interest. Exxon's Valdez environmental woes, J.P. Stevens's labor difficulties, and Ralph Nader's pronouncements about certain cars all affected, to some degree, the consumers' purchasing of products and the price of stocks.

Lawyers who can assist corporate clients in dealing with the media bring extra value and enhance their client relations. This does not necessarily mean the lawyer will speak with the media. The lawyer who is helpful in drafting a press release about a legal matter is of greater value than one who has no talent in this area. In this instance, helpful means to be able to review the release for legal accuracy while improving the positive "spin" that is put on all media releases.

RECOGNIZING WHAT IT TAKES TO PAY THE FEE

The corporate legal fee success equation is simple:

LOWER LEGAL FEES = BETTER BOTTOM LINE

This elementary concept is often absent from outside counsel's conscious state and sometimes is totally missed by corporate counsel.

Few lawyers stop to realize, if a business client makes 10 percent profit, for every $100,000 in legal fees the lawyer charges, the corporation's sales must be increased $1 million just to maintain the same dollar amount of profit. Even with the $1 million increase in sales, the payment of the lawyer's $100,000 invoice drops the percentage of profit because the revenue base is larger. If sales do not increase, the money paid for legal fees lowers the dollar amount of profits by the same amount. This robbing Peter to pay Paul is detrimental to the advancement of the corporation and is particularly distasteful to the executive working diligently to make the numbers.

The lawyer who openly acknowledges to executives and corporate counsel concern about the ratio of sales effort necessary to pay legal fees will substantially enhance corporate client relations, even if the amount of the lawyer's bills remains constant. It is the recognition of this executive's challenge and effort to assist the executive, not the outcome, that is appreciated.

CORPORATE COUNSEL GOALS

The goals of corporate counsel, while contributing to the general corporate goals, differ from those of other executives. To understand the goals of the corporate counsel, we must think a little bit about the corporate organizational structure.

Normally, the corporate counsel assigned to a particular matter will report to a number of higher-level corporate supervisors within or outside the law department. Similar supervisory levels are not usually present in law firms. If the law department is large enough to have supervisory lawyers, they report to the general counsel, and the general counsel usually reports to the chief executive officer (CEO) or chair of the board. The chair reports to the board and the board and chair together to the shareholders. Obviously, the number of layers of reporting within the corporation is directly related to the size of the corporation and, independently, the number of lawyers in the law department.

This arrangement is drastically different from the law firm in that an associate usually has to satisfy only the partner for whom he or she is working and not irritate the other partners. In the law department of a corporation, each level of management must satisfy at least the next two higher levels of management. Since, in most instances, the general counsel reports to the CEO or chair of the board, they are well aware of the general counsel's performance in substantive legal matters, as well as law department financial matters. They are also quite cognizant of the general counsel's performance and the impact it has on the corporation's goals.

The chair is accountable to the Board of Directors and the shareholders for every aspect of corporate performance. The fact that negotiations on a deal or litigation by the law department and outside counsel are influenced or determined by uncontrolled outside influences is not relevant. If these events turn out poorly, it is only the chair's relationship with the board that will spare her or him. The situation is the same for the general counsel and outside counsel.

Unlike the orientation of many lawyers in private practice, the corporate counsel is as concerned with lowering and controlling legal fees as with the substance of the matter at hand. The private practitioner may pull out all stops to win a legal point, even a minor one during discovery. The corporate counsel's managerial responsibilities expand that world to winning a legal point while at the same time spending no more than the budgeted amount for that matter.

For the above reasons, any private practitioner who reacts to a corporate counsel's inquiry about a bill with the attitude, "So what if it's high; that's the time it took," does not have the prospect of longevity for that corporation. Delivering legal services below budget thereby assisting the general counsel and business executives does.

Another goal of corporate counsel is to look good to the supervisors in the law department and the business managers. Saving money is only one factor. Certainly, winning the case or securing a better competitive position for the client is another facet. Outside counsel should attempt to understand the goals of corporate counsel before commencing work on any matter. One obvious way to obtain a better understanding is to ask corporate counsel what those goals are. Another way of obtaining information is to better understand the people in the hierarchical structure of the corporate organization. Yet another is to gain a greater understanding of the competitive position and the nature of the business in which the corporation is engaged.

COMMITMENT TO ETHICS

My experience has been that the commitment to ethics has permeated most law departments' legal and personnel actions. Some general counsel have had such widespread recognition among the executives for their ethical concerns that they have been designated Ethics Officer for the corporation. Ethics in the business of law is of great import to most general counsel and other lawyers in law departments.

Corporate relations opportunities may be created by outside counsel offering to present legal ethics seminars to corporate counsel and business people. These presentations should be participatory, rather than lectures. This format provides some assurance that outside counsel will not be viewed as talking at or down to the corporate audience. It is also a better learning environment.

Outside counsel could certainly develop client relations with a corporation by suggesting ethical means of winning sales competitions, improving competitive positions, avoiding executive embarrassment, keeping the corporate contacts informed of new developments in the law and ethical standards, preventing litigation and assisting the client (corporate counsel and business people) to "look good" by internal standards.

Each situation differs, so there is no generalized formula that may be uniformly applied to assist corporate counsel in achieving their goals. One thing is sure—the more you know about the business and the people who run it, the more likely you will be able to satisfy corporate and your corporate contacts' goals.

INTERNAL CORPORATE COMMUNICATIONS

The state of a law firm's client relations with a corporate client is determined in part by internal corporate communications. While outside lawyers may communicate with a certain individual within the corporation, most of the internal corporate communications about the outside counsel and the matters being handled are *ex parte*. That is, one corporate employee communicates with another about the legal matter and the job outside counsel is doing. This situation obviously differs dramatically from a lawyer representing an individual client.

Lawyers, in general, have a bad name. Until a lawyer accepts that unfortunate perception as a fact, the lawyer cannot deal effectively with client relations. The lawyer with excellent client relations has dug his or her way out of a negative image of the profession with which almost all clients start the lawyer-client relationship. If lawyers continually remember that we have a bad name, one is more likely to think of ways of overcoming this detrimental phenomenon. The object is to convince the corporate personnel that you are far better than their general impression of lawyers.

Within the corporation, lawyer bashing of both corporate counsel and outside counsel is a popular sport. Be aware that there are plenty of derogatory comments being made about outside counsel by the very individuals with whom the outside lawyer has the primary contact. In fact, it is the culture of many organizations, corporations included, that if the higher-ranking person bad-mouths a lawyer, the lower-ranking individual either remains silent or jumps into the fray agreeing with the higher-ranking person. This occurs even where the corporate contact believes and knows the outside counsel is doing a good job. Yes, we lawyers are necessary evils, but that reluctant admission itself is a reflection of the pervasive negative impression, which our profession has created.

"Deal breaker" is a label that is often pinned on lawyers. This comes principally from the lawyer's effort to protect the client through document language that frequently is unacceptable in the marketplace. Insistence to impasse by lawyers on many of the theoretical protections in a contract situation or wording of a particular clause in a specific fashion generates this type of description.

The problem arises because the lawyer is not thinking like the client. The client may in fact know that the language protections advocated by the lawyer are desirable, but there is no certainty that those protections will ever be used. So, the client makes the decision whether those crafty, wordy clauses will be included based not on a narrow view of the contract as a self-contained document, but rather on the realistic commercial risks and the apparent business opportunities that the signed contract will open or the opportunities the lawyer's insistence on clause language will foreclose.

This disconnect of the lawyer—corporate or private—from the client stems from two misconceptions. First, the lawyer believes it is her or his role to give advice and write protections against *every possible* downside. The businessperson wants the lawyer to provide insight from experiences with other clients and technical legal knowledge to contribute to finding an immediate practical solution or opportunity. Secondly, lawyers are envisioning and basing advice on an abstract possibility, "The Law," which is far less relevant to businesspeople because their world is the concrete of the present situation.

Lawyers can correct their corporate images by communicating that they know they were hired or retained to make the situation or deal better. Only by making it better can lawyers add value. Yes, at times that means pointing out all of the pitfalls and a bad deal is rejected. But more often, this means that if the law prevents or makes risky a lawsuit's legal outcome or a course of business, the lawyer has to do more than just say "No." At the very least, it is the lawyer's role and template for evaluating the situation to suggest more acceptable alternatives. In this way, the lawyer will add value by making the situation, deal and corporation better.

Many times we lawyers say or write to clients that if you do not follow our advice and you are sued, you will not have adequate protection. Isn't it interesting that no matter how dour our predication of adverse consequences, we virtually never add, "And I will NOT defend you." While a lawyer's focus may be solely or primarily on putting the client in the best defensive position to avoid suit, businesspeople are not basing their decision to enter into a contract or not on the chance they will be sued.

In addition, most astute business people know from experience that it is not the language in the contract that causes a person to sue or not to sue. Rather it is the personal relationships and circumstances of the business situation. If every union attempted to enforce every provision contained in the collective bargaining agreement against the employer or vice versa, no product would be manufactured and no customer serviced. Similarly, if the businesses on both sides of an agreement constantly raised each provision in a contract that had been technically violated, neither would have any time to pursue their business. Instead, they would create a business of pursuing each other, which generally is neither profitable nor pleasant.

Proof that the lawyer is not attuned to the businessperson in many a contractual matter is demonstrated by the fact that the lawyer is retained to negotiate the agreement (or formalize what has been negotiated) and to sue if the business deal goes sour. While the business is actually being conducted mostly under the contractual terms, the lawyer is rarely, if ever, requested to give advice on the implementation of the contract. This period of doing business as usual is the most important time for the clients—the time to make or lose money. The lawyer's lack of focus on the practicality of business and the futility of conducting trade under the strict interpretation of contractual clauses keeps the lawyer on the sidelines during the best of times for the client. This is unfortunate for lawyers become identified with difficult situations and bad times.

Lawyer-client relations could be advanced immeasurably by the lawyer, within ethical and legal limits, getting in step with the day-to-day practical thinking of the businessperson. This will increase accurate communications and understanding between the client and the lawyer. It is unlikely that a client will pay for a lawyer to become so informed. Thus, it is up to the lawyer to continually educate herself or himself about the client at no cost to the client.

The lawyer can also head off miscommunication by offering to provide, at no additional fee, an oral or written report on the matters being handled or an update of relevant law to those to whom his corporate client contact reports. This has the advantage to the outside and corporate counsel of touching all of the communication bases and exposing the other corporate decisionmakers to the lawyer's personality, rather than just the amount of the lawyer's bill or salary. However, such a report must be realistic, concise, and relevant to businesspeople and expressed in lay language that communicates clearly to the businesspeople.

In such a meeting, the lawyer must be prepared to listen intently and thoughtfully evaluate rather than instinctively stonewalling or shooting back with a defensive reaction. If the businessperson's concern or comments initially seem to be irrelevant, it is probably because the lawyer has failed to do his or her homework on several fronts: educating the client on the legal matter, understanding the corporate personalities, learning the business, and communicating effectively.

Facts, feelings, circumstances, and perceptions are all of the same value to most nonlawyers. Executives may be approaching a matter with an experiential background that leads to a conclusion far different from the one anticipated by the lawyer. Descriptions of what impressions were created by opponents are sometimes quite important to the corporate person because they may provide insight into a solution or the current business conditions. They may also be important to the legal strategy that is ultimately developed, if only the lawyer will pay attention to what is being said.

When making such a report, extreme caution must be exercised to assure that what counsel reports cannot be used to criticize the corporate contact or anyone else in the corporation. No fuel to internal competition for positions should be provided. To avoid such a situation, focus on the law, the uncertainty of court outcomes, and the necessity of concluding the agreement. Never defend yourself as inside or outside counsel by saying, "I didn't want to do it, but your corporate personnel insisted." Model Rule 1.13 provides additional guidance on this point.

The outside lawyer's key to not being sandbagged by *ex parte* internal corporate communications is to know the business, to understand the corporate people, to maximize the number of contacts with appropriate corporate personnel, and to communicate in their language.

DECISION MAKING: STRUCTURED VS. OPEN ENVIRONMENT

The law, the pleadings, the rules, and the facts confine the range of a lawyer's professional decisions. On the other hand, only the realm of business possibilities and the broadest constraints of the law limit the businessperson's decision parameters.

Lawyers in litigation generally deal with knowns and givens, and interpret the law and facts in accordance with events and decisions that have already occurred. It is a very structured discipline and a challenging one within which to work. Lawyers negotiating contracts and deals work within the parameters provided by corporate personnel and boilerplate language approved by the courts. Also, a difficult, but a known and controlled, limited set of rules.

Walking in the moccasins of the businessperson reveals that that individual must make decisions about what products are safe based on experimental research, without knowing whether later-developed technology and scientific theory may render them allegedly unsafe. What products promise to make X amount in sales are determined by unproven projections, not past occurrences and rules. Corporate types must determine how to deal with the personalities of the various people involved in every commercial activity. They are frequently called to adjust to unanticipated changes in market conditions and internal corporate considerations. When and how to roll out an advertising campaign that will spike sales upward has no certain rules guaranteeing success to those who comply. Managing so as to maximize the business with the available assets is yet another decision that must be made on the basis of open-ended considerations and future unknown events. This business decision making is a much more inductive process with a myriad of additional factors and far less structured than a lawyer's professional decision-making boundaries.

Although it is not an excuse for poor or dangerous commercial decisions, the businessperson's decision-making process appears to be future-oriented and based on judgments about many unknowns. The lawyer is basically looking at the past, at what has already happened or what is the existing law. The businessperson is deciding which fork in the road to take, while the lawyer is looking back and sometimes smugly saying that the businessperson should have chosen the other fork. That type of commentary from lawyers, while not infrequent, is neither helpful nor very perceptive concerning the difference in the nature of the two decision-making processes.

Although it might be difficult for the lawyers to admit, telling businesspersons that the decisions they have to make are tougher than the ones lawyers make could go a long way toward cementing their relationships. Understanding the businessperson's decision-making process and all of the factors that must be taken into consideration will dramatically improve the odds of winning the case or negotiating an advantageous agreement. Communicating the lawyer's appreciation for the client's difficult decisions will enhance the lawyer's standing.

If the lawyer empathizes with, rather than criticizes, the businessperson, the lawyer will be more likely to be retained again. Besides, the businessperson may know as well as the lawyer that the wrong decision was made. Nothing is gained by retrospective criticism of the businessperson's future-oriented decisions, except to undermine a viable lawyer-client relationship.

If lawyers avoid such traps in thinking about the business decision-making process, the relationship with the client will certainly improve.

SUMMARIZING CORPORATE RELATIONS

The best summary of points made in this chapter may be an outline of its sections:

1. Who Is the Lawyer's Corporate Client?—corporations are people;
2. Corporate Goals and Lawyer Service Quality—they must mesh;
3. Corporate Counsel Goals—understand and advance them;

4. Internal Corporate Communications—outside counsel should maximize direct corporate contacts at all levels; and

5. Decision Making: Structured vs. Open Environment—business decisions involve more uncertainties than legal decisions and, therefore, they are fundamentally different.

Many lawyers who have represented corporations for years never really understood corporate client relations unless and until they became a corporate counsel. There are only a few lawyers in private practice who truly know their corporate client. That can be remedied only by the desire and pursuit of a corporate client education by the corporate and outside lawyer.

The single summary principle that best describes developing excellent corporate client relations, is that lawyers need to focus on the future and not on the past because that is how businesspeople think. This can never be achieved if the lawyer—corporate or outside—does not immerse herself or himself in the corporate goals and daily business.

Mistakes are easy to see in everything after "everything" has transpired. The truth is that excellent lawyers aid corporations in making the best of wrong decisions, regrettable facts, and bad law. This is true for plaintiffs' lawyers as well. A backward-looking, criticizing discussion about what a businessperson did or didn't do is, for the attorney-corporate relationship, just that—backward. All superb lawyers, whether they represent corporations or not, satisfy clients with super efforts, understandable communications, and supportive actions that forge strong, forward-looking client relations.

CHAPTER 15

THE ADVANTAGE OF ALLIANCES

The accepted concept of law firm growth is to hire additional lawyers, add areas of practice, and open new offices, be they in different cities or suburbs. The prevailing business philosophy in the legal community seems to be that if a firm is all things to all clients and is everywhere, there is no opportunity for another firm to compete for or to steal a client. This is an outmoded concept for all law firms, except very large firms. For middle-sized firms, small law firms and solos, as well as corporate law departments, this growth concept is, for the organizations and their clients, counterproductive, inefficient, legally and financially risky, and physically detrimental to the lawyers.

In an earlier book (*Practical Planning*, ABA Law Practice Management Section, 1984), I described the practice of law in the United States as essentially being a cottage industry. Law firms and even lawyers within law firms compete to take in legal piecework without a genuine understanding of the benefits that come from a division of labor and an alliance with others. Individual lawyer control of clients seems to be the preferred vehicle for law practice. The fuel for this vehicle and counterproductive phenomenon is most frequently law firm compensation systems that reward digging up clients and hoarding work instead of serving clients better, faster and cheaper, regardless of which organization or who performs the work.

In my early teens, I earned a weekend train trip to Detroit by selling newspaper subscriptions. On that trip, we toured the Ford plant at River Rouge, Michigan. As a native of Pittsburgh, I was not overwhelmed as many tourists were with the fire and smoke of the Ford steel mill. I do recall, however, being intrigued and impressed with the fact that Ford made everything it needed for its cars at that single location, from the steel to the glass. That was total control . . . and it turned out to be fiscally disastrous.

Belatedly, decades later, Ford and the other American auto manufacturers discovered that it was cheaper and easier to buy component parts from specialty component manufacturers and assemble them, rather than manufacture everything themselves. By doing so, they were able to take advantage of specialization, more-efficient manufacturing processes, cost control by bidding, flexibility of smaller organizations, and multiple product sources. At the same time, they avoided capital investment, personnel problems, intensive research and development, single vulnerable source, turf kingdoms, and numerous staff functions necessary to support a large manufacturing operation of diverse products.

Look at your television. In spite of the label on the front of the television, you probably have no idea what company made the picture tube or the other critical internal parts. In all likelihood, you probably don't care who made the parts as long as the television functions properly.

When you think about it, any part of your decision to buy that particular television, based on a quality assessment, was probably made based on the corporate nameplate and consumer surveys. It is virtually certain that you did not care if the quality value came from parts that were all manufactured by the nameplate corporation or whether the nameplate corporation bought components from other manufacturers while retaining the responsibility for having a total quality product. Imposing and enforcing quality standards for subcontractors involves as much or more control than making the entire product.

APPLYING BUSINESS PRINCIPLES TO LAW PRACTICE

The advantages of component buying are not restricted to the manufacturing sector of the economy. Service organizations have also found that they can obtain more thorough cooperation than total control. Catalog sales businesses, while having separate toll-free telephone numbers, have turned over their phone order business to independent companies, which contract to perform the phone order-taking service for a number of businesses. Some health-care providers contract for everything from doctors, to laundry, to billing, to collecting, to computing and to maintenance services. Even public sector service providers such as schools and municipalities contract for snow removal, road repair, counseling, food service, and tax collection services. With the explosion of the Internet, astute businesses have turned to Internet experts to develop and maintain Web sites.

Law firms and lawyers seem to find it difficult to work in a cooperative fashion with other law firms, which provide service in different areas of the law (and even with lawyers within their own firm), other professionals, and their business clients. Although it takes energy, ingenuity, and creativity to work cooperatively with others, that is not a reason to continue to try to scarf up all of the business for one's self or law firm or to provide all support services with employees.

Producing every service element within the firm is also inefficient and fiscally detrimental to the law firm and individual lawyer. For one thing, this cottage-industry approach severely limits the profit opportunities to the number of hours a lawyer or firm can work and to the rates (hourly or contingent) competition will allow to be charged for the work performed.

If the firm's objective is to have more work without regard to profit, the exclusively homemade approach may indeed be the best course of action. Few large clients concentrate all of their work with a single law firm. Consider carefully whether there might be more opportunities to acquire additional work through alliances with other law firms and other professionals than when an organization does everything itself. If the cost of the services acquired is reduced, the savings will be appreciated by the client.

Strategically, general service law firms should think about and concentrate on developing areas of practice that are involved in virtually every business. Such areas as tax, environmental law, labor employment law, litigation, and commercial matters certainly qualify, and there are others. The well-known axiom that 20 percent of the entities control 80 percent of the business or process is applicable to the fields of law. Focus on that critical 20 percent of the fields of law practice and clients that generate 80 percent of your profits and forget attempting to be all things to all clients. Form alliances to cover the remaining fields of law.

More specifically, pursuing the same principle within a field of law, becoming known as the expert in the critical 20 percent of the legal matters that control 80 percent of the client representation within a particular industry, would seem to make good business sense to a law firm or an individual lawyer. For instance, becoming known in the labor and employment law field as an expert in National Labor Relations Board law on accretions to union bargaining units might be a nice, intellectually esoteric, Ph.D.-type reputation to develop. However, accretions to bargaining units were never a large part of the practice before the National Labor Relations Board, and in the past couple of decades, practice before the Labor Board has shrunk from being the mainstay of labor and employment law practice to a barely visible vestige for many firms. Therefore, expertise in this particular area does not seem to be commercially sensible. Clients do not become more loyal to lawyers offering services that are not needed by the clients.

Even a superficial study of the recent development of law practice prohibiting discrimination based on age, gender, national origin, and disability will demonstrate that more than 50 percent of the cases arise from allegations of an employer's age discrimination. Under these circumstances, leverage for a plaintiffs' or defendants' employment law practice could be obtained by becoming an expert in age discrimination. This reflects an obvious business observation and the long-known principle of supply and demand. Yet, many firms on the plaintiffs' or the defendants' side can't see that they could profitably position themselves by forming an alliance with a lawyer or firm that has expertise in age discrimination matters rather than just general labor law. When a sophisticated plaintiff or defendant has an enormous age discrimination problem, it will select a specialist.

Large full-service firms should critically analyze the profitability of each practice sector. This analysis must push beyond the typical statistics comparing revenues from the previous year and such things as realization rates (the amount of the full hourly rate times the hours worked divided by actual revenues results in the realization percentage). These only measure gross revenue growth and theoretical potential for increasing revenue if competition and clients would permit charging maximum hourly rates.

Instead, for each area of practice the firm should carefully total revenues for that field. Then all expenses to maintain that area of practice should be totaled, not an easy task since in all but the largest firms, lawyers, and legal assistants work in a number of areas. Common expenses should be apportioned on some reasonable basis. For instance, rent on a square foot basis with an adder for a portion of the common space with administrative, technical, and marketing costs allocated on the percentage of gross revenue generated by the practice area. The next step is to subtract the total legal field expenses from its gross revenue to determine net profitability for that field of practice.

When this exercise is completed for each field of practice, check the totals of all fields to be sure they equal the gross revenue and total expenses of the whole firm. Frequently, practitioners are astounded at the differential in profitability when compared among the fields of service a firm offers clients.

Obviously, the preceding calculations could set off a compensation argument within the firm that might cause the firm to explode. But, if there is little or no profit in providing service in a particular area of the law, doesn't this fact argue strongly for forming an alliance with another firm to provide the service? Unlike the retail grocery business, there are very few examples in the practice of law where a "loss leader" brings in more purchases from a client buying the bargain representation. Most clients are not impressed with the bargains offered by lawyers. The most notable exception is a matter undertaken on a contingent fee basis.

An unprofitable corollary to failing to form an alliance with a specialty firm for a low profit margin sector of your practice is acquiring a profitable boutique firm, which not infrequently becomes a loser in the larger firm environment. This usually occurs because the referrals from other law firms to the boutique dry up from the fear that the larger firm will take other work from the referring firm's clients beyond the former boutique's specialty. And in truth, that expansion of legal representation is a goal of the business plan of one-stop shopping.

Because the estate planning sole practitioner or boutique firm is highly profitable is no assurance that it will continue to be so if acquired by a larger firm. The business analysis must go much deeper, for one can not pick up a successful business, place it in a new foreign environment, and be guaranteed it will continue to throw off double-digit profits. The specialty practice, larger firm, and clients of both are very often far better off developing a strong alliance rather than making an acquisition.

From the small-firm perspective, contact with less-frequent users of legal services may be expanded through other lawyers. Alliances are advantageous. These statements are valid because you know that the more lawyers who recognize your special expertise, the more likely you will receive referrals from them in your super specialty. That will not likely continue if you become part of a larger organization. Clients who have retained a small firm for years are often suspicious that a merger with a larger firm will destroy the special relationship they have with their lawyer and increase fees. If a merger is effectuated, the client relations issues need to be recognized and addressed.

The advantage of alliances is almost universally low risk on the downside and is laden with low-cost upside potentials. The same cannot be said of unprofitable specialties or acquisition of boutique practices by large law firms because the client relations issues may render the merger unprofitable.

LAWYER AND LAW FIRM RESISTANCE

Why, then, do lawyers and law firms steadfastly refuse to apply well-established business alliance principles to their practices?

The reasons are twofold. First, lawyers are often narrowly focused on their own interests rather than those of the firm or the client. Second, lawyers are unable to address, satisfy, and resolve the client-relations issues that would result from a multi-firm representation of a single client. If the client relations issues were resolved, lawyers would become more focused on the client's needs and thus enable them to utilize more-effective business techniques.

In a litigation practice, the centralization or referral debate is sometimes resolved within firms for the wrong reasons. In many instances, a large law firm cannot effectively try a case for a client in a country courthouse because it lacks credibility with the judge and jury, which is necessary to successfully litigate. This problem is resolved by the large law firm affiliating with local counsel. This is virtually a no-risk situation with respect to the large urban law firm because it is highly unlikely that the local firm will take the client away from the large firm. In addition, good working relationships with local law firms can generate large project or sophisticated legal business for the larger firms. Clients pay more for this solution by having two sets of attorneys participate in the trial, but they usually accept the added cost without much resistance for it adds value.

Smaller law firms are far more reluctant to affiliate with larger law firms, even when a client needs representation by a larger firm. This reluctance has been created out of a sometimes justified fear of larger law firms stealing the smaller firm's better clients. If this occurs, it is not on a price competition basis (because the larger firm is usually more expensive), but rather by disparaging the limited range of services, depth of backup support, and/or the quality and competency of the smaller practitioner.

That is an extremely shortsighted approach for both sizes of firms and, more importantly, for the client. The best defense to prevent other lawyers from stealing clients from a smaller firm—or firm of any size—is to develop and maintain a strong alliance with the client through effective client relations. Then, clearly stated agreements between the two firms and the client will go a long way toward putting remaining fears to rest.

By way of example, if a smaller practitioner thought it was in the best interest of the client to work with a larger firm on a matter, that boutique lawyer could discuss the plan—without identifying the larger firm—with the client. If the client agreed, then the specific larger firm should be revealed to the client in case the client did not wish to work with that particular firm.

Then the boutique practitioner should discuss the terms of the joint representation with the larger firm. This should include everything from who is going to do what work on the project, to not doing any other work for the client, to fees. The boutique practitioner should attempt to negotiate fees for the client that are below what the larger firm would charge the client if the client walked in off the street. If successful, the smaller firm should make the client aware of the discount obtained. This will strengthen the relationship with the client. The boutique practitioner should then send a letter outlining the terms of the arrangement to the larger entity with a copy to the client. Through this type of alliance and these communications, the relationship the boutique or small general practice lawyer has with clients will be strengthened.

The agreement between law firms cannot and should not attempt to control which lawyer a client chooses for future projects. However, if all three parties agree on the scope and cost of this engagement, it is more likely that a satisfactory arrangement for future legal work will be forthcoming. There are many examples of such alliances lasting for years to the benefit of clients and both law firms.

Hopefully, a joint representation agreement will lessen the resistance of the two practices to forming an alliance. It will surely benefit the client, which has a very positive impact on client relations.

THE REFERRING LAWYER RELATIONSHIP

An extremely significant portion of the revenue that I brought to a medium-sized firm with which I practiced was generated by lawyers in other law firms referring their clients' labor and employment law work to me. Note well that I said other lawyers referred the clients' work and NOT the client. These other lawyers included solos, large firms, local, and out-of-town firms.

In these situations, it was my practice in the initial interview with the client whose specialized work was referred, to explain that I would perform the labor and employment work, but that if we discovered other legal problems during the course of dealing with the labor and employment law problem, I would send the client back to the referring lawyer. I made it clear that I would refer them back even if I or another member of our firm was highly qualified to perform the legal work needed. This made the client keenly aware that this was an alliance on a limited scope project, not a transfer of the client.

I then confirmed the limits of my representation to the client in writing after the initial interview and sent a copy of that letter to the referring lawyer. Throughout my limited representation of the referring lawyer's client, my client relations efforts were bifurcated between the referring lawyer and the client. I diligently attempted to cement relations with the client, not only with our firm and me, but also with the referring lawyer. I did this because I regarded my representation as limited and wanted the client to have a good impression of both firms and our profession. As with most good client relations practices, this was both the right thing to do and served as a very effective marketing tool with the referring lawyer.

During the course of my representation of the client (even when the client complained about the referring lawyer), I never made a remark or gave an indication that could be construed, or misconstrued, as being detrimental or disparaging to or about the referring lawyer or firm. In instances when I disagreed with the past advice given by the referring lawyer, I would not raise the issue with the client. Sometimes clients trapped me by asking what I would advise under certain factual circumstances. I supposed a hypothetical was being posed. Once I gave them an opinion, they would occasionally tell me that it was contrary to what the referring lawyer had told them. I would explain honestly that I might not have known all of the circumstances or the referring lawyer might have been approaching the situation from a perfectly logical but different viewpoint.

Tearing down the referring lawyer or the advice given by some other lawyer really is pointless. There is nothing that can be done to reverse what occurred. One never builds self to a higher esteem in the eyes of others by "dissing" someone else. Whatever the cause of clients' present attitudes about previous lawyers, successor lawyers' only practical option is to deal with the substance of the present situation in a way that is best for our client. Heaping criticism on a previous lawyer is not only dangerous because not all of the facts or advice can ever be acquired from a former client, but it also focuses the client on the past rather than on the only place resolution of the client's situation can be found: the present and future. As lawyers, our job is to help client's with what they presently face rather than to fuel clients' tendencies to blame lawyers or others for allegedly creating the current situation.

Feeding the negative attitude of a client about lawyers doesn't build client relations for anyone. It causes the client to be more suspicious of all lawyers, including you. Criticizing a referring lawyer is also criticizing the client for going to the referring lawyer in the first place. If the client is complaining to you about the referring lawyer, the client is very likely to tell the referring lawyer or others what you say. That is no way to build and maintain an alliance for the benefit of the client with either the client or the referring lawyer.

In a number of instances where I believed that a potential labor problem might have been handled in a less than ideal manner by the previous advice given by the referring lawyer, I called the referring lawyer and gently raised the possibility that the advice might have been given on a misunderstanding of the facts. I did not raise the possible misinterpretation of the law for I felt the other lawyer could make that assessment himself or herself. Almost always, I discovered that the client had failed to relay all of the facts to the referring lawyer. In other circumstances, I have alerted a referring lawyer when a client was dissatisfied with the service received and related the reason for the dissatisfaction. I did this to provide a road map to the referring lawyers on how to restore a workable relationship with their client. This further convinced referring lawyers that I recognized it was their client, not mine, which clearly demonstrated that I recognized I was in an alliance with them on the limited assignment I had been given.

In the course of handling labor and employment matters, a number of clients requested that I handle all of their legal work. While that would have been a certain short-term economic advantage, I refused, even when they told me they were going to fire the referring lawyer. You see, the referring lawyer would never believe that the client had decided independently to fire him or her and retain me. If I had begun representing the discharged lawyer's former client on matters not referred, the referring lawyer probably would have assumed that I had plotted for that lawyer's termination and to steal the client. That impression would foreclose any future client alliances with that referring lawyer and probably a number of others.

COMPONENT EXPERTISE

Perception is more powerful than fact. A perception that you took a client from another lawyer, who had originally referred a discrete piece of business to you, would be devastating for your relations with your fellow lawyers. They would talk about it with every lawyer who would listen. Actual and potential referrals from and alliances with them would dry up—that's a certainty.

One key to getting referrals from other lawyers is to assist them with their client relations. You must also practice astute client relations with those referring lawyers. But, no matter how charming you might be with other lawyers, if you do not advance their relationships with their clients and their practice, you will not receive significant additional referrals for very long.

MAKING ALLIANCES WORK

I'm sure one could think of a million reasons why this alliance-between-law-practices approach to client relations will not work. That's a no-brainer. The more challenging and rewarding endeavor is to sit down and list the possibilities of how it might work to the benefit of clients and practitioners.

First, list examples in which legal expertise is frequently needed in your geographic area and among your clients and potential clients. For instance, if you practice in a high-tech area such as near a university or in a Silicon Valley-type area, the demand for intellectual property services may be great among the businesses. However, if your client base is in personal injury matters, it may not make sense to list intellectual property as a specialty area frequently needed by your clients. If the demographics of your region reflect an aging population, estate planning may be needed.

Second, identify and segregate the skills in the listed expertise areas, which you enjoy and in which you truly excel. For instance, in tax it might be advice on mergers, in family law it might be negotiating settlements, or in litigation it might be trying toxic tort cases. We're not looking at the whole substantive legal field—the focus is on refined skills and tasks within the field. Honestly examine your personal professional achievements to isolate your precise expertise and what you like to do best—they are usually the same. The type of analysis for a lawyer with a real estate practice might include "Am I best at . . ." and "Do I most like researching the chain of title or dealing with the people at the closing?"

Third, determine which of your special skills are not possessed to the same degree by other lawyers or firms in your geographic area of practice. The geographic area may be the county, a portion of the county, or the nation. This step really requires an honest assessment of other lawyers and yourself. It should ultimately reflect which skills are needed and the degree of potential application of those skills. This process of identifying the practice that would offer you a competitive advantage is analogous to market research, but it really deals with how to best position yourself to build solid client relations while performing the aspects of legal practice that are satisfying to you. It's important in this step that the lawyer's ego doesn't interfere with the realistic assessment of his or her special skills and the competition. Many of us think we are really good in many areas of practice. To give some counterbalance to this ego-hatched perception, keep focusing on what you enjoy doing most.

Fourth, design a service plan and fee structure for your special skill that is profitable for you and compatible with the clients of the law firms you are targeting for referral business. With few exceptions, it makes no sense to try to interest a smaller law firm that represents small to mid-sized clients in a service that is being offered at two times the rate they charge their clients. Unless desparate, neither the lawyer who charges less than half that hourly rate nor that lawyer's clients will be interested.

If you conclude from this analysis that you must charge double the hourly rate to be profitable, this referral market is limited or nonexistent. That theoretical plan, no matter how desirable, is commercially unfeasible. It is time to start the planning process for possible alliances with other lawyers over again.

Fifth, design and implement a strategic alliance plan that will accomplish the following in the order that the elements are set forth:

- Refine the special skill;
- Further develop your expertise;
- Streamline the process you use in practicing your expertise by reducing the number of steps necessary to accomplish the end result;
- Obtain the necessary equipment to upgrade the assistance that technology can provide for practicing your special skill;
- Assure that assignments of the various elements of the service within your practice are to competent persons who will generate the greatest margin of profit for that element;
- Build into the practice of your special skill added value factors for both the referring lawyer and the consumer of the service (interim status reports, standardized initial letters, follow-up letters of thanks and so forth);
- Run a quality check with your own clients to determine whether the quality of your specialized services was what they expected, whether the time frame in which it was delivered was acceptable, whether your involvement with the client was sufficient, and whether the client has any suggestions for service improvement, and finally, make necessary adjustments.

Sixth, spread the word:

- Make your expertise known through bar association meetings, seminars, lectures, Web site, and newsletters to lawyers as well as clients;
- Let it be known that you are willing to use your skills in an alliance with other lawyers on behalf of other lawyers' clients;
- Illustrate through stories and anecdotes to other lawyers that you are no robber baron of clients;
- Demonstrate to other lawyers the practicality and profitability of referrals to and an alliance with you; and
- Constantly look for opportunities to raise the level of awareness in other lawyers of your ability to help them serve their clients and develop their client relationships without being a competitive threat.

Seventh, check for progress

- Goals and objectives should be checked on a regular basis to see if your program of alliances for client relations is progressing in accordance with your strategic plan (performance measurements should include counting the number of contacts, as well as monetary ones); and

- Through computerized bookkeeping codes, track the dollar amount of new business from alliances with referring lawyers and their clients.

- Allow sufficient time for the alliance process to work. But, don't extend a futile effort over a lifetime of practice. Set timetables for specific achievements. Generally, a minimum of two years is necessary to obtain a recognizable amount of business referred from other lawyers. Remember, not every lawyer on every day has the opportunity to refer the specialized type of business you're seeking. It pays to have continuous reminders to other lawyers about your specialty so that when lawyers do have potential referrals in your area of expertise, you will be on the top of the possible alliance list. This may be accomplished by advertising in the local legal journal or by sending updates on the law in your specialized area to potential referring lawyers.

- Using the benchmarks discussed, make adjustments to your strategic alliance plan based both on your successes and failures in obtaining business and assisting other lawyers with their client relations. Such modifications should take into account the additional knowledge you have obtained about your market from your initial efforts to crack it or to gain greater market share. These adjustments may include the ultimate—dropping your efforts to obtain alliances in a particular specialty. But, don't be impatient.

Success requires sufficient investment of money, a great investment of time, and continuous, vigorous effort. If you are short on any of these three elements or lack the commitment and discipline for a sustained, high level of implementation actions in each, either create a new plan or significantly extend the two-year period in which to accomplish the plan.

NEW CENTURY: NEW OPPORTUNITIES

The world has changed dramatically, from the last century. Corporations are collaborating in joint ventures and other commercial arrangements to capture larger shares of existing and new markets. Years ago, who would have speculated that the United States and Russia would be cooperating in a space program? Allies in the same business are frequently critical for success. Witness the ticketing cooperatives among arts organizations and airlines. The field of law is no exception to the advantages to be gained from cooperative alliances. As a profession, we need to institute changed behaviors to become a more active participant in this changed commercial world. By demonstrating that lawyers are forming alliances to benefit clients and by so doing foregoing maximizing their personal compensation, lawyers will improve their relations with clients.

NEW CENTURY: NEW DEMANDS

We started this chapter by talking about the automobile manufacturing business. That business has other analogies to the practice of law. As long as the American manufacturers of automobiles were competing only among like manufacturers and the market was growing, practically every manufacturer was expanding its volume of products sold and was making money. In a way, that describes the practice of law in the United States during the last couple of decades of the 1900s. For most, the legal competition was restricted to a county or region.

Now, in the new century, declining demand and foreign competition from lawyers in other towns, new law practice branch offices, banks, stockbrokers, accountants, financial advisors, title companies, high-volume/low-cost providers of legal services, do-it-yourself software programs, and corporate law departments have forever changed the world of the private practice of law.

This changed world demands a changed response from private practitioners and corporate law departments. One such creative response in private practice is to obtain referrals of specialized work. A new or dramatically improved skill to achieve that end is to utilize confidence you build in other lawyers and law firms to make yourself a part of an alliance for serving clients on specialized legal work. When you are part of an alliance, you must also persuade clients of others that it is in their best interest to continue to retain their current primary lawyers rather than engaging the competition—you—to do all of their legal work. You can accomplish this through a new dimension of sophisticated and coordinated client relations that forge lawyer and law firm strategic alliances that benefit clients, and ultimately their cooperating lawyers.

Corporate and government lawyers are required to form new alliances as well. To best serve their clients, these lawyers must analyze and recognize when it makes sense to bring services in house and when it is more advantageous to outsource them. Government and corporate lawyers must assure that their elected officials, supervisors, line managers, and executives become and remain part of alliances to provide client services. This will definitely advance client relations, which in turn drives appreciation for the job the lawyer is performing.

SUMMARY

This chapter has been sharply focused on alliances with other lawyers. Success in today's environment also demands alliances with professionals and service providers who are not members of the bar. For instance, estate lawyers can develop alliances with financial planners, banks, stockbrokers, insurance agents, and others who will benefit their clients. Patent lawyers can better serve their clients through alliances with engineers, academics, and scientists. Plaintiffs' counsel who forge alliances with unions, consumer organizations, investigators, and experts represent their clients better. All of these alliances are structured to improve the quality of service and usually lower price to the client. Today's client relations realities demand that lawyers seek all alliances that will be advantageous for clients and work to maintain good relations within all such alliances.

To optimize the benefit from an alliance, every client should be part of the alliance with all involved in the client's matter. There is no reason for lawyers to pretend that they do it all or that they know everything. Most clients who are consulted about alliances have more respect for lawyers who admit a gap in their expertise and advocate bringing in a more qualified person, whether the new teammate is another lawyer or not. Clients should be brought into meetings when selecting an expert and made part of the evaluation team of any reports submitted by experts retained by the other side. The client is in the best position to evaluate an expert's report because the client knows the practical aspects of the report's subject matter.

Client relations now requires a team consisting of both people within your practice organization and outside it. While the lawyer may be the head of the alliance, the lawyer must make clear to the client that the client is a critical part of this alliance. Even if the client declines to participate, the invitation will be appreciated. Lawyers who request and virtually demand client participation in alliances will almost automatically improve client relations.

Besides, well-executed plans for alliances make law practice more enjoyable by restricting the unending information on developing law and detailed facts which the lawyer must know and retain. Alliances further provide marvelous opportunities for client relations and professional friendships beyond the legal organization in which you practice.

CHAPTER 16

COMPARING CLIENT RELATIONS

Think for a moment about your observations as to how a regular patron at a restaurant or a frequent customer of a dry-cleaning establishment is treated compared with you, an infrequent user of the establishment. Most often, the entrepreneurs and employees of the establishments treat the regulars with a certain familiarity that grows into camaraderie.

The regular has a sense of being special at a truck stop when he walks in and, without him ordering, the waitress brings a cup of coffee with just the right amount of sugar and cream. A regular patron also treats the counter people in a special manner. The language used is short-hand communication, "The usual, please." The coded language in part is saying to the server in the diner, "You too are special because we have a special way we talk to each other."

As an infrequent customer under similar circumstances, I have often been curious to see what is served up as "the usual." If the infrequent patron orders the same thing from the menu, it takes the server and the infrequent or new customer a lot more words and time to get the meal ordered and served. This leads to the conclusion that communications between the provider and infrequent users of services require much more time, effort, and careful use of language than when regulars talk.

Spend a moment to think about how you speak to those you see every day in your family or at your work compared with relatives who live far away, suppliers, or other lawyers who work in your law firm but in a different city.

Comparative Communications with Clients	
Frequent-Familiar	*Infrequent-Unfamiliar*
Little introduction—short time frame; discussion of specific activity: "Who won your daughter's ball game last night?"	Introduction—longer time frame; generalized questions: "How's the weather?"
Get right down to business.	Ease into the business of the meeting.
More informal	More formal
Less uncertainty	Greater uncertainty

If we act on our knowledge of how people who frequently see each other and how people who infrequently see each other behave, lawyers will have much more successful client relations. With both types of clients, the lawyer must tailor his or her conversation and behavior to that which is expected by the client. However, lawyers, because they focus on the legal work instead of the client, regularly treat every client with the same behavioral patterns. This is not beneficial to positive client relations.

Tailoring behavior and conversation to different types of clients does not mean that the lawyer should mimic the client's behavior. In fact, the client may be coming to you because you behave differently than he or she does. This means that you should quickly figure out how the client expects you to behave. In all cases, you should be aware of the client's expectations, as learned from other life experiences, so that at least you do not inadvertently offend the client or stymie effective communications.

Now, let's examine the difference in client-relations goals between the frequent and infrequent client.

THE FREQUENT CLIENT

The worst thing you can do with a frequent client is make an assumption that you really do not need to spend any additional time on client relations. Other law firms and other professions are constantly attempting to woo your client and so you, too, must constantly work to maintain and further strengthen your relationship with the client.

Merely maintaining the client relationship, which created the desire for the client to return and reengage you for legal services, probably will not cause a client to look for a different lawyer. But, by limiting your message and efforts to the client, you have no doubt lost some golden opportunities. There is much more to be achieved with a frequent client. Minimally, the lawyer must openly discuss whether the client's goals have changed and how he or she can help achieve the client's evolving goals by doing additional work. Ponder for a moment the difference between what was stated in the previous sentence and the usual approach of asking the client to give the lawyer or firm additional work. It shouldn't be a matter of giving anything; the lawyer must be seen as the best professional to assist the client in a practical, cost-effective way.

Perhaps the most difficult task in client relations is to figure out how to raise the frequent client's level of satisfaction to a point where the client becomes not just satisfied, but an enthusiastic promoter of the lawyer and the law firm. A client has many opportunities to tell others about what a tremendous lawyer he or she uses. The client will not do that unless the services being provided and the fees being charged are so enthralling that the client can barely contain himself or herself. Plus, the relationship with the lawyer must be so good that the client is energized to brag about the lawyer as a person, rather than just talk about fees, services, and results.

This extraordinary level of client relations is extremely difficult to achieve and does not fit into any clear mold or formula. Its main ingredient is that the client feels a unique recognition by the lawyer who truly regards the client as special. To attain this relationship quality, the lawyer must be creative and sincere in developing the client relationship. Aspects of that relationship include personal, professional, business, and social.

Of course, the greatest danger with respect to frequent clients is that you take them for granted. Just because a client has never used another lawyer does not mean that you can be lackadaisical about returning phone calls or completing work. If you have set a high standard of intense client relations, you have created an expectation in the client that must be consistently met.

Please note that the client's expectation of your high level of attention is transferred to and imposed on everyone else in your office by the client. Your other lawyers and staff must be trained and required to respond to client needs as well or better than you do. If anyone in your office—lawyer or staff—is unable or unwilling to meet and maintain this standard, that person should be replaced.

The loss of such a regular client is greater than the loss of the infrequent client. The frequent client provides the steadier income and the formerly frequent client is much more likely to be personally bitter about the unacceptable treatment received than a one-time user of the law firm's services. Such a parting of the ways may very well motivate that former frequent client to make disparaging remarks in the community about the lawyer and the law firm.

In one person, the frequent client incorporates the best opportunity for repeat engagements and the most dangerous chance of a person speaking out against the person's former lawyer.

THE INFREQUENT CLIENT

With the infrequent client, the lawyer must concentrate on building the relationship. The foundation of this relationship must be set with solid stones that are all related one to another. Frequent communications, perception of high value by the client, lawyer availability, and reliability of performance by the lawyer are some of those solid building blocks.

The infrequent user of legal services may need more concurrent information about what the lawyer is doing and why the lawyer is doing it. This client is not usually as sophisticated in legal matters, the use of lawyers or the amount of their bills. Also, trust has not yet been built by frequent contacts into a strong lawyer-client relationship. Therefore, an explanation of what is involved in terms of lawyer skill, resources, knowledge, document drafting, procedural steps, and costs should be clearly and frequently explained so that clients will be reassured that they have received value when they are asked to pay their bill.

The single most important thing for a lawyer to achieve with an infrequent client is to create an open line of communication that is used by client and lawyer. Saying to the client to call anytime is woefully inadequate. Some of these communications may be "handholding," which is not usually regarded by lawyers or staff as a legal service. This may also mean that the lawyer will have to record certain time and show it as a "No Charge." However, if the lawyer views this time as an investment in a client, the client will come to realize that the lawyer is providing greater value to the client than is covered by the fees charged. That greater value eventually becomes the solid relationship with the client that the lawyer seeks.

NEW CLIENTS

Unless a lawyer or firm has won a beauty contest to represent a client on a certain volume of work, the lawyer doesn't know the first time a new client comes to the office whether the client will be a frequent or infrequent user of legal services. The client with a single legal matter doesn't even know if future circumstances will require a large volume of legal services. Becoming a named plaintiff in a class action, buying a business with numerous product liability claims, and seeking redress for an employer's alleged discriminatory acts are a few examples of unanticipated legal needs.

The best approach is to educate a new client on the value of a strong relationship with the lawyer. Start with the suggestions made for infrequent users, but invest enough time with the client so that the client graduates to the relationship sought in the frequent user section. This investment of nonbillable time should be made even if it is not justified by the size of the fee to be earned on the matter the new client brought to the lawyer. In this way, the lawyer will be developing the relationship with the client so that the client will feel comfortable coming to the lawyer with any future legal inquiry.

By understanding new clients' perceptions and expectations of their lawyer you are gaining two crucial insights. Obviously, the lawyer obtains information about what the new individual or corporate client thinks about and expects from lawyers. The other insight comes from the new client's general perceptions about lawyers, which probably reflects what others in the new client's sphere think too. This investment in time and interest may well yield useful information about the new client's family, social contacts, and business connections that will help the lawyer establish a client relationship with any referral the new client might make. It will also help the lawyer develop a fruitful relationship with the new client, because the new client's expectations are partially determined by those with whom the client is in contact.

Most of the specifics of building a solid client relationship with new clients are the same as what is reflected in other chapters, so they won't be repeated here. Suffice it to say that I have had clients come to me for representation and tell me another lawyer had represented them a few years ago, but they can't remember the lawyer's name. This lack of memory seems to say the lawyer didn't spend very much time with the client and didn't impress the client. If a lawyer skimps on time for client relations on a small matter, the lawyer squanders opportunities to represent the client and the clients' acquaintances on future big matters.

The area most frequently underserviced for new clients is client relations. Time pressures and billable hours frequently cause lawyers to minimize face time with clients, especially new ones. On real estate deals, paralegals handle almost everything. In litigation, associates do much of the legwork instead of the partner to whom the new client came. This efficiency for the sake of making money this month often cuts a lawyer off from a long-term client relationship. The percentage of time other professionals spend with the new client often exceeds that spent with the lawyer. If the lawyer denies the client adequate time to establish a relationship, the client will feel little compulsion to return. There is also little likelihood that a new client who never got to know the lawyer would recommend the lawyer to an acquaintance.

New clients are important. They offer new possibilities for a very satisfying client relationship. New clients have more potential to generate more business than the majority of your existing clients have generated. Existing clients, at least presumably, are already giving the lawyer as much business as they desire to do and are recommending the lawyer to others to the extent they deem appropriate. New clients potentially can help the law practice that is limited only by the lawyer's willingness to invest in client relations and the new clients' contacts.

SUMMARY

All the above elements are aimed at creating value cognizable to the client through the services and a relationship provided by the lawyer. Whether the client perceives the value of these efforts will depend upon how effectively all of the elements are integrated by the lawyer's sincerity. Some of the opportunities, the language, and the approach differ between infrequent and frequent clients, but the goal is certainly the same.

I am not trying to imply that frequent clients must be treated in a totally different way from infrequent or new clients. There are common elements in the chemistry of all relationships. Continual education about what is involved in lawyering is essential. Building and refining the lawyer-client relationship through service of all of the client's needs at a cost the client perceives to be acceptable is another shared element. Performing with quality by doing things right the first time and explaining what you have done and why it has practical value contributes to building every client's trust in the lawyer.

Most of all, as lawyers we must realize that to maintain and build our practices demands we invest time and energy in client relations with every client. Execution on this commitment is essential if we are to reasonably expect a return from clients that exceeds the payment of the last invoice.

CHAPTER 17

RETAINING CLIENTS AND AVOIDING FORMAL COMPLAINTS

THERE'S USUALLY ANOTHER CHANCE

While our society has become far more litigious in recent years, clients do not want to fight with their own lawyers to get a job completed to their satisfaction. Clients tend to retain lawyers with whom they do not have to argue or be concerned about the lawyer heading in a different direction than the one the client desires.

Let's view the atmosphere in which we practice as clients might see it. Complaints about lawyers, demeaning lawyer jokes, and abhorrence of high legal fees have become as American as apple pie. There is a dichotomy in clients between realizing they need a lawyer and intensely resenting that they have that need. Aggravating the situation is that clients have to pay substantial money for legal services, which they feel they are forced to buy. These circumstances practically guarantee that clients will be dissatisfied with the service, results, and fees. Neutralizing the preconceptions clients bring to lawyers' offices is a major undertaking. Clients expect to have a complaint, so they look for a cause.

Our societal psychology of "it's not my fault" also puts the lawyers and the services they provide in a no-win position. If everything doesn't turn out perfectly, and real life never does, the client blames it on the lawyer because it just couldn't be the client's fault. Thus, the facts the client creates, the client's testimony, and the client's insistence on particular contract provisions will rarely be the cause of failure. Instead the lawyer will frequently be to blame, as far as the client is concerned.

Although it is relatively unusual for clients to switch lawyers in the middle of a case, it is not unusual for them to choose another lawyer for a subsequent legal matter. In fact, they may deal with their bank, accountant, or insurance broker on future business matters rather than retaining a lawyer at all.

Clients switching to another profession for representation and problem resolution are even more devastating for the legal profession than changing from one lawyer to another. Nevertheless, this is becoming more prevalent, and the lawyers are not doing enough to stem this tide.

WHAT MAKES CLIENTS WANT TO FIGHT?

Even though clients would rather switch lawyers than fight, a minor matter such as a telephone expense charge might activate their fight reaction. If we know and address what causes clients to feel they are fighting with their lawyers, we will be better prepared to avoid arousing those intense client feelings that generate business for other lawyers and other professions or, even worse, that provoke litigation against lawyers.

The lawyer may not even be congnizant of the boxing match of which we write, because its ring may be contained in the client's mind. Sometimes, too, the audience for the broadcast of the fight's description is the client's friends or disinterested listeners. If the relationship with the lawyer is such that the client feels he or she cannot talk with the lawyer about the situation or that it would be a useless act, the client is likely to tell many people, but not the lawyer involved.

Remember, too, that clients are being encouraged to use more formal routes to register complaints. When I first saw them, I was shocked by a stack of client complaint notices (see Exhibit 17-1 for an example) in the dignified reception area of a large, respected Dallas law firm. I learned later that the availability of such notices was required. More recently, in a jurisdiction where it wasn't mandated, there were pamphlets in the law firm's waiting area detailing how to file a complaint against lawyers.

Upon reflection, I thought the placement of these notices in the reception area, whether by regulation or choice, was a stroke of brilliance. The client could never say that the complaint process was unknown. The firm conveys that it is confident it will handle clients in a manner that will give no cause for complaint. The lawyers and staff at the firm are put on notice that they have to fully satisfy clients and give them no cause to use the toll-free number on the notice.

Now, consider some specific areas in which client complaints may arise.

Example of Notice for Client Complaint Procedure

**ATTORNEY
COMPLAINT
INFORMATION**

NOTICE TO CLIENTS

The State Bar of Texas investigates and prosecutes professional misconduct committed by Texas attorneys.

Although not every complaint against or dispute with a lawyer involves professional misconduct, the State Bar's Office of General Counsel will provide you with information about how to file a complaint.

Please call 1-800-932-1900 toll-free for more information.

THE THEORY OF THE CASE

Have you ever heard an individual say, "That lawyer just is not handling my case properly"? You may even have had clients who came to you from other lawyers give you that rationale about their previous lawyers. In most instances, when we investigate how the case was handled, there certainly was no cause for a malpractice charge, but there may have been good cause to switch lawyers.

What, then, causes the client not to agree with the lawyer's approach to the case? Almost universally it turns out that the complaint is not about how the case is being handled or was handled, but rather how the client is handled.

In most of these instances, it is a lack of effective communication by the lawyer. If the client does not understand the salient points of law as they apply to the client's facts, the client will almost inevitably be distressed with the lawyer's actions. This misunderstanding leaves the client in the same position he or she was in before retaining a lawyer. With that perspective, the client is bound to think that the lawyer, at best, did not understand the case. The lawyer may be acting perfectly rationally and in accordance with ethical standards, precedent, and procedure. However, if the client does not know that, who is responsible or at fault? It surely can't be the client.

Secondly, if the lawyer failed to involve the client in the decision-making process, the client will feel that he or she has no control over the matter, the way it is being handled, or the results. Some methods of involving the client in their legal matters are discussed in Chapter 8, "Involving the Client in the Decision-Making Process." The lack of client involvement in the decisions that are made in the client's matter and the lack of client control provide the breeding grounds for much client dissatisfaction.

RESPONSIVENESS

"That lawyer never tells me anything. The only thing I get from him is bills to pay." A lawyer may be handling a client's matter in an efficient and effective manner. However, if all the client knows about it are the bills that are to be paid, who could blame the client for being angry? This also pertains if clients think, without factual foundation, that they are in the dark. The lawyer must understand and meet what the client perceives is the client's acceptable level of knowledge if the client relations obligations are to be fulfilled. This bar is substantially higher than the ethical and malpractice ones.

The client really has a legitimate need to know. The need to know is not only about the end result, but also about the process and progress. Think about it. If all you saw your lawyer doing was to spend a half day preparing witnesses and one day in a trial, wouldn't you be distressed if the verdict were adverse and the bill high? We need to be more alert to the fact that clients want to know when you are researching the law or talking to the lawyer on the other side of the case. The behind-the-scenes activities of lawyers are the ones least understood by clients and often the ones they most resent finding out existed only when they read the invoice. This need to know is not satisfied by an after-the-fact computer printout at the time a bill is sent or presented to the client.

Lawyers may be handling forty or fifty matters at one time. When you review your time records, you will notice that often there is no action taken on the case of which the client would be cognizant other than by the rendering of a bill. Be alert to these needs of the client and supply the necessary information before billing without the client's having to ask for it or being shocked by the bill. Oral progress reports from secretaries, administrative assistants, and legal assistants are usually quite satisfactory to clients. The nice thing about those reports is that they don't require any additional lawyer time.

Another frequent complaint of clients is that phone calls are not returned. Do you recall how irritated you were as a child when you asked your parent a question that seemed urgent to you, but your parent continued to read the newspaper or wash the dishes without immediately responding? That type of frustration is escalated in adults who are pushed by their schedules and do not hear back from their lawyers. No wonder people like the commercial that asserts, "If I don't return your phone call, you can rest assured I'm probably dead."

Although most lawyers regard the telephone as the bane of their existence, most clients regard it as the prime source of information and relief from legal-matter stress. From the client's point of view, a delayed response to the client's phone call convinces the client that the lawyer is avoiding the client for a catastrophic reason (a bad result, or not doing the client's work frequently pop into clients' minds) or does not regard the client or the client's legal matter as being important.

Many lawyers do not respond promptly to clients' phone calls because nothing of significance has occurred in the case and they are dealing with immediate matters for other clients. We must divorce ourselves from this reality. Instead, substitute the realization that the most important thing to each client is not the legal matter being handled by the lawyer. Rather, it is the recognition of the client as a person. The substance of the telephone call is not nearly as critical as the responsiveness to the client as a person.

E-mails create a more client-perplexing problem than the telephone. Both client and lawyer assume that the other has read an e-mail as soon as it has been sent. If it has not been read, the client's or lawyer's actions and decisions are being made on stale information and may be contrary to the intent and instruction of the other. If the e-mail has been read, but no response sent by the lawyer (a reply could be as simple as "I'll follow up"), the client without software to indicate when the lawyer opened the e-mail is left wondering if the message was even received.

Acknowledging receipt of an e-mail, agreement on a new direction, or disagreement about an instruction must be conveyed to a client. Failure to promptly read and respond to clients' e-mails may result in the client and lawyer singing from different sheets of music to the other side. Such discords are fatal in legal matters. All actions the lawyer can take to prevent this divergence in action, understanding, and perception is critical to the health of client relations.

I have been in the situation where the client has called to discuss something communicated by e-mail. I professed that I didn't know anything about it. The client was incredulous, saying, "I sent you the info in an e-mail an hour ago!" In these circumstances, I've opted to admit I hadn't read the e-mail or kept the conversation going while I pulled it up and read it. You want to avoid having to choose between these options. Both are detrimental to your relationship with your client and increase stress in you.

One suggestion to avoid such situations is to establish an e-mail policy that is discussed with all clients at the outset of representation on each matter and is summarized in the engagement letter. The communications would assure that every client understood how most e-mail messages are opened, read, and if and when a response could usually be expected. The client might also be instructed to call, as well as send an e-mail, if the message is urgent.

If you, as a lawyer, saw your client on the street and said, "Hello, Mr. Client," what would be your emotional state if the client looked you directly in the eye, turned his or her head away while slightly inclining the direction of the nose, and made no verbal response as he or she continued to walk down the street? I suggest to you that the client has the same reaction when we, as lawyers, fail to promptly return telephone calls and e-mail messages. It is not the failure to complete the exchange of information that is the big problem; it is the apparent personal rejection.

Another area in which we must be careful to be responsive is to the substance of the client's questions. When a client asks a question of a lawyer, the client expects an understandable, meaningful answer. Legalese is not the client's native tongue. Also, those answers should not be couched in terms of "on one hand it could be this, and on the other hand it could be that." A client could get a more definitive answer from a Ouija board.

Obviously, not all questions can be given an absolute "yes" or "no." However, it is much more satisfying to the client if the lawyer answers as though speaking to a reasonably intelligent adult, discusses the alternatives and competing influences, and describes percentages of opportunities or risks, and the cost of each. Then, when the client has been educated, suggest a direction and ask for the client's blessing, buy-in, or alternative direction.

One effective technique is for the lawyer to follow the answer with a question to the client. Merely ask, "Is that responsive to your question?" If informed that the answer was not responsive, ask the client to rephrase the question or state what is of concern or not understood. Do not leave the subject until the client confirms that you have been responsive and that response is comprehended.

QUALITY OF SERVICE

Some clients will fight with lawyers or switch to other service providers based on the quality of service received. In this discussion, I am not referring to lawyers who have failed to meet minimum responsive legal ethical standards for services, such as missing a filing deadline. Those lawyers deserve to be disciplined appropriately either by the significant increase in their malpractice insurance, by the local disciplinary and/or ethics board, through appropriate litigation, or all of the preceding means.

When clients fight about the quality of service, they are almost never complaining about the substantive legal decisions the lawyer has made. Almost always the root of the problem can be traced to a failure of the lawyer to properly communicate with a client.

That failure to communicate could involve the theory of the case, the timetable upon which actions would be taken, the lack of responsiveness by the lawyer, or the amount charged. The legal intricacies of a matter rarely enter into a client's evaluation of quality of service. If the client understood the technical legal aspects of a case, the client would never retain a lawyer because the client could handle the matter alone and less expensively.

The simple conclusion is that to avoid the fight-or-switch syndrome with clients, lawyers need to communicate promptly and responsively.

FEES

Have you ever stopped to think why some clients search out lawyers with cheaper fees than their current lawyer, while other clients almost brag about how expensive their lawyers are? What makes the difference?

The difference resides in whether the clients perceive they are getting more value than the fees they are paying.

This is the same theory as a retail sale. If I desire something offered in the department store that costs $15 and I purchase it and it proves to have the benefits of what I thought I was purchasing, I will be satisfied with my purchase. However, if I were able to find the same item in a discount store or on sale in the department store for $10, and I still thought it was worth $15, I would be happy and enthusiastic about my purchase. Similarly, if I spend $5,000 on legal fees for a benefit that I perceive to be worth $10,000, I will be delighted to brag about how much I paid in legal fees. However, if I paid $5,000 and received a value or benefit that I perceived to be worth $2,000 or less, I will regard my lawyer as overpriced. I will resent the fact that I have been taken, especially when I knew of no option to get the service cheaper.

The lawyer's and law firm staff's time does not necessarily equal value to the client. If a client does not receive value, as defined and perceived by the client, in return for the fees charged, the client will switch or fight. A consumer's value of legal services is set only by the client's perception of the worth of those services. The price the lawyer assigns to the service is irrelevant. Value to the client may even be independent of effort, time, and result. Dealing with and influencing the client's perception of worth is therefore a critical part of client relations.

In most instances, the client will have to be taught the value of legal services. Lawyers erroneously assume that the value of their services is as obvious to clients as it is to them. This just can't be when the client doesn't understand the necessity of all the effort the lawyer is expending or the impact of those efforts on the result. Thus, client education during the course of the matter will enhance client understanding and appreciation of the value of the service when the bill arrives.

The root of most fee disputes is planted in the initial discussion with the client. Quoting hourly rates is insufficient because the client has no concept of how many hours it will take to complete a matter. Therefore, it is impossible for the client to have a notion of the amount of the total bill. Quoting an hourly rate with an aggregate fee cap may be extremely dangerous from the law firm's standpoint, because this matter may very well turn out to be more complex than initially described by the client.

Sometimes a combination of those approaches works best. Quote hourly rates with a limit and a clear understanding that the limit may be insufficient to conclude the matter. The lawyer and client enter into an agreement that as the monetary limit is approached, the lawyer will notify the client and the lawyer and client, together, will make a decision on the future course of action.

This approach will protect the client from paying more than antici-pated and the lawyer from putting in more work on the matter than for which he or she will eventually be paid. It also sets the foundation for a series of positive decisions by both parties to continue the relationship on clearly agreed-upon financial terms.

HOW TO AVOID DESTRUCTIVE FIGHTS WITH CLIENTS

A lawyer cannot win a knock-down, drag-out fight with a client over qual-ity of service, fees, or the lawyer's performance. The veracity of this state-ment holds even if the lawyer prevails in a court action. In fact, the only time a lawyer should enter into a knock-down, drag-out fight with a client is if it concerns a serious malpractice allegation that would or could affect the lawyer's license to practice by censor, suspension, or disbarment.

If the lawyer wins the knock-down, drag-out fight, the lawyer still loses. The lawyer obviously loses a client and the confidence of other members of the community to whom the former client speaks. If the local media pick up the dispute, the damage to the lawyer's reputation is more widespread. The lawyer loses the respect of other members of the bar and bench and sometimes the members of the lawyer's firm. The lawyer loses money paid to another lawyer for fees to defend an alleged ethical violation or pursue collection of billed fees. The lawyer loses focus on the practice of law and servicing other clients. It simply is a no-win situation for the lawyer, no matter how correct he or she might be.

Compromise, though we are less able to make it when disputed mat-ters affect us personally rather than clients, is the only reasonable course of action when clients come after lawyers. The ironic fact is that lawyers control practically every circumstance that is necessary to prevent nasty battles with clients. Let's consider a few of those situations.

EXPLANATION

If the lawyer clearly explains up front what is going to happen, what it is going to cost, and keeps the client updated, there is little likelihood of a battle. When things change because of later-discovered facts, new law, or a realization of an honest initial misunderstanding, the lawyer must immediately notify the client and fully disclose and discuss the matter with the client. Then a mutual decision about a future course of action must be made. Even if the course of action is for the client to switch to another lawyer, it is a good result for the initially retained lawyer because the mutual decision minimizes the possibility of a later drawn-out battle. The lawyer first retained is well advised to go the extra mile to cooperate with the client and the replacement lawyer.

Admittedly, some clients are quicker on the uptake with respect to explanations than others. However, from a professional service standpoint, the client who does not fully understand deserves our patient and detailed explanation. From a practical standpoint, that same client is most likely to sue a lawyer or to retain a different lawyer if the full explanation is not understood. So, the additional time a lawyer takes to explain the situation is not at all wasted. Besides, as a professional counselor, this is your duty.

Uncertainty and unwelcome surprise are two events with which the human psyche has great difficulty. A fuller discussion of how to avoid inflicting those circumstances on a client and stimulating the resultant emotional response is detailed in Chapter 10, "Uncertainty—For Lawyer and Client." Even if it is not billable, we lawyers owe it to ourselves, and our profession, to explain so as to reduce uncertainty and protect clients from an unwelcome surprise.

OPEN-DOOR ATMOSPHERE

Too frequently lawyers create an atmosphere in which communications are channeled in one direction: from the lawyer to the client. Even when the lawyer does not attempt to convey his or her superiority in knowledge or station in life, many clients approach lawyers feeling inferior to or intimidated by them.

A client is far less likely to retain a different lawyer or file a complaint against a lawyer if that lawyer successfully creates an open-door atmosphere for the client. When the client feels comfortable discussing his or her concerns with the lawyer, it is less likely that the client will misunderstand and seek help elsewhere. It is also more likely that given another opportunity to understand what concerns the client, the lawyer will be able to convince the client that things are under control. Don't deny yourselves these opportunities by being closed to open two-way communication with the clients.

Clients have discussed such things with me as being dissatisfied with an associate's performance, being treated rudely on the telephone by a secretary, being absolutely frustrated by my own failure to return phone calls, and the amount of the bills. Of course, they were never charged for this discussion time. In fact, I should have paid them.

In one instance, a client alleged that I had interpreted the law incorrectly and had given him advice that amounted to malpractice. I immediately retained another lawyer to research the law and review my advice. I was angered and concerned even though I believed I was correct. The research determined that I clearly was correct and the client was way off base. In spite of that determination, I significantly compromised the fee. The reduced fee rectified the client's perception, even though objectively it was not justified by the facts.

Incidentally, the client insisted I continue to represent him on the matter. As you might imagine, I had zero interest in doing so. Despite my feeling and with the urging of my partner, I chose to see the matter to conclusion for we thought that was the best way to protect against further unfounded accusations. Fortunately, that proved to be the case. Just as clients choose to continue to be represented by lawyers with whom they'd rather not be associated, lawyers must also make similar practical decisions about clients.

Except for the above incident involving alleged malpractice, instead of being upset or defensive about the clients' voicing complaints to me, I was thankful to clients for the complaints. The complaints provided an opportunity to deal with the clients' concerns in a fashion in which I could resolve the issue that was bothersome to them. In all these instances, I was able to retain the clients and learn how to improve service to them. Also, many times the clients talked within the community about how I listened to what they said and took action upon their comments. New clients did comment that they heard from existing clients that I was "a good lawyer and would listen." They expressed this as though if you listened and were a lawyer, you were a good lawyer. We must pay attention to this!

It seems the old saying—we have two ears and only one mouth, which is why we should listen twice as much as we speak—applies to lawyers in client relations.

FEE DISPUTES

Successful businesspeople make compromises every day. They have learned that to compromise a dispute is far cheaper, less distracting to their goals, and measurably more profitable than to enter a battle royal that will burn bridges and destroy future opportunities. With compromise, market share is retained or expanded. Based on this experiential data, the decision for the businessperson centers on the terms of the compromise, not whether there will be one.

Lawyers must learn that collecting every receivable, which was billed for every minute, especially where there is a dispute about the quality of representation, is not an end to be pursued. Graceful compromise preserves the same advantages in the legal marketplace that businesspeople recognize. Entering into a suit or a protracted argument to collect for every moment of time billed is, at best, shortsighted. If it were precisely tallied, one might actually be fighting over the value of time when your associates went down the hall to the bathroom or the time when you went for coffee. Success of legal fee collection litigation most often carries with it the fallout of lost clients, additional costs, decreased income, lost opportunities, bad reputation, and misplaced priorities.

Please don't assume from this that I advocate giving away rightfully earned fees. I constantly rode my partners about recording and billing their time and collecting their receivables in a timely fashion. In some instances, I have found a phone call to a client about an overdue bill, an explanation of the charges, or an offer to work out a payment plan resulted in the full payment of the receivable.

Clients who are strapped for money frequently don't want their lawyer to know they have a financial problem. Many of them believe they have to pay a bill in its entirety or not at all. Your unsolicited offer to work out a payment schedule almost always eases the client's cash-flow problem and improves your cash flow. It also avoids embarrassing the client and builds a better lawyer-client relationship. These offers conclusively demonstrate to the client that you are supportive in more than the legal matter. This is reassuring.

Lawyers who demonstrate some flexibility resolve most fee disputes quickly and amicably. When you are deciding how to deal with fee disputes, take off your hard-working lawyer's hat and put on the hat of a businessperson who wants repeat business. This will assist in appropriately adjusting your view of the situation. Your client will also be appreciative.

SUMMARY

Clients usually expect something to be wrong with their lawyer or the handling of their case. We must accept the fact that clients may look for miscues and, if perceived, would rather switch than fight with their lawyers. Lawyers can best minimize the desire of clients to switch by effective, thorough communication on the legal and business aspects of the lawyer-client relationship. Ignoring complaints, dealing with complaints ineffectively, and not pursuing rapport-building opportunities are chief causes of both the fight and switch reactions in clients.

When the client wants to fight, the lawyer's victory will almost always be found in compromise.

CHAPTER 18

"ALL ABOARD"— THE SERVICE QUALITY TRAIN

Assurance of quality service or positive client relations is not passed automatically from one lawyer generation to the next. Witness those thriving practices that have been purchased from a venerable, client-oriented solo practitioner who is retiring. Many fail to retain their economic vigor because the client relations bond has been broken or the purchaser was unable to make the necessary commitments to keep the clients engaged with the same intensity of client relations. Awareness and training in client relations are essential to avoid this devastating outcome.

When complaints about Miami cab drivers were running rampant, taxi companies instituted a five-hour course called "Miami Nice." The course simply taught cabbies how to act nicer to passengers. It quickly reduced the complaints by 80 percent. Even the American Management Association was receiving a substantial number of complaints about servicing its membership. Three hours of training reduced the number of complaints by 82 percent. Obviously, a little bit of training can do a whole lot of good.

The saying, "If at first you don't succeed, try, try again" is great to apply in most client relations circumstances. For instance, a survey has revealed that salespeople usually make 80 percent of their sales after their fifth call in a day. Client relations improvement training should be continuous and may be found to bring measurable improvement only after a number of refinements in training techniques are tried over a period of time.

Absolutely, it will be really tough to get all of your partners and associates on board the service quality train. Have you considered that even if you did accomplish getting them aboard, there would still be a big crowd left standing on the station platform? That nonlawyer staff is as much needed as the partners and associates to cement effective client relations. A successful client relations–service quality team includes, at a minimum, the following:

Receptionists	Messengers	Information Specialists
Legal Assistants	Law Clerks	Investigators
Secretaries	Librarians	File Clerks
Paralegals	Office Managers	Research Assistants
Proofreaders	Marketing Directors	Billing Clerks
Bookkeeping-Accounting	Administrators-Executive	Administrative Assistants
Communication Directors	Word Processors	Cleaning Personnel
Controllers	Systems Administrators	

All of these job classifications and any others you have in your practice, regardless of whether they are employees or independent contractors, have potential to make contributions to the quality of service given to clients, even if they have no direct client contact. All connected directly or indirectly with your practice need to constantly strive to do their best in client relations. Their functions are integrated and must all work cooperatively to have an efficient client-service team.

Some have written that the service quality process is a top-down process. It is true—the top people in the law firm, law department, solo practice, or government office must set the policy and direction. They must also demonstrate their commitment to the process by their actions. They must identify the goal to be accomplished and the resources to be committed to the project.

The top management's function might be defined as follows:

1. Set the goal;
2. Specify the minimum and maximum resource commitment in terms of money, people, and time;
3. Designate how progress is to be measured (accountability); and
4. Provide resources, examples, encouragement, and reinforcement (leadership).

Having all of the above essentials from the top management of the organization doesn't guarantee a good service quality program. The most effective service quality–client relations programs are instituted from the top down and implemented from the bottom up.

Implementing from the bottom is necessary because the client's perception of service quality frequently is driven as much or more by support staff than by lawyers. Unfortunately, it is often hard for support staff (and for lawyers) to understand and accept their key role and potential for contributing to the clients' service quality team. This pertains whether you are a solo or a member of the world's largest law firm.

THE IMPORTANCE OF SUPPORT STAFF

A few examples of how the support staff affects service quality perceptions of clients might serve to clarify this concept.

If a lawyer is unable to return a phone call and a secretary calls to tell the client the lawyer is out of the office and asks when the lawyer might get back to the client, the client is reassured that the organization cares. Staffpersons who take the initiative to say the lawyer is in trial but may be calling in, and offer to relay a message, are much appreciated by clients. The bookkeeping-accounting department contributes by ensuring that the correct bill is going to the client, payments are accurately credited, and promptly obtaining resolution of any questions about charges. Clients, as we all know, are sensitive to billing and if they are inadvertently charged for a service for which they have already paid, they will be doubly unhappy. Even if they eventually get the billing mistake rectified, clients will think lax standards are acceptable throughout that law practice.

THE RECEPTIONIST

Years ago, in a relatively small firm, when we hired our first businessperson as a firm administrator, he knocked me off my feet with an early observation. He stated that when he had been in sales and was calling on different businesses, his first impression of the business came from the receptionist who answered the phone and greeted the visitors. He recalled how the receptionists who conveyed that they cared about callers and visitors gave the business a far superior image than businesses with gum-chewing, magazine-reading, "I-can't-be-bothered" receptionists. The use of his name really impressed him when he went into different offices.

I could understand all of that. He then pointed out that we used our receptionist position as the entry-level position for the newest and least-knowledgeable employee in the law firm. She was unfamiliar with the work and uncertain as to whom was who in the firm. Most disconcerting was she didn't know the clients. By the time she was getting to know the clients, we usually promoted her to a secretarial position where she had less client contact. But, if a recently hired receptionist didn't have the skills to become a secretary, we left her as the receptionist. Consequently, the receptionist job became a high turnover position for all but the less competent.

Our administrator continued, "Clients like to know who they'll be talking with when they call and who they'll see when they visit. Clients are thrilled if the receptionist can identify their voice on the phone before they state their name. There is no way that can happen the way you run people through the receptionist position. You should hire a highly skilled receptionist and pay that person well to stay in that position. Your clients will love it."

Of course, he was right. Think of those offices where you are immediately recognized. It makes you feel good and puts you at ease. We changed our musical chairs receptionist policy. Interestingly, not only did the clients notice and appreciate the change, but also all of the folks in the firm felt it aided the internal organization and brought some previously unknown degree of calm to the outer office for them. As a result of having the greatest opportunity for brief but frequent client contact, the receptionist may be the Most Valuable Player on your service quality–client relations team.

LEGAL SECRETARIES

Now, let's take a look at a secretarial service quality breakdown that occurred in my practice, which I dearly hope never occurs in your office. In a critical case that was shortly coming to trial for an important client, I decided it was essential to let the client know the strengths and weaknesses of our case so that the client would be fully prepared to make decisions in the ongoing settlement discussions. I set forth with great detail the weaknesses as well as the strengths of our case. This was a case that was referred to me by another lawyer in another law firm, and so it was my habit to send a copy of correspondence to that referring lawyer. There were standing instructions in the file to send such copies.

My secretary knew that she was always to send a copy to the lawyer who referred her or his client's work to us. She routinely got an address from the file, typed an envelope with the referring lawyer's name and address on it, inserted a copy of my letter to the client, and mailed it. Unfortunately, the name and address she copied from the file on this particular occasion was that of the opposing lawyer rather than the referring lawyer. While the opposing lawyer was absolutely ethical and gracious about returning the letter to me with a note, saying "I don't think this was intended for me," the quality of service had significantly been reduced by the secretary's mistake. Simultaneously, the level of my embarrassment rose to new heights.

All people in the legal organization have an opportunity to contribute positively or negatively to the quality of service received by the clients. Some people—at the top, middle and bottom of the firm— just don't recognize positive and negative opportunities, their frequency, or the magnitude of their importance. Everyone should be encouraged, and actually required, to participate by being active in quality improvement.

Some years ago, I bought a new suit and was struck by the number of quality checks and the obvious level of participation the management had built into the suit-manufacturing process. In virtually every pocket, one or more workers in the suit assembly process placed a slip certifying the quality of their work. The "tickets" are shown in Exhibit 18-1 so that you get the feel for the number of checks that were performed.

For the detail-oriented lawyers among you, I have no idea why there are sequential numbers missing. Either they were used only in more-expensive or vested suits, some quality inspections weren't done, some quality standards weren't met, or the certifying confetti was still in the suit after numerous wearings and cleanings. In any case, the sleeves haven't fallen off and the suit seems to be fine.

Ask yourself, "What quality checks do I have for the legal work and client relations activities we perform?" As importantly, "What evidence do we provide to clients that any quality checks have occurred?" If the client doesn't get a quality check slip and doesn't know about the quality check, why would the client be willing to pay for undocumented quality checks? Without some physical indicator, there is no way the client knows you care about the quality of the legal work being performed for the client. The only thing the client knows is how much time you put in, which has nothing to do with the quality of the work product.

Make no mistake about it: secretaries are very important to how well your office functions and to the clients' and potential clients' impression of your law practice.

While speaking on the same educational program as another corporate counsel, I was thunderstruck by the brilliance of his approach to evaluating whether to engage a lawyer to represent the insurance company where he was general counsel. Besides assessing the lawyers by investigating their reputations with opposing counsel, reviewing their trial records and evaluating their briefs, he added an unusual, if not unique, step. The

Clothing Inspection Tickets

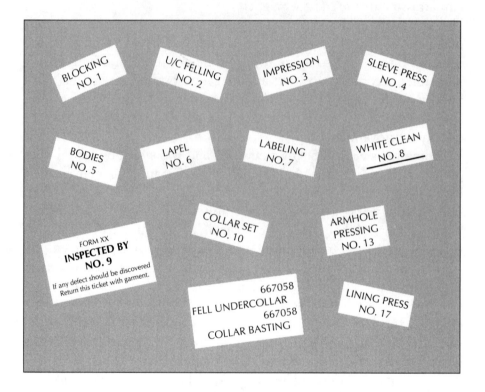

general counsel described his process as always including a visit to the lawyer's office rather than having the "beauty contest" in his office. His purpose was to see if the office was organized and efficient.

The primary gauge of the level of organization and efficiency in the law office was whether the legal secretaries displayed those qualities. He spent time observing them work and talking with them about the scope of their responsibilities. By gathering this information from secretaries, he credibly concluded he could determine if the whole office was organized and whether the lawyer could represent the insurance carrier with competent, efficient, quality work.

This insightful corporate counsel reasoned that if the secretaries weren't well organized, clients' matters couldn't be handled in a cost-effective manner. Brilliant! Think about it. When you as a lawyer have a well-organized secretary, you practice law much more efficiently. Cost of legal services and quality of representation certainly tilt in favor of the client if lawyers work with well-organized secretaries and other staff who are given appropriate responsibilities. As you may suspect, the speaker is a very, very successful corporate counsel.

The point of this is to remind you that with greater participation comes greater pride in the finished work product. This will also translate into better service quality. I'm NOT suggesting a set of rubber stamps to be impressed on every pleading, Agreement of Sale, and letter reading:

```
                          Inspected By:

        No. 5   Secretary:   John
        No. 4   Paralegal:   Richard
        No. 1   Associate:   Chloe
        No. 2   Associate:   Ward
        No. 4   Partner:     Kimberly Q. Rainmaker
```

At a minimum, you can and should have appropriate accountability methods within the organization that measure and recognize the quality an individual puts into each task. Secondly, it pays to make clients aware of the checks your office uses to assure it is turning out a quality product for your clients.

Gluing the client to the lawyer and the law practice cannot be achieved without the secretaries and the rest of the staff being fully on board.

QUALITY MEASURES

Output and number of mistakes per unit of output have been measured by industry for many years. Often, this ratio is used as a measure of quality with the object of reducing the number of mistakes and thus positively affecting the ratio. In the legal service business those calculations are relatively easy to complete for secretarial work. The ratio is harder to apply to lawyers' work but not impossible. For instance, the number of drafts it takes a lawyer to arrive at a final document is one measure. Reduction in the number of drafts saves the solo, law department, or firm the time of people in the organization and thereby increases the profit in private practice or frees the time to do other work in government and corporate law departments. It also delivers the product quicker and cheaper, which improves the client's service quality. There are many other possible measures, which may be more appropriate for and have greater impact in your office.

Even if the law organization does not have such a service quality program, individuals within these organizations who adopt one for their own use will soon find their workload more manageable, their satisfaction level higher, and their work life less stressful. Doing the right things to satisfy the client's needs correctly the first time is its own reward in many different ways.

Ultimately, the best judge of quality is the person who pays for it. Client surveys, as simple as an oral question or several pages of written queries, will be a better gauge of client satisfaction than assuming or guessing how the client feels about the service being provided. "What did we do well?" "How can we improve?" These straightforward inquiries usually provide a wealth of information to improve your processes and your client relations. Interestingly, a comment is rarely made in such surveys about the "quality" of a document. Most of those observations pertain to typos or the lack of them. This is additional confirmation that client's quality criteria are far different from those of lawyers.

Unless people believe, they will not act. Belief in a client-relations program is a critical element to a successful one. A capable but under-performing child must first believe he or she can do better in school or another activity before the child will ever be able to perform commensurate with his or her capabilities. If law offices and law department staffs do not believe in striving for top-quality representation and client relations, that improvement is possible, and if they don't understand on a personal level that they can make a difference for themselves and the practice, behaviors will never change.

As individuals, we become what we believe we are. We need also to know that actions implementing desirable beliefs are recognized and rewarded. Those recognitions and rewards are needed to reinforce the discipline to continue behaviors that support those beliefs. Individuals will respond by actively seeking other desirable behavior, that is, other improvements in quality client relations.

We opened Chapter 2 with one of the great techniques of sports training: visualization. Athletes are encouraged to visualize a perfect performance. This has been found to be critical for the athlete obtaining the execution of that perfect performance. The visualizer sees how to make the physical moves, then through instruction and practice comes to believe he or she can do it. Finally, using repetition and practice the athlete causes the body to duplicate the visualized moves. For instance, an ice skater must visualize a jump before he or she can do it. A mechanical execution of moves illustrated in a manual is not enough; the athlete must visualize himself or herself making these moves before they can be expertly, or even smoothly, executed.

Likewise, if the management—it matters not if it's the managing partner, the legal administrator, or a senior administrative assistant—tells a junior staffperson to carefully proofread everything before giving it to the lawyer, you will find in many cases that even where there is tacit compliance, there will still be mistakes. Why? One explanation is that the proofreader has not visualized how important his or her role is in either the substantive work or in the client relations process. If it is futile or an individual doesn't understand that the action makes a difference, it doesn't matter to an individual. Perhaps, the proofreader has not understood or visualized what personal action and attention it takes to accomplish quality proofreading. In essence, the staffperson has not internalized the method, the importance, and the value of proofreading.

Internalizing the value of proofreading means that the proofreader believes and has internalized the fact that she or he is an important part of servicing the client and has visualized the best method to accomplish the most foolproof way to ensure that no mistakes will appear on the paper. Rarely will a page produced by individuals who have internalized these values and envisioned the importance of their roles contain a typographical error.

INTERNALIZING THE VALUE OF SERVICE

How do you get someone to internalize the value of the superior quality of service? I truly don't know. Everyone is different so it requires a different approach for every individual to reach a common goal. However, I do know a few principles and methods have worked for a number of people.

My wife, Mary, has often said to me, "Well, I'm no mind reader," when I say I thought she should have known what I wanted. Fortunately, the frequency of such comments has declined over the years of our marriage. Either she has become a better mind reader or I have gained more confidence to say what I wanted and to be clear about it.

There is no doubt that we all love to have our behavioral expectations anticipated and fulfilled. Unfortunately, this serendipitous experience is infrequent. And, in an organization where instead of two persons there are many, fulfillment of unexpressed desires or requirements becomes even more unlikely. Obviously, more formal methods of communication and behavior modification are required as the number of people seeking a common behavior increases. The method of communication that worked so well when the firm had two lawyers is likely to fail when it has grown to ten lawyers.

If you hit the bull's-eye on a target but could not see the target, the accomplishment was achieved through dumb luck. In order to move group behavior to a higher level of service quality, the leaders of the group must clearly define the target. They must spotlight that target so all can see it, whether viewing it from the senior partner's office or the file clerk's chair.

Many leaders in law firms and law departments will respond to this request to define client services quality by taking one Supreme Court justice's approach to pornography: "I can't define it, but I know it when I see it." Maybe you will know it. That, however, will not provide any assistance to others in your organization who are struggling to define the term so that they can get with the program. Besides, everyone in the organization must share the same definition. Otherwise, with each pursuing an individual definition of quality there are likely to be countervailing efforts resulting in only accidental institutional progress in quality improvement.

Similarly, communicating a definition such as "We want to be known as the most service-oriented professional organization in town" is of little practical use. Each person in your organization attributes an individual meaning to this generality and pursues a unique and divergent role on this service quality team. A specific, not a generalized, direction as to how to change their behavior is required if each is to contribute significantly to improving service quality for clients.

Usually, when initially discussing improvements in client service, neither lawyers nor staff will be able to define specific actions they should take to improve client relations. This stems from the fact that no matter how badly you think another in your organization is servicing clients, that other person usually thinks he or she is doing a fine job. This is just as you do when thinking about your own client relations. It is often helpful to hear directly from clients.

INVOLVING KEY PEOPLE

As a leader of change or key contributor in an organization, if you do not convert grandiose goal statements to spelled-out, specific step-by-step expectations of and commitment to behavioral changes for each person working in the organization, there is little chance that those individuals will ever understand what is desired, let alone be able to accomplish it. Organizational improvements result from a critical mass of individuals within the entity changing behaviors, not from generalized quality improvement slogans. The change plan is the vehicle by which the organization gets most of those willing to change to pursue coordinated implementation actions.

Further, if the leaders and supervisors of these individuals don't involve each employee in defining an improved service standard for the employee's job, the individual is unlikely to internalize the desired behavioral change. Many an individual at every level of an organization has visualized improved service quality for his or her job long before being asked by management how it could be improved.

For instance, many lawyers, doctors, and accountants have become convinced that they could better serve their clients by purchasing or leasing a variety of technologically superior machines and software. I recognized the vast improvements in service that could be gained by switching from typing to word processing in the 1970s. Convincing my partner to spend what was then a significant amount of money on new equipment was not the easiest advocacy job I ever undertook. It was accomplished and he eventually enthusiastically signed on. On behalf of our law firm, I purchased an automatic typewriter with very limited word memory and processing capabilities. The limited capabilities kept the cost down. As the salesman pitched to me on the lower cost (compared to a mag card machine), he also sold me on the expanding capacity feature, which would cost us only when required for future needs. The equipment could be upgraded to much more sophisticated word processing capabilities with additional modules with what is now known as software. I selected this "major breakthrough in technology" from a manufacturer whose main source of income was from oil and gasoline. In a very limited way, the breakthrough worked—I think the memory capacity was 800 characters.

After a couple of months the secretaries told me this thing was a toy and they needed greater capacity. I called the salesperson who had sold me on the idea of adding increased capacity at a low cost when it was needed. The response I got from dialing the salesperson's number was a recording: "The number you have dialed is no longer in service. Calls are being taken at 555-1212." Not only was the phone not in service but also the scarcity of imported oil had rocketed the domestic price, so the petroleum company had dropped out of the word processing business to concentrate on making profits from retail gas pumps instead of keyboards.

If I had initially involved the secretaries, the ones who were going to use the equipment, they would have saved our firm that investment.

They would have spotted the fatal flaw that the system was too limited to be very useful. Then they would have told me. I tried to make decisions about equipment to be used by people whose jobs I didn't know except in a very macro sense. This parallels lawyers trying to tell clients what they have to do when they don't know the individual's situation or the company's business.

I did not learn my lesson and this temporary setback did not stop me on my goal to service clients better through greatly improved technology. Undaunted, and unfortunately, unchanged from my first learning experience in technology, I selected a stand-alone word processing machine that looked much like the "work-saving" mangles sold to housewives in the 1940s and 1950s to save them from the drudgery of using an iron. This thing had unlimited storage capacity (mag cards), so I felt very confident I had not repeated my mistake. Besides, it was manufactured in Europe. The salesperson said I was purchasing technology with a worldwide reputation. This company had its own sales and service department, for which I was grateful. I ordered one, announced it to the lawyers and staff, and regaled them with how we could use this gray wizard to produce documents faster for our clients and save the secretaries and word processors work on revisions.

The installation day arrived. The office air was alive with expectation and excitement. The staff and lawyers gathered around to admire the machine and see new horizons explored before their very eyes through a demonstration by the installer. The technician finished the assembly and adjustments. His demonstration of the machine's capability was impressive. Then our best word processor sat down at the machine as though she were a concert pianist about to perform. She placed her talented fingers on the keyboard with a smile of anticipation. She banged out a sentence. She gasped, turned to me with a look of horror, and said, "Mr. Ewalt, the keys are placed differently than on our American typewriters!"

My stomach dropped to the level of my toenails. All eyes of the assembled turned on me. Some of the lawyers' gazes seared through my head like hot pokers through butter. How was I to know that the Europeans arranged the letters on their keyboards differently? Just at that moment our crack typist said to me, "Oh, but don't worry, I can learn this keyboard real quick." Indeed she did, and saved me "real quick"!

The point of these real-life experiences in law firm and client service improvements is to illustrate the folly of having any process improvements driven and made exclusively from the top down. Initiative, commitment, evaluation, encouragement, participation, and resources should come from the top. The specific steps must be a joint decision between those at the top and those who are expected to implement the improvement. Had I known this principle in the 1970s, our typists would have saved me from buying an oil company's typewriter with less "memory" than what was in their heads and a European word processor requiring crazy fingering.

While legal administrators and executives hired by professional organizations provide some assurance that such lawyer-caused fiascoes don't occur, they are not fail-safe. The leadership of the legal organization must maintain constant vigilance to assure that the administrators always involve the implementers in service quality decisions before a decision to change equipment or a process is made. This involvement of the implementers will reduce mistakes, increase commitment, save money, and speed adoption of the process. In short, it will enable the organization to actually improve client service.

When I was in the law department of a corporation, one of my responsibilities was for litigation across the United States and some additional cases in foreign countries. The volume of litigation, and other matters, being handled by the law department was tremendous. The Deputy General Counsel recognized that significantly upgrading our computer system was the most economical way to manage the ever-increasing workload.

Those charged with evaluating the technology options took an enlightened approach. They came to the department managers and asked what information we needed to manage the people and legal matters. Then they went to the secretaries and administrators to find out how much of that information we were currently capturing. They deduced what additional information needed to be gathered. The processes and technology necessary to obtain all of the requested information was then designed by nonlawyer managers, accountants, secretaries, administrators, information specialists, and computer consultants. This bottom-up design process assured that the implementation phase went smoothly and had buy-in from those who had the day-to-day responsibility for gathering the information. The managers accepted the new system because they got the information they needed.

Our internal corporate clients, the General Counsel, Chief Financial Officer, and Chief Executive Officer were pleased because we were able to strengthen the predictability of the financial consequences of the litigation and other matters. If only the lawyer-managers had designed the system, the implementation period would have been many times longer and the probability of the reports being satisfactory to our clients, greatly reduced.

Here is another illustration of the benefits of getting everyone on board. Earlier in my career, a small firm with which I was practicing agreed to purchase an older solo practitioner's workers' compensation practice when the solo made it known that he wanted to reduce the amount of time he spent practicing law. The practice consisted exclusively of representing insurance companies that insured employers against workers' compensation injuries and losses.

This solo practitioner had a secretary who, in addition to typing, arranged for all of the workers' comp hearings. Today she would be known as an administrative assistant or paralegal. She was very highly paid, and we had no need for an additional secretary. However, the solo practitioner adamantly insisted that as part of selling his practice, she would have to be hired with no reduction of her high rate of pay. The projected immediate economics of the solo's practice were not such that the highly paid secretary could be covered. As a firm, we also fretted about what word of her salary would do to our lower-paid secretaries' morale. Even more frightening was what it might do to our secretaries' pay expectations and the existing salary scale.

At a partnership meeting there was a great split as to whether we should proceed with the deal or not. Some of the partners were opposed. Others wanted the practice for the potential and thought it was worth acquiring in spite of the inordinate compensation paid to the secretary. Still others seemed to just want to practice with their old friend. After much debate, we made a bare majority decision to buy the practice.

The former solo whom we banked on bringing the insurance companies' loyalty and business to our firm died a very short time after we bought his practice. We five partners were all frightened that we would lose all of our investment in his practice because we had not had enough time to build alliances with the insurance companies.

When we called the insurance companies to inform them of the death of the former solo practitioner and to explain (plead) that we would still like to serve as their counsel, we were taken aback by the response. Every insurance company asked us if the highly paid secretary was going to remain with the firm. We responded that we did not anticipate any change, and their response was that as long as she remained they would not drop our law firm for another. The insurance carriers said that she was the most efficient, courteous, competent, caring person that they dealt with anywhere in the United States. She arranged for hearings, prepared cases, and made them look good by assisting in setting reserves and achieving better settlement results than anticipated. True to their word, not a single insurance company switched law firms. We suddenly and dramatically found out why she was so well paid by the former solo practitioner—she was his client relations specialist . . . and his practice.

Some corporate clients are now requiring a computer interface between themselves and the law firms they retain. When faced with that prospect, my response has been, "It's okay with me if you get it worked out with our computer people." Instead of my getting into the middle of the technology—and getting it all fouled up—I get the systems administrators from the corporation and law firm together to work out the details. If our systems administrator fails to take a cooperative approach, it is very bad for client relations. So, the instructions to the systems administrator are simply, "Make it work and be nice." Smaller firms may have to engage an outside consultant for the interface. If so, the instructions should be the same.

These illustrations should clearly prove beyond any reasonable doubt that secretaries and other staffpersons in the law firm and law department have an important role to play in client quality assurance and client relations. Just like clients, they need to be involved in decisions to maximize their commitment and contribution to the practicality of implementing changes.

Your whole organization, whether it be a government legal office, corporate law department, law firm, or solo practice, must be client-oriented. Weak links in that chain are devastating to the very purpose for which the organization exists. If the receptionist has a bad day and is not pleasant with a client, the client reacts negatively to the whole organization, including you, the lawyer.

Support staff are critical because lawyers need help eliminating impediments to a client calling or coming to see them. If contact with the staff encourages clients to use legal services, the staff adds significant value to the organization through good client relations.

HIRING HELP

One of the greatest and most enjoyable challenges that I have been privileged to undertake in my professional career is starting a two-person law practice with a very fine individual, Ted Brooks. Gratefully, our practice grew rapidly and we soon saw the need for an additional lawyer. The specific needs and thus duties for the third lawyer were to do the research and writing support work that we did not have time to do because of our ever-expanding client contact time.

We hired an individual who had an excellent academic record capped by his service on the law review of his nationally recognized law school. Our intent was that the individual would be used exclusively in backroom law firm operations. Researching and writing were his intended limits of responsibility. Shortly after he was hired, he had to be pressed into service to cover for Ted and me when we had irresolvable conflicts in our schedules thanks to our rapidly expanding client base and increasing demand from existing clients.

The clients reacted poorly to the new associate. At the same time, our practice continued to grow at such a rate that there was unrelenting pressure on us to use him more and more in client-contact situations. It became apparent to us that we could not grow if we were unable to use this lawyer and every future associate in client-contact situations. We also became painfully aware that a few clients were threatening to take their business elsewhere if they had to deal with this associate one more time.

This unfortunate situation existed because Ted and I had misjudged our needs and the essential requirements of every practice. Belatedly, we realized that our real primary need was for an associate who would be appreciated by our clients and who could also research and write. Think how much more valuable it would have been if, instead of an associate, we had hired a administrative or legal assistant who engendered the client reaction that the workers' compensation practice's secretary was able to elicit from the insurance companies.

What lessons about hiring can I convey to you to assist in your service quality or client-relations team effort?

First, when considering hiring a support staff person, an associate, or a lateral-transfer lawyer, visualize the reaction of three of your key clients upon meeting that person. Even though your technical needs might be served well by that person, if you think the interpersonal reaction will be negative or even neutral, do not hire that candidate. Everyone in your office must augment continually improving client relationships.

Second, keep in the forefront of your mind that no purely library type or technical type need apply for any position in your organization. This maxim is true whether the individual will ever meet a client or not. It also pertains regardless of the size of the organization. In a large organization where the chances of an individual coming into contact with the client are remote, you still do not want this type of individual on your team. These academic or technocrat individuals usually are not service-oriented. While they may "get their hours in," those hours are likely to be of lesser immediate value to the client, which, in the long run, makes them of very limited value to the legal service organization. Further, hires lacking people skills will not contribute to team cohesion within your office structure.

Additionally, if individuals are not people-oriented and service-oriented, they probably are not coachable in client relations. Even if one is not in contact with clients on a day-to-day basis, a client-oriented person is far more likely to suggest and adapt to improvements that will further client relations. This will advance the law organization, not just the individual. Becoming a contributing member of your service quality team should be the salient criterion for working in your organization.

TRAINING

Everywhere between hiring and discharge or retirement there should be a significant commitment to training individuals. Government organizations and corporations are usually much more oriented toward training than law firms. Nevertheless, the need for training and development in client relations is universal.

Client surveys that show 24 percent of the clients who leave law firms do so because of unadjusted fee disputes. Lawyers and staff should be trained in how to comfortably adjust fees, just as they are trained to seek and complete additional work. They must realize and internalize that their practice will grow chiefly through referrals of new clients made by existing clients. Marketing has to be incorporated into relations with existing clients. This is something much more than romancing potential clients until you get them in the door, then only addressing their legal work. Service quality and client relations must be smoothly flowing with no fits and starts. All must continuously explore ways to serve clients better and to develop stronger relationships with them.

Formal training in communications, interpersonal relationships, and other people-to-people techniques is important. Probably even more important is to catch someone doing something good for client relations. Publicize that within the organization; reward it with days off or money or additional recognition; mention it in a letter to the person's supervisor and/or to the client. Be sure the person you are rewarding receives a copy of all such correspondence and appropriate recognition.

We will not all become super rainmakers, but we should at least all be able to engage in the process of mist making. Such things as keeping in touch, expressing thanks, performing work on time, establishing frequent preventive legal communications and asking clients for feedback on how you and the firm or department are doing are all things that everybody can do. They all contribute to an effective, proactive client-relations program.

Simple things that take only a few minutes, such as clipping articles about the client's industry and sending them to interested clients, demonstrate that the lawyers and the law organization are interested in the client and the client's business. Attaching a note to a clipping about a client and stating that you are pleased to see the client is doing so well in such a competitive industry is encouraging to the client and much appreciated.

Asking staff members how billing or processing of documents or generally communicating with the client could be improved is another step in the right direction. Most of the time, lawyers are so concerned about the legal aspects of a matter that they are unable to devote sufficient attention to process improvement. Seek and obtain the assistance of staff in this area. They are capable of more than they feel you want them to do. Process improvement—reducing the steps and speeding the time delivering the product to the client—produces the double benefit of servicing the client and increasing profit (or reducing cost in government law departments).

Steal ideas from successful retailers. Employees of top service-oriented retailers are uniformly thoroughly trained and execute customer relations matters well. Oftentimes, they do not give the answer the customer seeks, but they are always courteous. That means the customer rarely has a complaint against anyone personally even though the customer may still be upset with the product or service provided. If a dissatisfied individual has no complaint about the personal treatment received, the chances of the individual accepting the employee's answer or not pursuing a complaint about the lawyer in another forum are increased immeasurably.

For a few, these client service efforts come naturally. For most, the opportunities for building client relations must be spelled out. For all, improvements in whatever they are doing for client relations are possible. Training is the universal vehicle for improvement.

DISCHARGING PEOPLE WHO DO NOT UNDERSTAND CLIENT RELATIONS

On some occasions during my career I have attempted to work around a nonclient–oriented person. This has always turned out to be a mistake; do not make it.

If there is any truth to the premise that client relations and service quality build the professional reputation, and that reputation is built on what the client thinks and feels about you and your organization, the key differentiating business element is building the client relationship. This differentiation has been labeled *branding* by some writers. In law practice, if the quality of client service is high enough, clients and potential clients will buy services of that organization—and not consider other suppliers—because the name of the organization has been established as a brand name in client service quality.

When an individual lacks the capacity or the will to build client relationships, whether in the role of partner, associate, shareholder, or staff, the individual is a detriment to your department, firm, or practice. This is a truth for staff that has no client contact for they become an impediment to communication and cooperation within your organization. The road to establishing a client service brand is a difficult one and all need to help one another in traveling it.

The key is to people your organization with individuals who are intent on and enjoy building relationships with the clients. Through these people, the client will be (1) conditioned to recognize competence, and (2) made to understand that the relationship with the lawyer and the organization is more important than the result on any one particular legal matter.

In making this statement I am assuming basic competence of each individual for the technical aspects of the job. I am not advocating a flim-flam client-relations program with legally incompetent gladhanders. That, in itself, both marks and masks legal incompetence, which cannot be tolerated in any form by any element in the legal profession.

If one discovers that someone incompetent in client relations has been hired, the steps of evaluation, coaching, discussion, training, warning, action plan, reevaluation, and discharge if adequate improvement is not made, are all recommended. Occasionally, individuals are able to make acceptable improvement in a short period of time. Everybody in your organization should understand that client relations is not an on-again, off-again endeavor and that a high level of performance on the client-relations front is expected and must be constantly practiced.

The time frame for giving someone an opportunity to improve in the service quality process should be limited, while at the same time adequate to provide a reasonable opportunity to make the necessary behavior modifications. The specific limits on time are necessary for the organization to guard against the individual causing significant, long-term harm to the client-relations reputation, and therefore to the organization.

The actual length will vary with the circumstances. For instance, if your organization gets 30 percent of its receipts from a client who says that a particular person "offends me; if you don't get rid of him, I'll take my business elsewhere," the time frame probably needs to be pretty short—maybe about half an hour. Yes, I do mean that under certain egregious circumstances, a breakdown in service quality is cause for immediate, summary discharge of a lawyer or staff member.

There are many individuals who are legally competent and personally friendly but who are still unable to develop positive client relations. For example, clients have complained about a lack of decisiveness in some associates. Some very bright associates who have done extremely well in law school, but have tried to carry the law review and law school examination Socratic process into practice, have this syndrome. Usually, the opinions of these persons are characterized as advising that maybe the client could do this, or maybe the client ought to do that. When that type of lawyer asks me expectantly, "What did the client think about my answer?", I ask, " What would you think if you came to a professional for an answer and guidance and got neither?" The same holds true for staff responses to clients and lawyers.

In other instances, individual lawyers have been bright and articulate with a good presence but failed to return phone calls, did not produce according to client instructions or expectations, took too much time to complete projects, and/or did not perform on time. Even if an individual with those shortcomings has extraordinary research talents, writes well, and possesses good analytical abilities, that lawyer is not acceptable to clients. Whether clients tell you or not, the lawyer needs to be separated from your organization if significant improvement is not forthcoming in a reasonable period of time.

Please note, these comments do not include lawyers or staff who have a difficult time with one client. That may be a genuine personality clash and not evidence that a person lacks client relations skills. Rushing to judgment based on a single client's complaint may be very unfair to the accused and cause the organization to separate a valuable contributor. When true personality clashes have occurred, I have made reassignments of lawyers serving particular clients. That usually resolved the situation.

I recall two instances in which clients complained and I refused to discharge or transfer the lawyer. The first was when a client told me that he wanted a different lawyer because didn't want a "woman lawyer" representing his business. I inquired as to whether the client had any complaint about the quality of the advice, and the client answered, "No." I told the client that the lawyer was a very good one, that I would not change her, that what he was saying was unlawfully discriminatory, and that he should adjust his attitude to be fair. I suggested that he judge her on the advice she gave him instead of her gender. Since this was a corporate client, he couldn't reveal his discriminatory attitude, so he did work with her. Six months or so later he told me that she was really helpful.

About a year later, because of some changes in personnel, I announced a reassignment of the lawyer to a different business. The client called me to complain about her reassignment. I spoke with her and she said she too would like to continue with that client. I restored her assignment to represent the business unit that initially rejected her solely on her gender. Clients can be educated, and lawyers must insist on what is fair regardless of the client relations risks.

The second instance where I refused to transfer a lawyer arose when the client complained on several occasions about a number of small oversights that irritated the client. I investigated and got back to the client saying that I didn't think the matters were of consequence and that the lawyer was carrying an extremely heavy load. The client continued to raise such issues. One complaint of potential consequence was that the lawyer didn't present a certain piece of evidence in a proceeding. When I checked with the lawyer, he confirmed that he hadn't presented the evidence that would have been helpful. He added that he couldn't present it because the client, in spite of being asked for every written record during preparation, didn't give it to him and he never saw the document until after the hearing.

It finally dawned on me that the client wasn't really complaining about the quality of lawyering, but was disguising his prejudice against African-American lawyers. I refused to provide a different lawyer. I called the client and told him I understood that he had not given the document to the lawyer until after the hearing. He confirmed that. Since I didn't have any hard evidence of discrimination and the lawyer wasn't adversely affected, I didn't confront the client on the discrimination issue. But, I told him that I thought something else was at the root of his complaints and if there were more complaints they had better be valid or I'd have to search for the root of them. The client was well aware of what I meant.

I then candidly discussed the situation with the lawyer and told him to alert me to any indication that he was being treated unfairly. Neither the lawyer nor I ever received any more complaints. Obviously, this was not a situation where a lawyer lacked client relations skills.

True deficiencies in client relations will show up in a variety of circumstances. Usually, more than one client will complain and the person will not get along well within the law office. At times, larger law departments or firms transfer someone who is having difficulty with clients to another department or section. Client relations ability is needed and is constant, regardless of the department or field of law. Changing an individual's practice area or department will not even address, let alone correct, client relations deficiencies. You cannot hide individuals who are deficient in such skills.

Regardless of whether your organization is large or small, every one of your clients and potential clients has a choice of many legally competent practitioners within almost every competitive area—geographic and substantive. Put yourself in the place of the client. If the client for the same expenditure of money can retain a lawyer who is legally competent and more oriented toward service quality and client relations and practices in an organization that is client-oriented, isn't that client going to consistently choose the client-focused organization over one not oriented toward the clients? You would if you were a client and so will your clients.

In fact, once a client discovers that an organization and lawyer are client-oriented, the client will pay more money for that type of relationship rather than save a few dollars with another lawyer or law firm. Thus, developing good client relations is not only a positive for obtaining more business, it is a strong defense against the competition stealing your clients.

The basic rule for deciding the timing of when an individual should be discharged from an organization is that if it is a matter of technical legal competence development, the individual should be given a longer opportunity to develop than if the issue is poor client relations. Tolerance for poor client relations should be much shorter than for poor research and writing skills. There will be no research or writing to do if there are no clients.

EVERYONE IS ESSENTIAL

If your staff's function in client relations is limited to addressing Season's Greetings cards, ordering fruitcakes, or wrapping gifts at the holiday season, it is time for a change. A well-functioning, effective client-relations program is not possible without the commitment and involvement of every individual in the law firm or law department.

Thus, the concept of client relations is not and cannot be restricted to entertaining clients. The concept of client relations must be defined as having a total quality service relationship with a client. The more points of contact the client has with your organization and with which the client is pleased, the stronger the relationship. Therefore, it makes eminently good sense to get everybody in the legal organization on board and actively involved in bettering client relations in every way.

CHAPTER 19

GETTING YOUR REPORT CARD

The final grade in any solo or law firm client relations course of action is whether your practice is growing, remaining static, or declining in terms of numbers of clients and gross revenues. For corporate law departments it is reducing costs, winning cases, closing deals, and preventing lawsuits. In government legal functions it includes increasing compliance with statutes, designing practical regulations that generate compliance, winning cases and, of course, reducing costs.

However, in all types of law practice there are interim indicators that will give you opportunities to accelerate what you have been doing or to change direction to improve your approach to client relations that will greatly affect your final grade.

ELICIT THE CLIENT'S OPINION

Have you ever told a client that there is a problem with the client's business? I have, but I have expressed it as a concern for the client's welfare. I have also complimented clients on how well their business was being run, especially when I had previously reported a problem and it was corrected.

The president of a grocery chain that I represented proudly told me he had a competitive edge because his stores were providing carry-out service to the customer's car as an additional benefit to customers. When I shopped in one of his stores and saw the part-time, carry-out person trying to avoid eye contact and pretending he didn't see me with my arms loaded down with bags, I let the president know. The kid just didn't want to do what he was being paid to do. I didn't tell the president what time or on what day I was in the store because I didn't particularly want to get this young person into trouble. The president stated that he would speak with the manager of the store. The next time I shopped at the store, two different people were offering to carry my bags and neither had any idea that I was the general counsel for the corporation.

Telling your clients about issues in their places of business and how you tell them will greatly influence whether and how clients will tell you about the operation of your law practice. It is essential that we encourage client feedback if we are going to be able to attain greater client satisfaction.

This same president of the grocery chain reported to me that he was dissatisfied with one of our associates who was working on some of his legal issues. The dissatisfaction was not in the legal scholarship, but rather in failing to follow up on things the associate promised to do and not returning phone calls. Although I was at first defensive, I quickly realized that if the client had not cared about my practice as he saw that I cared about his business, I might never have found out about his dissatisfaction until he went to another law firm.

I investigated the president's complaint by determining what work had not been completed and discussing the situation with the associate. After hearing both sides of the story, I could tell this associate's relationship with the client would not work. Although the associate did not admit it, he had fallen down by not meeting performance commitments on a number of occasions. Even more grievously, the associate never called to let the client know that the deadline would not be met or when the client might expect to see the work product.

I called the client and made a deal that that associate would never work on any of the client's matters again. The client was fully satisfied, even though there was no change in the legal sufficiency of the documents being drafted. Because the technical legal competency remained the same in the replacement associate, this proved that the relationship was the most important consideration for this client in choosing and remaining with a particular lawyer or law firm. After being given several additional opportunities to meet the level of service we provided our clients, the associate was discharged for failing to do so.

This type of oral report card from clients is most helpful for improving client relations; it may well be complimentary as well as critical. The vital element in the process is that you are hearing about your practice from your practice, your clients.

If you have an associate or partner who has stated that he or she will improve client relations and does not show marked improvement in a reasonable amount of time, from the client's point of view, you have no choice but to make a change in the lawyer who represents the client. If more than one client expresses dissatisfaction and there is insufficient improvement in the client-relations aspect of a lawyer's practice, there is no place for that lawyer in your organization. This is true whether in private practice, in government service, or in the corporate environment.

In all law practices we have clients and they must be serviced and satisfied by every member of the organization. If you find yourself thinking or speaking about any member in your organization with the gist of your comments being that the person is not good with people, you had better take a closer look. Figure out why you are saying that and offer a plan to help the individual to improve; failing that, separate the person. Similarly, don't consider hiring someone who fits your requirements for academics, experience, and skills but will not be good with clients.

THE CLIENT SURVEY

Another approach to receiving interim report cards is the client survey. Much has been written about client surveys. I believe they have a very important function, but they do not supplant face-to-face communication with the client.

It is even wise to couple your billing mailings with the insertion of your client relations survey. Clients are more likely to fill out and return the surveys—and you are more likely to get honest opinions—if they fill out your report card along with their check. Your response rate will be higher if the survey accompanies the bill. The final advantage is that it reduces postage costs to mail surveys with bills.

The client survey is also an excellent behavior modification instrument for the law office whether it is a solo, firm, corporate department, or government office. If those in the office know what the clients are going to be asked on a survey, they will modify their behavior so that they will get high marks from the clients. This certainly works for businesses accepting phone orders when their operators know that the call "may be monitored for quality purposes." A properly designed survey form serves as an excellent client service training tool as well as a feedback mechanism.

Instead of discussing in detail the pros and cons of client surveys, I have included a copy of a short one here so that you may determine if it, in whole or in part, would be useful in your practice.

Client Survey

1. Did you feel welcome the first time you walked into the office? Why?	Yes	No
2. Did the receptionist tell you her/his name and call you by your name?	Yes	No
3. Did someone offer to:		
Take your coat?	Yes	No
Provide you something to drink?	Yes	No
Tell you how long you would have to wait?	Yes	No
Tell you that if you needed anything, just ask?	Yes	No
4. Did the lawyer take time to listen to everything you wanted to say?	Yes	No
5. Did the lawyer:		
Ask what goals you wanted to achieve?	Yes	No
Tell you how the lawyer was going to try to achieve your goals?	Yes	No
Obtain your input and approval on the course of action?	Yes	No
Tell you how long the process would take?	Yes	No
Tell you how fees were charged?	Yes	No
Estimate your total bill?	Yes	No
Explain that you would be making decisions about your case?	Yes	No
Use your name when conversing with you?	Yes	No
Keep you informed of developments?	Yes	No
Promptly respond to your requests, including returning your calls?	Yes	No

6. Did we meet your expectations?
   A. Yes, very well, in the following areas:
 	
   B. Somewhat, in the following areas:
 	
   C. No, improvement could be made in the following areas:		

Thanks so much for taking the time to answer these questions. We will review your answers and strive to make appropriate changes to serve you and other clients better.

If you want to give us your name and phone number, we may call you to seek further advice. We will also discuss any action we are taking to improve our service to clients. We again thank you for selecting us as your lawyers and helping us improve our client service.

OPTIONAL: _____ (name) _____ (date)

                _____ (phone)

                _____ (case/matter)

A REPORT CARD

Effective client relations require careful strategic planning, team commitment, expenditure of sufficient assets (time, correct staffing and money), and constant follow-up. Haphazard approaches and intermittent implementation may actually damage relations with your clients because you will be creating client expectations that go unfulfilled. If you and your organization are not going to actually institute an enhanced client-relations approach correctly, you would be better off not changing what you are doing now, for your clients have grown accustomed to being ignored or treated however you have treated them in the past.

We were told in high school that our final grades would go on our permanent record and affect us the rest of our lives. Law practice is a continuum allowing for change as long as you practice. At any time

---

REPORT CARD

My Name _____   My Grade ☐

My Company, Law Firm, or Government Agency _____   It's Grade ☐

Course: CLIENT-SERVICE RELATIONS

Grade and Description

A = Outstanding Plan, Effort and Execution, Creative Approaches, Many Repeat Engagements, Clients Telling Others How Good the Lawyer Is, Rapidly Growing Practice, Steadily Increasing Receipts and Compensation

B = Organized Effort, Intense Execution of Approaches, Some Repeat Engagements, Clients Largely Satisfied, Growing Practice, Sporadically Increasing Receipts and Compensation

C = Some Effort, Routine Approaches, A Few Repeat Engagements, Some Client Satisfaction, Practice Holding Its Own, Receipts and Compensation Static

D = Occasional Effort, Routine Approaches, Rare Repeat Engagements, Clients Not Particularly Satisfied, Practice Declining, Receipts and Compensation Slightly Less

E = No Effort, Rare Repeat Engagements, Clients Complaining in the Community, Practice Shrinking, Receipts and Compensation Decreasing

Teacher: _____ My Clients

---

you choose, you may improve your client relations grades or you may let them deteriorate. However, my hope is that you will continually earn an A in client relations because that grade will truly affect you far more than any classroom grade or result on any particular legal matter.

You may determine the current state of your client relations efforts by using the report card set out on page 257 for an honest self-assessment. The grades reflect criteria that apply both to you as an individual practitioner and to the organization in which you practice law. Please grade both yourself and the overall organizational client relations effort.

Your most telling report card is whether your practice progresses in terms of the number of clients, amount of repeat business, as well as higher levels of satisfaction for both clients and those who practice law with you.

CHAPTER 20

A SUMMARY OF VALUABLE EXPERIENCES IN CLIENT RELATIONS

Many nuggets of client relations truths I have observed or learned over the years seem to be universal. They resist being categorized by a chapter title. Since these distillations of ideas and concepts apply to all other chapters, I've assembled them here. They summarize many of the concepts that are spelled out in greater detail in the chapters.

These conclusions from client relations experiences provide quick reminders that there are a few concepts that bridge many of the specifics. Just by following this summary, you will be able to advance far down the road of beneficial client relations.

TREAT THE CLIENT LIKE A RELATIVE

You don't agitate a difficult mother-in-law when you want to develop or maintain a loving relationship with your spouse. Similarly, don't agitate any person who works for or is part of your valuable family of clients.

TRAIN EVERYONE IN CLIENT RELATIONS

The entire legal organization must be well trained in client relations. Each person in the office must know and practice business courtesies.

All must know what to tell the client in an emergency, such as when the lawyer is unreachable. Reducing the client's uncertainty in emergencies starts with the proper training of a legal services delivery team and thoughtful communications to clients. Law firms should train and demand that all who are employed by the firm perform well in customer service—it keeps clients coming back. A client with a sense that a secretary, paralegal, or other staffperson will help them in an emergency is more comforting than the legal team may realize. Assuring clients that assistance in an emergency will be available may also be achieved as easily as giving the client your home phone number.

CONCENTRATE ON CURRENT CLIENTS

Management studies in a variety of industries have clearly established that the success rate of getting new business is far more productive among existing patrons than programs to attract new patrons. Also, the cost of acquiring more business from existing patrons is much less than obtaining a like amount of new business from new patrons. Besides, current clients usually have more legal business to refer and, if well satisfied, will tell others about your services. If you do an excellent job of relating to your clients, they will become your most effective ambassadors to the folks who have not yet become your clients.

TAKE CARE IN COMMUNICATING

Many lawyers are so intent on conveying information that they don't think about how the client will hear it and react. They fail to consider the best way of communicating.

Instead of "We're going to use a trust in your estate plan," a lawyer could say, "If we create a trust in your estate, we can avoid $36,743 in taxes, which we can eventually get to your grandchildren. What do you think about that approach?" The difference is between paternal or dictatorial ("Here's what we're going to do") and participatory, ("This is what I recommend as your lawyer; does this meet your objectives?"). Usually, the resulting decision will be the same as far as the ultimate content of the estate plan. The key difference is that the client is a partner with the lawyer in a participatory environment and feels better about himself or herself, which ripples into a better feeling for the lawyer as well.

The means of communication is likewise important. Much as it is used, e-mail is a cold, impersonal communications vehicle. If the content may have an emotional impact, the most effective communications tools in descending order of preference are: face-to-face, telephone, longhand note, typed letter, and e-mail.

AVOID DISPARATE TREATMENT

If the law organization has a lawyer skilled in client relations—usually also an outstanding rainmaker—that person sets the standard on how the client expects to be treated. If the matter, in whole or part, is serviced by another lawyer or staffperson not similarly skilled in client relations, the client probably will be disappointed in the services performed by the other and consequently with the firm. See that all persons in the organization are skilled in at least maintaining, if not creating, excellent client relations. Standards set high by one person in your office will be accepted by the client and expected from all.

With personal and small business clients, pay attention to the spouse as well as the direct client—he or she may be the power behind the throne. With corporate clients, treat all people well—you never know who will get promoted, laid off, or become a key manager in another company.

Being late may demonstrate to yourself how busy you are, but to the client it shows you aren't organized, don't care, or don't think the client is as important as another client or matter. Stay on schedule; it is a test every client knows how to grade.

DON'T CRITICIZE OTHERS: YOU DON'T ALWAYS KNOW WHO THEY ARE!

Once, when I represented a savings and loan at a mortgage closing, I criticized the seller's real estate agent for some major lapses in preparing for the closing. The criticism was more than objectively justified because her lack of preparation caused additional work for others and a delay in the closing date. Later, a valued client told me his wife said I really embarrassed her in front of her real estate client. I replied that I did not even know his wife and no one with the name of Mrs. Client had ever been in a closing with me. My client told me her name. I recognized it immediately. How was I to know she was married to my important client and using her maiden name in the real estate business? Instead of criticizing what she did in the past—failing to prepare for the closing—I should have kept my mouth shut and devoted my attention exclusively to solving the problem for my savings and loan client, even if it meant doing extra unpaid work.

Criticizing another lawyer during a social conversation or after you have taken over representation of the lawyer's former client is very unwise. What is to be gained other than salving your ego? For one thing, such attacks often make the client feel foolish for selecting that lawyer or not recognizing poor legal services sooner. Even more frightening is that you might be called on the basis of your derogatory comments to testify in a malpractice proceeding brought by the former client. Another detriment is that it does our profession no good. You have the client; concentrate on resolving the client's problem rather than pointing out another lawyer's shortcomings. Criticism just doesn't pay.

OPEN UP TO THE CLIENT

Many lawyers reveal nothing about themselves or their personality to their clients. They are as sterile as a hospital operating room and sound like Jack Webb on Dragnet: "The facts, Ma'am, just the facts." These practitioners usually don't care about their client as a person. Although such lawyers may be very proficient in the procedure and substance of the law, they probably won't establish the kind of client relationships that will enrich their satisfaction from practicing law. Without the lawyer revealing a personal side and encouraging the client to reveal more of his or her personality, a valued personal attorney-client relationship cannot exist or grow.

Most service business is obtained by the prospective purchaser first trusting the seller and then gaining confidence in the service being offered. Repeat business may be obtained with relatively less price sensitivity if a relationship of trust is solidified during the first encounter between the service provider and client-customer. Revealing your human side will accelerate the development of a profitable and enjoyable relationship.

HELP THE CLIENT UNDERSTAND

Doctors who describe medical conditions to their patients in obscure medical terminology do not satisfy patients as much as doctors who speak in understandable layperson terms. Lawyers shouldn't mask their thought processes in technical legal terminology and case cites. A client's confidence in your legal ability can grow only when the client understands the rationale and wisdom of your recommendations from what you say, write, and do. Obtaining a good result often leaves the process of understanding elsewhere. Lawyers need a reassuring "bedside manner" just as much as successful doctors do.

BENEFIT FROM THE LESSONS OF LAW SCHOOL

Client relations is not a subject that is featured in the law school curriculum. Nevertheless, law school taught us many things that are useful in our practice of law. However, lawyers must be careful not to misapply what they learned in law school, especially when it comes to client relations:

- Remember how they taught you to think in law school, but forget how they taught you to speak and write.
- Those who come to the bar thinking and behaving like least-favorite law professors will have few rave technical reviews and few clients.
- Extensive research and strings of case cites are not important to the client, but a practical solution is.
- Numerous very successful legal practitioners did not graduate at the top of their law school class. Perhaps successful practice is predicated more on people skills than analytical legal talent. The ideal is a pleasant combination of scholarship and relationship skills.
- Footnotes don't impress clients because clients aren't used to reading written materials containing them and usually don't even read them.
- Sterilized appellate-type opinion letters to clients are not as helpful in practice as awareness of and explanations based on all of the factual dynamics. Explain situations to clients in terms of facts and analogies, rather than legal theory from case precedents.

I assure you, the grades your client awards will not be predicated on the brilliance of your legal analysis or the sophistication of your language, but rather on the strength of your relationship.

PAY ATTENTION TO DETAIL

In the eyes of a client, a lawyer's brilliance comes from attention to detail. Forget not, the most important detail is the client.

CONSIDER CLIENTS' PERCEPTIONS

Clients' perceptions, not the facts of your relationship with them, determine the result of your client relations efforts. If you are pursuing a client relations effort, always consider and act on the following clients' perceptions:

- Clients are like juries—they may not know the law, but they can sense a lack of veracity, confidence, and sincerity.
- Clients' perceptions of lawyers are based on factors other than technical legal competence.
- Client confidence grows more from the relationship with the lawyer than from performance or result.
- If all the client is shown by the lawyer is the lawyer's formal side, the connection between client and lawyer cannot progress beyond formality.
- Fees are always too high when the only visible return is legal services without personal interest in the client.
- Clients initially think lawyers are different, and usually not in a good way.
- Failure of a lawyer to answer a client's phone message or correspondence is promptly translated by the client to mean that the lawyer doesn't care about him or her.
- Caring only about a legal matter and not the client is demeaning to the client and ultimately fatal to the health of your practice.

REJECT HARMFUL PERCEPTIONS

The following lawyer attitudes are sure to damage client relations:

- I don't have time to spend with the client because I have to make my billable hours commitment.
- If the clients knew the real me, they wouldn't like me.
- Lawyers can control the conversation and impress people if we keep the topics legal. (On the contrary, clients are overwhelmed or bored by excessive technical legal talk.)
- I like the practice of law—except for the clients.
- My billable hours are more important than the total amount of the client's bill.

Replace those perceptions with these client relations maxims:

- A lawyer's decision to sell tomorrow with today's bill may fetch a very handsome sum, but it will always turn out to be not enough.
- Burning any bridge is unwise, but torching one with a client is foolhardy, for many other bridges, seen only by the client, are simultaneously destroyed.
- Providing it is ethical, a lawyer's fee compromise with a client to maintain a relationship is more profitable than being right.
- The client controls who will represent it tomorrow; the lawyer's fate is so determined.
- A law organization may be on call, but it should regularly let the client-coach know it is ready to come off the bench and give the client-coach its best when needed.
- The legal organization is responsible for identifying some client needs; the client will evaluate whether and by what means to satisfy those needs.
- Often the lawyer does not know when she or he will be next at bat because the client-manager doesn't telegraph strategy: be visible and be prepared.
- Growing a financially sound law practice is a long-term proposition. The best short-term measurements of progress are relationships and market share, not gross receipts or profits.
- Extraordinary hustle, long hours, and demonstrated enthusiasm usually buy another chance.
- Solid client relations creates tomorrows for lawyers.

A TELLING ANALOGY

You want to celebrate a special occasion and choose the person closest to you to take to the best restaurant in town. There are just enough other patrons to create a pleasant din, but the place isn't full. The décor is at once inviting and comfortable. The conversation you share is intimate and meaningful. No wait staff paid attention to you for a half an hour. When they did, the water you requested never appeared. You waited an hour and fifteen minutes after ordering for your food to be served. The presentation and taste of the food are magnificent. Your guest was served the wrong dinner, they forgot to serve the coffee you ordered for after dessert, and after you asked for your bill you waited thirty minutes for it.

What would your reaction and that of your guest's be? One might argue that the product, the food, was perfect so you should be well pleased. I don't think most people would be so generous in their opinions. Bad service can ruin a good meal and good service can make an average meal very pleasant.

Bad service, not paying attention to the person paying, and failing to follow up on requests has a universal negative impact. Inevitably bad service, which is a product of not caring about those being served, results in disappointment, resentment about paying, resolve not to return, and a strong probability that the customers will tell others of their dissatisfaction.

Lawyers must realize that poor service leads to bad client relations and will surely rain the same reactions and consequences on them as it does on restaurants treating their customers poorly, as well it should.

CONCLUSION: RETURN ON YOUR INVESTMENT IN CLIENTS

You may be asking yourself, "Yes, but if I do all this 'stuff' on client relations, where am I going to find the time to practice law?" You're not alone. However, until you realize that this client relations "stuff" is practicing law, you probably will never take time to practice law.

Excellent client relations is the key element in long-term and short-term law practice satisfaction and growth goals. How do I know? I started practicing law in 1966. I have been a lawyer for the federal and local governments, a solo practitioner, an associate and partner in a small law firm, a partner in both a mid-size and large law firm, and in the top management of a global corporation's law department. All of these positions involved very different clients and somewhat different types of law. I have approached each with vigor and enthusiasm and, I believe, a relatively high degree of recognized competence. Each position required that I play a different role as a lawyer to best serve the clients. I always tried to play the part that I consistently allowed the client to write.

The only constant has been my abiding commitment to service my clients' legal and other needs by giving whatever it took to create excellent client relations. Building a practice in this fashion takes more time, effort, and energy. It pays off in the long run in money and, more importantly, in personal satisfaction. I know this because the result for me was a continuing increase in my personal satisfaction with my law practice while my annual financial compensation grew too.

The key to your practice, and your enjoyment of it, is truly superb client relations. It is also critical to improving the image of the legal profession.

I have stated my case for putting your practice emphasis on client relations. Now it is time for you to decide on the level of personal satisfaction you want from being a lawyer and the fate of your practice. You do this by choosing to act on improving client relations or by permitting fiscal opportunities and personal satisfactions to pass you by. Get aboard . . . and have a good ride!

—————ABOUT THE AUTHOR—————

Henry W. Ewalt earned a bachelor's degree cum laude from Allegheny College, a small liberal arts school, and a master's degree in political science and J.D. from the University of Michigan.

He returned home to Pittsburgh, Pennsylvania, where he has practiced law with the National Labor Relations Board, with small, medium, and large law firms, and as Associate General Counsel, Litigation and Employment Law, for Westinghouse and CBS. He currently has a solo practice that includes offering services as a consultant and mediator.

Management has been a consistent interest of Henry's. In addition to many years of active participation in the ABA's Law Practice Management Section, he has applied his knowledge as president of a law firm and as a member of the executive committee in law firms, law departments, and non-profit organizations.

Henry has facilitated law firm strategic planning retreats, assisted on change management issues, and provided advice to law firms on governance, direction, and marketing opportunities. He has spoken across the country on management topics. Previously, he authored *Practical Planning*, a how-to book for law firms interested in strategic planning.

Henry's interest in clients has been consistent throughout his career. While a field attorney at the NLRB, he was prosecuting a party charged with federal statute violations. After extracting a settlement favorable to the government, Henry was asked by the accused if he would be the accused party's lawyer. As Henry tells the story, he replied that as a government lawyer he could not represent the party, but that if the party held off engaging a lawyer for a couple of weeks he'd be glad to do so for he had submitted his resignation to the NLRB. Indeed, that individual did become Henry's first client.

Demonstrative evidence of the strength of the client relations that developed between Henry and his first client came a few years later. The client opened his wallet, pulled out one of Henry's business cards to which he had taped a quarter, and said to Henry, "This is for my one phone call if I ever land in jail."

INDEX

Selected Books From...
THE ABA LAW PRACTICE MANAGEMENT SECTION

The ABA Guide to International Business Negotiations. Explains national, legal, and cultural issues you must consider when negotiating with members of different countries. Includes details of 17 specific countries/nationalities.

The ABA Guide to Lawyer Trust Accounts. Details ways that lawyers should manage trust accounts to comply with ethical & statutory requirements.

The ABA Guide to Legal Marketing. 14 articles—written by marketing experts, practicing lawyers, and law firm marketing administrators—share their innovative methods for competing in an aggressive marketplace.

The ABA Guide to Professional Managers in the Law Office. Shows how lawyers can practice more efficiently by delegating management tasks to professional managers.

Anatomy of a Law Firm Merger. Considering a merger? Here's a roadmap that shows how to: determine the costs/benefits of a merger, assess merger candidates, integrate resources and staff, and more.

Billing Innovations. Explains how billing and pricing are affect strategic planning, maintaining quality of services, marketing, instituting a compensation system, and firm governance.

Changing Jobs, 3rd Edition. A handbook designed to help lawyers make changes in their professional careers. Includes career planning advice from dozens of experts.

Compensation Plans for Law Firms, 3rd Ed. This third edition discusses the basics for a fair and simple compensation system for partners, of counsel, associates, paralegals, and staff.

The Complete Internet Handbook for Lawyers. A thorough orientation to the Internet, including e-mail, search engines, conducting research and marketing on the Internet, publicizing a Web site, Net ethics, security, viruses, and more. Features a updated, companion Web site with forms you can download and customize.

Computer-Assisted Legal Research: A Guide to Successful Online Searching. Covers the fundamentals of LEXIS®-NEXIS® and WESTLAW®, including practical information such as: logging on and off; formulating your search; reviewing results; modifying a query; using special features; downloading documents.

Computerized Case Management Systems. Thoroughly evaluates 35 leading case management software applications, helping you pick which is best for your firm.

Connecting with Your Client. Written by a psychologist, therapist, and legal consultant, this book presents communications techniques that will help ensure client cooperation and satisfaction.

Do-It-Yourself Public Relations. A hands-on guide (and diskette!) for lawyers with public relations ideas, sample letters, and forms.

Easy Self-Audits for the Busy Law Office. Dozens of evaluation tools help you determine what's working (and what's not) in your law office or legal department. You'll discover several opportunities for improving productivity and efficiency along the way!

Finding the Right Lawyer. Answers the questions people should ask when searching for legal counsel. Includes a glossary of legal specialties and the 10 questions to ask before hiring a lawyer.

Handling Personnel Issues in the Law Office. Packed with tips on "safely" and legally recruiting, hiring, training, managing, and terminating employees.

HotDocs® in One Hour for Lawyers. Offers simple instructions, ranging from generating a document from a template to inserting conditional text and creating custom dialogs.

How to Build and Manage an Employment Law Practice. Provides clear guidance and valuable tips for solo or small employment law practices, including preparation, marketing, accepting cases, and managing workload and finances. Includes several time-saving "fill in the blank" forms.

How to Build and Manage an Estates Law Practice. Provides the tools and guidance you'll need to start or improve an estates law practice, including

How to Build and Manage a Personal Injury Practice. Features all of the tactics, technology, and tools needed for a profitable practice, including hot to: write a sound business plan, develop a financial forecast, choose office space, market your practice, and more.

How to Draft Bills Clients Rush to Pay. Dozens of ways to draft bills that project honesty, competence, fairness and value.

How to Start and Build a Law Practice, Millennium 4th Edition. Jay Foonberg's classic guide has been completely updated and expanded! Features 128 chapters, including 30 new ones, that reveal secrets to successful planning, marketing, billing, client relations, and much more. Chock-full of forms, sample letters, and checklists, including a sample business plan, "The Foonberg Law Office Management Checklist," and more.

Internet Fact Finder for Lawyers. Shares all of the secrets and shortcuts of conducting research on the Net, including how to tap into Internet sites for investigations, depositions, and trial presentations.

Law Firm Partnership Guide: Getting Started. Examines the most important issues you must consider to ensure your partnership's success, including self-assessment, organization structure, written agreements, financing, and basic operations. Includes *A Model Partnership Agreement* on diskette.

Law Firm Partnership Guide: Strengthening Your Firm. Addresses what to do after your firm is up and running, including how to handle: change, financial problems, governance issues, compensating firm owners, and leadership.

Law Law Law on the Internet. Presents the most influential law-related Web sites. Features Web site reviews of the *National Law Journal's 250*, so you can save time surfing the Net and quickly find the information you need.

Law Office Policy and Procedures Manual, 4th Ed. A model for law office policies and procedures (includes diskette). Covers law office organization, management, personnel policies, financial management, technology, and communications systems.

Law Office Staff Manual for Solos and Small Firms. Use this manual as is or customize it using the book's diskette. Includes general office policies on confidentiality, employee compensation, sick leave, sexual harassment, billing, and more.

The Lawyer's Guide to Creating Web Pages. A practical guide that clearly explains HTML, covers how to design a Web site, and introduces Web-authoring tools.

The Lawyer's Guide to the Internet. A guide to what the Internet is (and isn't), how it applies to the legal profession, and the different ways it can—and should—be used.

The Lawyer's Guide to Marketing on the Internet. This book talks about the pluses and minuses of marketing on the Internet, as well as how to develop an Internet marketing plan.

The Lawyer's Quick Guide to E-Mail. Covers basic and intermediate topics, including setting up an e-mail program, sending messages, managing received messages, using mailing lists, security, and more.

The Lawyer's Quick Guide to Microsoft® Internet Explorer; The Lawyer's Quick Guide to Netscape® Navigator. These two guides de-mystify the most popular Internet browsers. Four quick and easy lessons include: Basic Navigation, Setting a Bookmark, Browsing with a Purpose, and Keeping What You Find.

The Lawyer's Quick Guide to Timeslips®. Filled with practical examples, this guide uses three short, interactive lessons to show to efficiently use Timeslips.

The Lawyer's Quick Guide to WordPerfect® 7.0/8.0 for Windows®. Covers multitasking, entering and editing text, formatting letters, creating briefs, and more. Includes a diskette with practice exercises and word templates.

Leaders' Digest: A Review of the Best Books on Leadership. This book will help you find the best books on leadership to help you achieve extraordinary and exceptional leadership skills.

Living with the Law: Strategies to Avoid Burnout and Create Balance. Examines ways to manage stress, make the practice of law more satisfying, and improve client service.

Marketing Success Stories. This collection of anecdotes provides an inside look at how successful lawyers market themselves, their practice specialties, their firms, and their profession.

Microsoft® Word for Windows® in One Hour for Lawyers. Uses four easy lessons to help you prepare, save, and edit a basic document in Word.

Practicing Law Without Clients: Making a Living as a Freelance Lawyer. Describes freelance legal researching, writing, and consulting opportunities that are available to lawyers.

Quicken® in One Hour for Lawyers. With quick, concise instructions, this book explains the basics of Quicken and how to use the program to detect and analyze financial problems.

Risk Management. Presents practical ways to asses your level of risk, improve client services, and avoid mistakes that can lead to costly malpractice claims, civil liability, or discipline. Includes Law Firm Quality/In Control (QUIC) Surveys on diskette and other tools to help you perform a self-audit.

Running a Law Practice on a Shoestring. Offers a crash course in successful entrepreneurship. Features money-saving tips on office space, computer equipment, travel, furniture, staffing, and more.

Successful Client Newsletters. Written for lawyers, editors, writers, and marketers, this book can help you to start a newsletter from scratch, redesign an existing one, or improve your current practices in design, production, and marketing.

Survival Guide for Road Warriors. A guide to using a notebook computer (laptop) and other technology to improve your productivity in your office, on the road, in the courtroom, or at home.

Telecommuting for Lawyers. Discover methods for implementing a successful telecommuting program that can lead to increased productivity, improved work product, higher revenues, lower overhead costs, and better communications. Addressing both law firms and telecommuters, this guide covers start-up, budgeting, setting policies, selecting participants, training, and technology.

Through the Client's Eyes. Includes an overview of client relations and sample letters, surveys, and self-assessment questions to gauge your client relations acumen.

Time Matters® in One Hour for Lawyers. Employs quick, easy lessons to show you how to: add contacts, cases, and notes to Time Matters; work with events and the calendar; and integrate your data into a case management system that suits your needs.

Wills, Trusts, and Technology. Reveals why you should automate your estates practice; identifies what should be automated; explains how to select the right software; and helps you get up and running with the software you select.

Win-Win Billing Strategies. Prepared by a blue-ribbon ABA task force of practicing lawyers, corporate counsel, and management consultants, this book explores what constitutes "value" and how to bill for it. You'll understand how to get fair compensation for your work and communicate and justify fees to cost-conscious clients.

Women Rainmakers' 101+ Best Marketing Tips. A collection of over 130 marketing from women rainmakers throughout the country. Features tips on image, networking, public relations, and advertising.

Year 2000 Problem and the Legal Profession. In clear, nontechnical terms, this book will help you identify, address, and meet the challenges that Y2K poses to the legal industry.

TO ORDER CALL TOLL-FREE: 1-800-285-2221

Order Form

Qty	Title	LPM Price	Regular Price	Total
_____	ABA Guide to International Business Negotiations (5110331)	$ 74.95	$ 84.95	$_____
_____	ABA Guide to Lawyer Trust Accounts (5110374)	69.95	79.95	$_____
_____	ABA Guide to Legal Marketing (5110341)	69.95	79.95	$_____
_____	ABA Guide to Prof. Managers in the Law Office (5110373)	69.95	79.95	$_____
_____	Anatomy of a Law Firm Merger, Second Edition (5110434)	74.95	89.95	$_____
_____	Billing Innovations (5110366)	124.95	144.95	$_____
_____	Changing Jobs, 3rd Ed.	*please call for information*		$_____
_____	Compensation Plans for Lawyers, 3rd Ed. (5110452)	84.95	99.95	$_____
_____	Complete Guide to Marketing Your Law Practice (5110428)	74.95	89.95	$_____
_____	Complete Internet Handbook for Lawyers (5110413)	39.95	49.95	$_____
_____	Computerized Case Management Systems (5110409)	39.95	49.95	$_____
_____	Connecting with Your Client (5110378)	54.95	64.95	$_____
_____	Do-It-Yourself Public Relations (5110352)	69.95	79.95	$_____
_____	Easy Self Audits for the Busy Law Firm	*please call for information*		$_____
_____	Finding the Right Lawyer (5110339)	14.95	14.95	$_____
_____	Handling Personnel Issues in the Law Office (5110381)	59.95	69.95	$_____
_____	HotDocs® in One Hour for Lawyers (5110403)	29.95	34.95	$_____
_____	How to Build and Manage an Employment Law Practice (5110389)	44.95	54.95	$_____
_____	How to Build and Manage an Estates Law Practice	*please call for information*		$_____
_____	How to Build and Manage a Personal Injury Practice (5110386)	44.95	54.95	$_____
_____	How to Draft Bills Clients Rush to Pay (5110344)	39.95	49.95	$_____
_____	How to Start & Build a Law Practice, Millennium Fourth Edition (5110415)	57.95	69.95	$_____
_____	Internet Fact Finder for Lawyers (5110399)	34.95	39.95	$_____
_____	Law Firm Partnership Guide: Getting Started (5110363)	64.95	74.95	$_____
_____	Law Firm Partnership Guide: Strengthening Your Firm (5110391)	64.95	74.95	$_____
_____	Law Law Law on the Internet (5110400)	34.95	39.95	$_____
_____	Law Office Policy & Procedures Manual, 4th Ed. (5110441)	109.95	129.95	$_____
_____	Law Office Staff Manual for Solos & Small Firms (5110445)	59.95	69.95	$_____
_____	Lawyer's Guide to Creating Web Pages (5110383)	54.95	64.95	$_____
_____	Lawyer's Guide to the Internet (5110343)	24.95	29.95	$_____
_____	Lawyer's Guide to Marketing on the Internet (5110371)	54.95	64.95	$_____
_____	Lawyer's Quick Guide to E-Mail (5110406)	34.95	39.95	$_____
_____	Lawyer's Quick Guide to Microsoft Internet® Explorer (5110392)	24.95	29.95	$_____
_____	Lawyer's Quick Guide to Netscape® Navigator (5110384)	24.95	29.95	$_____
_____	Lawyer's Quick Guide to Timeslips® (5110405)	34.95	39.95	$_____
_____	Lawyer's Quick Guide to WordPerfect® 7.0/8.0 (5110395)	34.95	39.95	$_____
_____	Leaders' Digest (5110356)	49.95	59.95	$_____
_____	Living with the Law (5110379)	59.95	69.95	$_____
_____	Marketing Success Stories (5110382)	79.95	89.95	$_____
_____	Microsoft® Word for Windows® in One Hour for Lawyers (5110358)	19.95	29.95	$_____
_____	Practicing Law Without Clients (5110376)	49.95	59.95	$_____
_____	Quicken® in One Hour for Lawyers (5110380)	19.95	29.95	$_____
_____	Risk Management (5610123)	69.95	79.95	$_____
_____	Running a Law Practice on a Shoestring (5110387)	39.95	49.95	$_____
_____	Successful Client Newsletters (5110396)	39.95	44.95	$_____
_____	Survival Guide for Road Warriors (5110362)	24.95	29.95	$_____
_____	Telecommuting for Lawyers (5110401)	39.95	49.95	$_____
_____	Through the Client's Eyes (5110337)	69.95	79.95	$_____
_____	Time Matters® in One Hour for Lawyers (5110402)	29.95	34.95	$_____
_____	Wills, Trusts, and Technology (5430377)	74.95	84.95	$_____
_____	Win-Win Billing Strategies (5110304)	89.95	99.95	$_____
_____	Women Rainmakers' 101+ Best Marketing Tips (5110336)	14.95	19.95	$_____
_____	Year 2000 Problem and the Legal Profession (5110410)	24.95	29.95	$_____

*Handling
$10.00-$24.99 .... $3.95
$25.00-$49.99 .... $4.95
$50.00+ $5.95

**Tax
DC residents add 5.75%
IL residents add 8.75%
MD residents add 5%

Subtotal	$_____
*Handling	$_____
**Tax	$_____
TOTAL	$_____

PAYMENT

☐ Check enclosed (to the ABA) ☐ Bill Me
☐ Visa ☐ MasterCard ☐ American Express

Account Number _____ Exp. Date _____ Signature _____

Name _____ Firm _____
Address _____
City _____ State _____ Zip _____
Phone Number _____ E-Mail Address _____

Mail: ABA Publication Orders, P.O. Box 10892, Chicago, Illinois 60610-0892 ♦ Phone: (800) 285-2221 ♦ FAX: (312) 988-5568

E-Mail: abasvcctr@abanet.org ♦ Internet: http://www.abanet.org/lpm/catalo

Source Code: 22AEND499

 **THE SECTION OF LAW PRACTICE MANAGEMENT**

CUSTOMER COMMENT FORM

 ABA

Title of Book: _____

We've tried to make this publication as useful, accurate, and readable as possible. Please take 5 minutes to tell us if we succeeded. Your comments and suggestions will help us improve our publications. Thank you!

1. How did you acquire this publication:

☐ by mail order   ☐ at a meeting/convention   ☐ as a gift

☐ by phone order   ☐ at a bookstore   ☐ don't know

☐ other: (describe) _____

_____

Please rate this publication as follows:

	Excellent	Good	Fair	Poor	Not Applicable
Readability: Was the book easy to read and understand?	☐	☐	☐	☐	☐
Examples/Cases: Were they helpful, practical? Were there enough?	☐	☐	☐	☐	☐
Content: Did the book meet your expectations? Did it cover the subject adequately?	☐	☐	☐	☐	☐
Organization and clarity: Was the sequence of text logical? Was it easy to find what you wanted to know?	☐	☐	☐	☐	☐
Illustrations/forms/checklists: Were they clear and useful? Were there enough?	☐	☐	☐	☐	☐
Physical attractiveness: What did you think of the appearance of the publication (typesetting, printing, etc.)?	☐	☐	☐	☐	☐

Would you recommend this book to another attorney/administrator? ☐ Yes ☐ No

How could this publication be improved? What else would you like to see in it?

_____

_____

_____

Do you have other comments or suggestions? _____

_____

_____

Name _____

Firm/Company _____

Address _____

City/State/Zip _____

Phone _____

Firm Size: _____ Area of specialization: _____

We appreciate your time and help.

Fold

BUSINESS REPLY MAIL
FIRST CLASS   PERMIT NO. 16471   CHICAGO, ILLINOIS

POSTAGE WILL BE PAID BY ADDRESSEE

AMERICAN BAR ASSOCIATION
PPM, 8th FLOOR
750 N. LAKE SHORE DRIVE
CHICAGO, ILLINOIS 60611-9851

Fold